Barbara Hogenboom

MEXICO AND THE NAFTA
ENVIRONMENT DEBATE

The Transnational Politics of Economic Integration

International Books, 1998

ISBN 90 5727 014 5

Keywords: Mexico, NAFTA, environmental policy, regional integration, international relations, NGOS

Cover design: Marjo Starink
Cover photograph: Tom Jacobi, ABC Press Amsterdam
Desk Top Publishing: Hanneke Kossen
Printing: Drukkerij Haasbeek

International Books, A. Numankade 17, 3572 KP Utrecht, the Netherlands,
tel. +31 30 2731840, fax +31 30 2733614, e-mail: i-books@antenna.nl

Contents

Preface

Only after having written one myself, have I come to realize how much work there is behind the innumerable books that are released year after year. As most writing is an individual activity, and writers work in silence and isolation, the efforts made remain largely hidden. Equally, a considerable share of the pleasure and satisfaction of writing remains hidden, although preferably a book should reflect these feelings of the author. I hope this one does. Another thing that is bound to remain largely unknown is the importance of all sorts of support from other persons. A preface is simply too limited and partly too public to fully express one's gratitude. This being said, I would like to shortly mention the most valuable contributions.

This book could not have been written without the fieldwork research in Mexico, the United States and Canada. Spread over four trips in three years, I spent in total more than six months in North America. During these visits I gathered a great deal of written material (documents, studies, newspaper and magazine cuttings), and interviewed over sixty persons in NGOs, government agencies, business interest organizations, and international organizations, while speaking to many more. I am very grateful to all the people who helped me in this respect, especially to those who, without knowing me, put their trust in me and allowed me to go through their files, or provided me with confidential information. In addition, these contacts gave me a sense of the real world of politics in each of the countries, and the influence of different cultures and perceptions.

The visits to North America also enabled me to establish numerous academic contacts. First, by presenting a part of my research at international conferences in Washington DC, Chicago and Toronto I received useful comments, which helped me further accentuate my ideas and analysis. Second, I had interesting discussions with several colleagues in the three countries, many of whom supported me by providing me with information and contacts. I am especially grateful to Sofía Gallardo, among other things for enabling me to make use of the facilities of the *Centro de Investigación y Docencia Económicas* (CIDE) in

Mexico City. Financial assistance for these visits was provided by the Dutch Organization for Scientific Research (NWO), the Faculty of Political and Socio-Cultural Sciences (PSCW) of the University of Amsterdam, and the Canada Foundation. Another organization I would like to mention here is the J.E. Jurriaanse Foundation, which financially supported this publication.

At home, in the Netherlands, I have experienced continuous and precious support from various persons. Alex Fernández Jilberto has been the supervisor I would have wished for. With his cheerful daily encouragement I have undertaken more activities than I had planned without delaying this book. Gerd Junne and Jean Carrière provided me with ideas for my research and gave me useful feedback on my writings. Several other persons read and commented on draft texts over the years. I would particularly like to thank Kees Biekart. Jolle Demmers not only read everything I wrote, she is also my great Mexico mate. Finally, as in everything I do, I have experienced the boundless love and support of Nic, Beatrice, Janneke and Pien.

List of Abbreviations

ACN	Action Canada Network
AMCHAM	American Chamber of Commerce of Mexico
APEC	Asia Pacific Economic Cooperation
ART	Alliance for Responsible Trade
BECC	Border Environmental Cooperation Commission
BEP	Border Ecology Project
CANACINTRA	*Cámara Nacional de Industria de Transformación*, National Chamber of Transformation Industry
CCE	*Consejo Coordinador Empresarial*, Coordinating Business Council
CEC	Commission for Environmental Cooperation
CFE	Comisión Federal de Electricidad, Federal Electricity Commission
CMHN	Consejo Mexicano de Hombres de Negocios, Mexican Council of Businessmen
COECE	*Coordinadora de Organismos Empresariales de Comercio Exterior*, Coordinating Organization of Business Agencies of Foreign Trade
CONADE	*Comisión Nacional de Ecología,* National Ecology Commission
CTC	Citizens Trade Campaign
CUFTA	Canada-US Free Trade Agreement
EDF	Environmental Defense Fund
ENGO	Environmental Non-Governmental Organization
EPA	Environmental Protection Agency
FDI	Foreign Direct Investment
GATT	General Agreement on Tariffs and Trade
GDP	Gross Domestic Product
INAINE	*Instituto Autónomo de Investigaciones Ecológicas,* Autonomous Institute for Ecological Research
INE	*Instituto Nacional de Ecología,* National Institute of Ecology
ISI	Import Substitution Industrialization

NACE	North American Commission on the Environment
NADBANK	North American Development Bank
NAFTA	North American Free Trade Agreement
NGO	Non-Governmental Organization
NRDC	Natural Resources Defense Council
NWF	National Wildlife Federation
OECD	Organization for Economic Cooperation and Development
PAN	*Partido de Acción Nacional,* National Action Party
PEMEX	*Petróleos Mexicanos,* Mexican Oil Company
PGE	*Pacto de Grupos Ecologistas,* Pact of Ecologist Groups
PRD	*Partido de la Revolución Democrática,* Party of the Democratic Revolution
PRI	*Partido Revolucionario Institucional,* Institutional Revolutionary Party
PROFEPA	*Procuraduría Federal de Protección al Ambiente,* Office of the Attorney General for Protection of the Environment
PRONASOL	*Programa Nacional de Solidaridad,* National Solidarity Programme
RMALC	*Red Mexicana de Acción frente al Libre Comercio,* Mexican Action Network on Free Trade
SARH	*Secretaría de Agricultura y Recursos Hidráulicos,* Ministry of Agriculture and Water Resources
SE	*Subsecretaría de Ecología,* Sub-ministry of Ecology
SECOFI	*Secretaría de Comercio y Fomento Industrial,* Ministry of Commerce and Industrial Development
SEDESOL	*Secretaría de Desarrollo Social,* Ministry of Social Development
SEDUE	*Secretaría de Desarrollo Urbano y Ecología,* Ministry of Urban Development and Ecology
SMA	*Subsecretaría de Mejoramiento del Ambiente,* Sub-ministry of Improvement of the Environment
SSA	*Secretaría de Salubridad y Asistencia,* Ministry of Health and Assistance
TNC	Transnational Corporation
UGAM	*Unión de Grupos Ambientalistas,* Union of Environmental Groups
UN	United Nations
US	United States
USTR	US Trade Representative
WWF	World Wildlife Fund

Introduction

In the night of 1 January 1994, the North American Free Trade Agreement (NAFTA) came into effect. With Mexico, the United States (US) and Canada, the NAFTA forms the largest regional trade block in the world. Proponents of the agreement claimed that it would encourage economic growth in each of the three countries, particularly in Mexico. The Mexican government presented integration in the North American market via liberalization of trade and investment as the only viable option for development. Other Latin American countries viewed Mexico's entry into NAFTA with anxiety, and hoped that the agreement would shortly be converted into a Free Trade Agreement of the Americas. In short, among proponents of economic liberalization NAFTA was perceived as Mexico's gateway from the Third to the First World, and it was presented accordingly.

That same night of 1 January 1994, an armed indigenous revolt took place in Mexico's southern state Chiapas. The revolting *Zapatistas* demanded democracy, land, and justice, and declared that Mexico's marginalized poor had nothing to gain from NAFTA. The peso crisis at the end of that year struck another blow to the myth of NAFTA's securing Mexico's development. Mexico proved not to be the trustworthy emerging market foreign investors had taken it for, and with fleeing capital its prospects for rapid growth collapsed. In the aftermath of this crisis, former President Carlos Salinas de Gortari did not obtain the expected chairmanship of the World Trade Organization (WTO). Instead, Mexico's architect of NAFTA is the first ex-president since the Mexican Revolution who has become an exile.

Indeed, Mexican extremes abound. To name just a few, social inequality is among the highest in Latin America. An abundance of natural resources is combined with the most polluted metropolis in the world. Despite an undemocratic, corrupt state system that is infiltrated by an increasingly powerful drugs mafia, Mexico is a major recipient of World Bank and other international credits. And this list can easily be extended.

Mexico's political system has heavily contributed to these extremes. Among this system's characteristics are a centralist government, a revolutionary ideology of national progress, corporatist relations with major social sectors, co-optation and repression of opposition, control of the media, and illegal election practices. In this context, the Institutional Revolutionary Party (PRI) has been able to govern Mexico for nearly seventy years, and has blended with the Mexican state into a hardly separable whole. This state-party system has dominated political representation at the level of civil society, and has largely resisted calls for democratization. It also allowed Mexico's political elite to follow a strategy of neoliberal economic restructuring that caused severe hardship among the Mexican lower and middle classes.

The ability of the PRI to absorb the political debate was also shown with the NAFTA plan. While the agreement was likely to have considerable impact on the country's future development, the NAFTA issue attracted only limited attention. Opposition parties and non-governmental organizations (NGOs) that protested against the NAFTA plan and attempted to initiate a nation-wide debate found that they were unable to compete with the pro-NAFTA propaganda spread by the government and the media. In contrast with the US, in Mexico NAFTA hardly became an issue of political mobilization.

Before we continue, it needs mentioning that the cracks in Mexico's state-party system seem to become larger and more numerous. The elections of July 1997 resulted in the end of the PRI's majority in the House of Representatives and the victory of left-wing opposition leader Chuauthémoc Cárdenas as the first elected mayor of Mexico City. These events point to a tendency of opposition parties' beginning to obtain some genuine political influence. It is nevertheless too early to assess how democratization will evolve, and at what pace. As Mexico's political system is based on numerous strong chains of economic and political interests, and the system is strongly interwoven with a cultural and historical background that reinforces undemocratic practices, institutional change is likely to be only the start of a long process of democratization.

— Assessing the effects of the NAFTA environment debate —

Although Mexico made a relatively early start with a formal environmental policy, for many years it was a low government priority. With minimal resources, enforcement of legislation was poor. On the other hand, the Mexican government adopted environmentalist discourse and encouraged the foundation of environmental organizations. These strategies to direct and control the growing environmental consciousness and concerns among Mexican citizens were only partly effective. In the mid-1980s, the weak protection efforts of the government were increasingly criticized by environmental groups. The government was embarrassed by these attacks, in particular when they were linked with opposition to the political system. With a few limited policy improvements and subtle repression, the Mexican government attempted to silence protesting organizations.

The NAFTA plan led to a new dynamic in the political struggle over Mexico's environmental policy. Economically, rather than being something new the agreement implied a reinforcement of historical relations. Politically, however, this (first) case of a developing country entering an industrialized free trade zone met resistance. Especially in Mexico and the US, there was much concern about further economic integration of such unequal countries. Many environmental organizations worried about the impact of the expected rapid growth in Mexico, and about the effects on each of the three countries of free trade in a context of diverging levels of environmental protection. These diverging levels were also of concern to labour unions and protectionist forces in the US, fearing for unfair competition from Mexico-based industry. As a considerable number of members of the US Congress lent a ready ear to the demands of this heterogeneous group of NAFTA critics, Mexico's weak environmental policy enforcement turned into a major issue. The excessive ecological degradation and health hazards caused by rapid industrialization in Mexico's border region with the US proved to be the Achilles' heel of the Mexican government.

The Mexican government was thus faced with a completely new pattern of political pressure with respect to its environmental policy. NAFTA was an important project for the process of economic restructuring initiated by Mexico's political elite of technocrats. Critics of NAFTA were establishing transnational relations and their ideas had considerable political leverage. If NAFTA was to become real, this criticism had to be effectively dealt with. In contrast to previous environmental politics, on this matter the Mexican government did not stand alone, as the US government, and to some extent private sector organizations, also made efforts to respond politically to the issues raised. The transnational political interaction between and among the main critics and proponents of NAFTA with respect to environmental matters that took place between 1990 and 1993 is here termed the transnational NAFTA environment debate, or in short the NAFTA environment debate.

The central question this study aims to address is: *How did the transnational NAFTA environment debate affect environmental politics and policy in Mexico?* To answer this question, it is useful to distinguish between possible direct effects and indirect effects. First, the transnational debate itself might have affected politics and policy through changing views, interests, roles, relations and activities of political actors. Second, the final outcome of the debate, the so-called NAFTA package, might have similar effects. Important political actors that need to be incorporated in this analysis are domestic and foreign government agencies, environmental and other NGOs, private sector organizations, and multilateral banks. The answer to the question of the NAFTA debate's effects on Mexico should provide a better understanding of the impacts of transnational politics in the context of economic integration, as will be explained below.

— The political economy of the NAFTA environment debate —

This study is linked to the wider discussion of the impact of globalization and regionalization processes on the control of citizens and governments over the course of economic, political, social, ecological and cultural developments. Although far from being a new phenomenon, globalization has over the past few years increasingly become the issue of political and academic debate. The most important reason for this recent attention is the changing nature of globalization due to the world-wide revaluation of market forces over government control, after the international economic crises of the 1980s and the virtual disappearance of Communist regimes in the early 1990s. Presented as the recipe for renewed economic growth, the rise of neoliberalism has changed the character of globalization. While previously Keynesian models of development aimed at welfare by readjusting the market to public interests, neoliberal development models pursue almost the opposite. Within this context, market forces are increasingly adopted as leading principles for government policy, and rather than setting limits to the market, governments have become its major advocates.

Economic integration of countries and liberalization of the private and public sectors have profound effects. State structures are changing to become more responsive to international demands, while governments are increasingly reluctant to interfere in the market. In Mexico, the previous economic model and the legitimacy of the state-party system were cast in terms of national values and national development, whereas the current model is based on international values and international integration. World wide, economic and social relations are affected by increasing international competition and decreasing government protection. Socio-economic polarization has increased globally as well as within many countries since neoliberal economic restructuring has gone hand in hand with a loss of employment, real income and social security of smaller or larger groups within civil society. Resistance to these tendencies has had little impact as economic liberalization and a "reduced state" have been successfully presented as inevitable.

Though globalization is a commonly applied term, it does not seem to be an accurate designation to describe the currently dominant patterns of world-wide change. Whereas speculative capital indeed primarily seems to globalize, other flows do so to a far lesser extent. For information flows, languages and weak infrastructure still inhibit a truly 'world wide web'. Moreover, economic and political integration are predominantly regional processes. Trade in goods, foreign direct investment and plant relocation increase much faster regionally than globally. Also labour mobility is primarily regional. Regionalization is generally still a more efficient, easy and safe strategy for companies and governments than globalization. The primary reason for the greater success of regionalization is that, despite the emerging consensus on economic liberalization, global integration initiatives have proved to be laborious and slow. Economic liberalization has so far largely resulted in integration within regional blocks that compete with one another. As a consequence, for countries that are not inside the European, Asian or North American block, association seems urgent for future development.

Despite the evident importance of regional integration, regionalization is not a useful term to replace globalization for characterizing the above mentioned trends since it is too restrictive. From a political (science) perspective, more than the geographical reach the trend towards a growing external influence on domestic processes is crucial. In many political economy studies, this trend is called internationalization. However, in this book the terms transnational and transnationalization are used deliberately instead of international and internationalization. The reason for this is that in a political context 'international' sometimes refers to inter-state affairs or politics of states and international organizations. 'Transnational' is more extensive, including non-state actors and any cross-border relation, which are central to this study. Political transnationalization takes place when political debates increasingly surpass the national level and political actors expand their activities and relations to non-state and state actors in other countries. Transnationalization of a certain field of policy implies a process in which policy-making becomes based more on external ideas, interests and pressure than before.[1]

---

1   The term transnational relations emerged in the 1970s, but lost its attraction in the early 1980s, when security issues came to dominate international politics. Since the end of the Cold War and the rise of other concerns, the usefulness of the idea of transnational political activity has been rediscovered. Currently, theorization of transnational politics is linked to discussions of the state, state-society relations, civil society and the intertwining effects of domestic and external factors (Peterson 1992: 371-5).

An assessment of the effects of the NAFTA environment debate is ultimately a case study of current global power structures and the possibilities for people to control their lives and their surroundings. Economic and political transnationalization renders the world more complex. Political transnationalization provides new avenues for influence, but these avenues are complicated as power structures become less clear. Simultaneously, environmental degradation requires a regulation of economic activities at the local, national and international level. Due to regional and global integration, economic processes become less controlled by the state, even more so because of the neoliberal character of current economic integration. As a consequence, national democratic mechanisms are losing their effectiveness, so far largely without being supplemented by structural avenues for citizen input at the regional or global level. Lessons in how to deal with limitations and options for citizen influence are therefore much needed. On the other hand, in the case of a country with an authoritarian political system like Mexico, transnational relations may also allow for new avenues to achieve democratization.

— Structure of this study —

As mentioned above, this study centres on the question of how the transnational NAFTA environment debate affected environmental politics and government policy in Mexico in the period 1990-1993. Focusing on the transnational NAFTA politics from the Mexican perspective, this book does not analyse the whole NAFTA process in the US and Canada. Since US NAFTA politics were decisive for the regional process, much reference is inevitably made to what happened there, but to support the analysis of transnational processes, and without the intention of being complete. Assessments of the Canadian NAFTA process are only included when they help to provide insight into the regional NAFTA processes, or if they are of special interest for Mexico. As Canadian actors were selective in their interests in the NAFTA debate, in some sections of this book they are only briefly touched upon.

While Mexico's environmental policy is an important issue of analysis, this study focuses on the interaction between transnational and national politics. The environmental policy of the Mexican government is thus primarily of interest as the outcome of political struggle, both at the national and the transnational level, and serves as a tool for understanding political change. A problem with assessing Mexico's environmental policy is its incoherency. As a result of the lack of priority given to ecological degradation by the Mexican government, there has been a considerable gap between policy on paper and in practice. In many instances, implementation of legislation and formal programmes has been weak, and actual efforts and results are hard to estimate.

Effects of the transnational NAFTA environment debate could be expected at any domestic political level, but this study is predominantly concerned with Mexico's federal politics and policy. Evidently, many initiatives for environmental protection stem from lower levels of government, as well as outside the government from citizens and NGOs. Here, the focus is on effects at the federal level, because of Mexico's centralist political system and the generally central responsibility of the state in environmental protection.

The information used for this study has been derived from different sources: documents from government agencies, NGOs, private sector organizations and other institutions that were produced in the NAFTA environment debate, information gathered in over sixty interviews with persons who were involved in the debate, and studies by other scholars. Information from interviews provided interesting background information and sometimes salient details. Interviews with Mexican government officials and other insiders proved useful to fill some gaps caused by the lack of useful and reliable documents of government agencies. As many interviewees requested or expected confidentiality, reference will be made not to their name but only to their position and the date of interview. Annex 1 gives a list of the interviewees' affiliations and dates of interview.

Prior to the analysis of the NAFTA environment debate, this book starts with two extensive introductory chapters on the Mexican context: one on the political economy of neoliberal restructuring, and the other on the evolution of environmental politics and policy. Chapter 1 describes the economic and political restructuring process that started during the presidency of Miguel de la Madrid Hurtado (1982-1988). Pushed and encouraged by multilateral banks and the US, and under pressure of a sequence of economic and financial crises, the Mexican government gradually came to adopt an economic liberalization strategy. Restructuring also occurred at the institutional level and within Mexico's political elite, where a group of young technocrats came to dominate. Under President Carlos Salinas de Gortari (1988-1994) these changes were consolidated, and their implications began to become clear. In particular, impact on presidential power, electoral processes, and avenues for political participation of social sectors and NGOs will be analysed.

In chapter 2, the evolution of environmental politics and policy in Mexico is reviewed. From the early 1970s until the early 1980s, the environment was of concern to a fairly limited number of scientists and NGOs, and government measures were largely symbolic. This changed with the administrative and regulatory reforms of President de la Madrid and his programme for popular mobilization on the environment. The combination of growing environmental activism and weak policy performance caused major political tensions in 1988. President Salinas would subsequently aim to obtain an environmental image. Apart from providing a historical background, this chapter describes the situation of Mexico's environmental politics and policy at the time the NAFTA environment debate started.

Quite unexpectedly, President Salinas and President George Bush announced in June 1990 that their countries were pursuing a free trade agreement, an initiative that was joined a few months later by Canada. With the Canada-US Free Trade Agreement already in force, and the limited Mexico-Canada ties, the plan was expected largely to serve Mexican and US interests. Apart from some expected losers, several US economic sectors and large Mexican companies were expected to gain from free trade and investment flows. Chapter 3 studies not only the interests linked to the NAFTA plan, but also the early critical environmental assessments of the plan. Trade and investment liberalization were expected to increase and to change production and consumption patterns. Moreover, a free trade agreement limits environmental policy freedom since environmental measures may hinder trade flows. Especially the issues concerning Mexico will be addressed.

Chapter 4 studies the organizations that brought the environment into the heart of the NAFTA debate. In late 1990, Mexican, US and Canadian NGOs started to criticize the NAFTA plans, and found sufficient common ground to establish transnational relations. These relations were an important source of information and supported NGOs in exploring the environmental issues linked to North American free trade. In a few months' time, environmental organizations in the three countries developed a list of concerns that they wanted addressed in the trade negotiations. This first, exploratory phase of the NAFTA environment debate lasted until May 1991, when environmental organizations were split into a moderate and a critical camp. As we shall see, a strategic move by the Bush administration caused a lasting division among US environmental organizations, which would have considerable transnational consequences.

The environmental critiques received considerable media, public and political attention, and when numerous members of the US Congress proved susceptible to environmentalist ideas, NAFTA proponents needed to react. Bush's strategic response involved a promise to deal with some of the environmental concerns and bought temporary support from Congress. From then onwards, the Mexican and US government speeded up bilateral border projects, while working together to improve Mexico's image in the US. Chapter 5 analyses these efforts and the arguments developed by NAFTA proponents that the agreement would not harm the region's environment nor the rights of governments to stringent environmental policy. Transnational environmentalist criticism thus provoked the major actors behind the NAFTA plans to develop a transnational position on the environment too. Moreover, a strong transnational lobby was set up.

Chapter 6 deals with the second and third phase of the NAFTA environment debate. It explains the clash between environmental NGOs and NAFTA proponents on the environmental provisions of the trade agreement and the environmental side agreement. An overview will be provided of the total set of environmental arrangements incorporated in and linked to the agreement, and the reactions to this NAFTA package. The immediate effects of the NAFTA environment debate on Mexico and on the contents of the agreement are also analysed in chapter 6. Mexico's environmental politics and policy changed considerably during the NAFTA debate, and an assessment is made of the influence of the NAFTA debate on these changes.

Finally, in the concluding chapter we return to the question of the effects of the NAFTA environment debate on Mexico's environmental politics and policy. This discussion concerns not only the immediate impact, but also the broader implications over a long time span. The most essential elements of the NAFTA environment debate, the NAFTA package and the changes in Mexico's environmental politics and policy are reviewed from the perspective of the economic and political restructuring process that Mexico gone passed through over the past years. This final analysis provides an understanding of the fundamental ways in which economic integration and transnational politics were linked, and how the transnational debate may affect Mexico's future.

CHAPTER I

Economic and Political Restructuring in Mexico

Mexico's participation in a free trade agreement with the US was an important step towards consolidating its economic restructuring programme. This programme was initiated after the debt crisis that hit Mexico in 1982. From the mid-1980s onwards, economic liberalization was the main policy objective of the Mexican government. The government sought economic cooperation with various countries and regions, but with the US above all. Whereas integration of Mexico in the US economy goes long way back, the signing of an agreement has reinforced this process and has embedded Mexico's policy of liberalization. This first chapter serves as the background to the analysis of the transnational debate on the North American Free Trade Agreement (NAFTA) and the environment, and the debate's effects on Mexico. It aims to provide the conceptual and empirical basis for understanding the economic and political changes in Mexico that preceded the NAFTA debate, and the global processes of transnationalization.

Describing the context of a political process that encompasses a multitude of political actors, economic developments, and interests at the national and transnational level is destined to be too long and yet incomplete. Therefore, the period to be studied here is restricted. The focus lies on the *sexenio* (six-year presidential period) of President Carlos Salinas de Gortari (1988-1994), who was predominantly responsible for the implementation of the restructuring programme, with various references to his predecessor President Miguel de la Madrid Hurtado (1982-1988).

This chapter discusses the various dimensions of Mexico's restructuring process. We start with the end of the story, the tumultuous last year of Salinas' presidency: 1994. A succession of political and economic disasters turned NAFTA's first year into a major Mexican disillusionment. Section 1 describes these political and economic events, and considers their relevance for this study. Next, in section 2 an attempt is made to come to grips with the nature of economic and political transnationalization world-wide and in Mexico. The third section deals with the introduction and consolidation of economic liberalization under de la Madrid and Salinas. Section 4 will then analyse the ways in which these economic changes have been linked to shifting roles of the Mexican state and the president. The consequences of all these changes on civil society and the private sector, and their political reactions to these changes, will be studied in section 5. Finally, conclusions will be drawn on the connections between these tendencies and their significance for the following chapters.

— 1.1 The 1994 experience —

In 1994, Mexico went through a succession of troubled events. The date of commencement of NAFTA, 1 January of that year, coincided with the occupation of several towns in the state of Chiapas by the Zapatista Army of National Liberation (EZLN), the *Zapatistas*. Their demands were both political and economic: democracy, greater local autonomy, and more federal support for the impoverished indigenous population. Even though after a few days the *Zapatistas* retreated to the jungle, they had impressively shown the extent of dissatisfaction among the poor of Mexico. A long process of negotiations between the Zapatista Army and the federal government began.

In March, Luis Donaldo Colosio, the PRI candidate for the presidential elections, was killed. This happened at an election meeting in Tijuana, Baja California, in front of a large crowd and several cameras. Only three months later the secretary-general of the PRI, José Francisco Ruiz Massieu, was murdered. Both assassinations were surrounded by many rumours and contrasting information, and were handled unprofessionally by the police and federal institutions. Instead of providing clarity, the official commissions that were created to investigate the incidents added to the confusion and uncertainty. More than anything else, the dealings of these commissions demonstrated the existence of fundamental conflicts within the PRI.

The problematic succession of Colosio similarly showed the lack of cohesion troubling the PRI. Ernesto Zedillo de Ponce León did not seem to have much support in the party and especially Manuel Camacho Solís, former mayor of Mexico City and at that time negotiating with the *Zapatistas*, was eager to contest Zedillo. Zedillo's weak charisma and persuasiveness came to the fore in his election campaign, in particular when compared to the candidate of the right-wing National Action Party (PAN), Fernando Cebolla. Zedillo was a weak candidate for presidential elections and his victory should be attributed more to the PRI's electoral machine than to his personal qualities.

THE PESO CRISIS

Before the end of the year, this political crisis was matched by a financial crisis that shocked both Mexico and the world. On 20 December, less than three weeks after the installation of Zedillo's cabinet, Mexico's Minister of Finance, Jaime Serra Puche, unexpectedly announced a 15 per cent widening of the exchange rate band of the peso, which allowed for a controlled devaluation of the overvalued currency. Only two days later, this measure turned out to be insufficient as capital was leaving the country at an enormous rate, and Mexico's Central Bank did not have the resources to continue supporting the exchange rate. Consequently, the government announced a floating exchange rate. The devaluation of the peso seemed unlimited as the exchange rate to the dollar fell from 3.45 on 21 December 1994 to 6.33 on 30 January 1995 (*Time* 13/11/95: 25). Simultaneously, Mexican shares fell considerably, while Mexican interest rates on loans had already gone up to 40 per cent at the end of December (*Financial Times* 28/xii/94: 15).

At an early stage, Serra Puche was fired for mismanagement, while the *Zapatistas* were blamed for causing the crisis, but the real causes were more structural. The direct cause was a combination of an overvalued peso and a balance of payments deficit which rendered Mexico incapable of paying back its short-term public debt. This problem stemmed from an unresolved long-term tension between exchange rate policy and macro-economic policy that had characterized the Salinas *sexenio*. President Salinas had attempted to have both low inflation rates and exchange rate stability. Inflation control and the inflow of external capital gave rise to the overvaluation of the peso. As a consequence, consumer imports were high at the cost of the demand for domestic products. Simultaneously, the high exchange rate of the peso limited options for expanding export. This situation contributed to decreasing levels of economic growth, falling from 4.5 per cent in 1990 to 0.4 per cent in 1993 (Lustig 1995: 375). A rise of the real exchange rate and a lack of productivity growth added to low growth rates. Despite international admiration for Salinas' economic restructuring policy, economic growth hardly surpassed the population growth rate (Krugman 1995: 40, 42; Lustig 1995).

Several other elements contributed to the peso crisis. Mexico is known for its relatively low levels of internal private savings, leaving the country more dependent on external capital than other countries. Between 1990 and 1994, the need for external capital was not a problem since foreigners were eager to invest in this emerging market, which seemed to be doing so well, but this external dependency turned into vulnerability at the time of growing political tensions. The assassination of Colosio and Massieu and the Zapatista revolt changed the perception of Mexico abroad. An external factor adding to this vulnerability was the rise of interest rates in the US (Lustig 1995).

These processes culminated in 1994, the year of the presidential elections. The balance of payments deficit (equalling $28 billion in 1994)[1] was to a large extent financed by external capital which had to be secured. However, two of the logical but politically unpopular mechanisms of achieving this, namely an interest rate rise or a peso devaluation, were unthinkable as they would severely harm the chances of the PRI candidate. In order to protect the inflow of foreign investment, the Mexican government aimed to reassure foreign investors by 'dollarizing' the short-term public debt. The government greatly extended the availability of *Tesobonos*, short-term government bonds that are indexed to US dollars but paid off in pesos (Lustig 1995).[2]

Traditionally in Mexico, devaluation takes place after the presidential elections and shortly before the new President comes into office. This act does no harm to the outgoing President (who is constitutionally obliged to give up involvement in Mexico's politics at any level), and it gives the newcomer a clean start. Salinas, however, broke with this precedent and did not use his last days in *los Pinos* (Mexico's presidential residence) to devalue the peso. Probably, he was unwilling to accept a stain on his image as the successful economic reformer because of his prospect of becoming president of the World Trade Organization (WTO). As a result, his successor Zedillo was left to deal with the overvalued peso.

Evidence suggests that it was first Mexican capital that fled the country. Compared to foreigners, Mexicans probably need less signals to recognize fluidity, despite the optimistic official messages. After the devaluation, foreign investors too learned about Mexico's real economic situation. Until then, Mexico's entry to the General Agreement on Tariffs and Trade (GATT) in 1986, and to NAFTA and the Organization for Economic Cooperation and Development (OECD) in 1994, were internationally held as guarantees of the success of its economic reforms. The late, sudden and unexpected devaluation of the peso and the revelation of the problematic financial situation of the Mexican government severely harmed the rosy image. Investors were shocked and frustrated to find out the truth, and felt wronged by Mexico's leaders. Surprisingly, even among top officials of the International Monetary Fund (IMF) there was a sense

---

1   The dollar sign refers to US dollars.
2   The share of Tesobonos as a percentage of the total of short-term government bonds held by foreigners increased from 6 per cent in December 1993 to 70 per cent in December 1994. Simultaneously, the value of capital invested in Tesobonos rose from $2 billion to $29 billion (Lustig 1995).

of frustration at the government's misleading information on the economic advances (interview with Onno Ruding, *Management Team* 15/XII/95: 60, 62; Lustig 1995: 282; *The Economist* 26/VIII/95: 12, 69).

INTERNATIONAL SUPPORT

The peso crisis turned rapidly into an international issue. Many shareholders were removing their capital from emerging markets world-wide, and exchange rate instability occurred in the rest of Latin America and in Asian and European countries. Despite the evident interest of the US in Mexico's stability, US President Clinton was unable to get Congressional approval for a $40 billion financial injection for Mexico. Instead, through an executive order he arranged a $20 billion package of loans through the Exchange Stabilization Fund of the Treasury. The international financial community also came up with funding to stabilize the international financial markets, although only after serious disputes. The warnings of IMF president Michel Camdessus of "a true world catastrophe" did not convince unwilling European countries, and he had to force them to not oppose a $17.8 billion support package for Mexico by threatening to resign (*Financial Times* 8/11/95). Without this unequalled international support, Camdessus argued, the peso crisis would become the starting-point of a world-wide withdrawal of investment in emerging markets. In addition, European Central Banks were made to join a $10 billion credit to Mexico by the Bank of International Settlements. In short, at the end of January 1995, despite strong resistance, the international community provided Mexico with over $50 billion of loans to deal with the peso crisis (*Financial Times* 1/11/95: 6).[3]

The background to the international commotion over the seemingly very Mexican crisis is the global domination of the so-called 'Washington consensus' since the early 1990s. The Washington consensus is the new view of development held by the US government, the IMF, World Bank, and important think tanks, investment bankers and finance ministers. This view takes free trade and low inflation as the recipe for economic growth. Paul Krugman argues that the Washington consensus was not sustained by empirical evidence, but that for some years the reasoning was 'self-supporting'. With the major

---

3 European countries doubted the systemic threat of the peso crisis, and argued that they were forced to pay to prevent financial losses of US banks and institutions. Moreover, the expensive international 'life-boat' for Mexico was criticized as a moral hazard for providing an example of the international community's being willing to clear up someone else's mess.

public and private financial leaders favouring free-market and sound monetary policy in developing countries, the emerging markets were internationally perceived as a good investment. This enthusiasm was partly a speculative bubble, but nonetheless reinforced the conventional wisdom that the new policy worked. Moreover, a political economy cycle came into being in which developing countries could be persuaded that the new policy was financially rewarding. And for some time, due to the speculative bubble and the conventional wisdom, it was (Krugman 1995: 28-37).

With the peso crisis, Mexico for the second time influenced the Washington consensus. At the beginning of the 1990s, Mexico was presented as the role model of developing countries' ability to move up towards a position among industrialized nations. Although in reality Mexico's trade liberalization of the late 1980s did not have immediate results on the National Product, and the 1990 debt reduction did not make that much of a difference either, international investors were convinced of the coming success. With this gap between Mexico's reality and the perception of foreign investors, a confidence shock was inevitable. The peso crisis, then, made the speculative bubble burst and immediately harmed the world-wide euphoria on emerging markets. Whereas trade liberalization and low inflation rates are still promoted by institutions like the World Bank as the best means for development, the fading of a direct financial pay-off of such policies will render them politically less self-evident (Krugman 1995: 29, 38-40, 43).

RESEARCH IMPLICATIONS

Although one should not make judgements based on these political and economic crises alone, the experiences of 1994 provide us with several indications of Mexico's political situation at the time of the NAFTA debate. First, the assassinations of Colosio and Massieu and the subsequent investigations showed serious discord within the PRI and the perversity of various powerful persons.[4] Information on this discord is limited but points to a crumbling internal cohesion, in particular because of conflicts over Salinas' restructuring policy (and the lack of short-term economic returns). Secondly, the ways in which some of the problems came into being and evolved indicate that a small elite, and most

4 This assessment is supported by a range of scandals that occurred after 1994, in particular Carlos Salinas' exile, and the involvement of his brother Raúl Salinas as well as high government and PRI officials in narcotics and fraud.

importantly the President, can play a determining role in Mexico's politics. Consequently, personal positions and relations of the political elite need to be considered when studying these politics.

The 1994 events also shed a light on the nature of modern Mexico's interdependence of politics and economics, and the interaction between national and international processes. The continuous mutual influence of politics and economics shows the need for incorporating major economic developments in an analysis of political processes in Mexico. Likewise, the peso crisis has illustrated that understanding Mexico's political situation requires taking into account its international integration, whereas studying the internal politics is equally a prerequisite for an insight in Mexico's international relations. These tendencies support the choice for an international political economy approach towards analysing the effects of the transnational NAFTA environment debate on Mexico.

Due to the international interests that were linked to Mexico's economic well-being, Mexico received unprecedented foreign financial support despite considerable resistance to such a package. Primarily, the heavy US financial penetration of Mexico was at stake, followed by the possible trade and migration consequences of a new Mexican crisis on its northern neighbour. Although President Clinton could not convince the Republican-dominated Congress to lend $40 billion, by circumventing Congress he nevertheless made the US contribute heavily to the support package. With less success, several European countries attempted to stay on the side-line. They questioned the threat of the peso crisis to financial markets world-wide and did not want to pay for irresponsible behaviour of Mexico's political elite, but the IMF exerted sufficient pressure for them to give in.

The fact that with the peso crisis the Mexican elite transferred part of the burden to the international community is of great political importance. The seemingly endless chain of economic crises since the mid-1970s has left the majority of Mexico's population poorer and more vulnerable. The peso crisis implied a virtual end to consumer imports (for the middle-class), and further decreased the living standards of the poor. But now, for the first time, foreigners felt just as cheated by the Mexican government as the Mexicans did. Moreover, the peso crisis indicates that the financial liberalization of developing countries not only renders them more vulnerable to international processes, but that, vice versa, the international community is also becoming more vulnerable to the policies of these countries. Last but not least, the political and economic crises that hit Mexico in 1994 contradict the image of its restructuring process as pictured by its internal and external proponents. Evidently, the status of a First World country and a democratic system was premature.

— 1.2 Processes of transnationalization —

For a profound understanding of the importance of NAFTA for Mexico, the economic restructuring process that laid the foundation for Mexico's NAFTA entry should be assessed within the context of broader international developments. This does not imply that Mexico's restructuring was simply imposed from the outside. Basically, any state policy is the result of domestic and international pressures, shaped by the political elite. In this respect we may think of the state as a transmission mechanism, which in reacting to external stimuli internalizes these stimuli (Palan 1994: 61). It is interesting, then, to analyse the interaction between the state, domestic pressures and external influences.

In the late twentieth century, this interaction has been affected by a set of more or less world-wide changes that have been lumped together as globalization. Cox (1991) provides a useful analysis of globalization as the synthesis of six major interlinked developments. The first development is the internationalization of production. Second, the state is also in the midst of an internationalization process in which adaptation to the world economy has replaced domestic development and welfare as the prior logic of policy-making. Third, a new pattern of uneven development has come into being. Using the typology of a Third World no longer seems adequate since these countries have been divided into a group that is able to become part of global production as providers of cheap labour and/or natural resources, and another group that is virtually excluded. Fourth, transnational finance has expanded rapidly since the 1970s, and both governments and corporations have come to depend more on transnational private banks. In the context of the international economic crisis and debt problems, governments have become more susceptible to the conditions of these bankers. A fifth element of globalization is the migration taking place from South to North. And finally, monetarism and supply-side economics are dominating the mind-set of governments around the globe (Cox 1991: 336-40).

Although these elements of globalization are all applicable to Mexico, not each of them will be addressed below. The inadequacy of the typology of a Third World is evident, with Mexico being among the developing countries that are included in global production. Also the pattern of South-North migration fits the Mexican case well, despite the many US patrols and fences at the border. These two issue will not be discussed any further. The analysis below pays attention to the processes of transnationalization of production and finance, and the domination of adaption to the world economy and monetarism in government policy. General theories of internationalization or transnationalization are linked to assessments of Mexico's role in this process. As argued in the introduction, when referring to processes involving non-state actors the term transnationalization is preferred to internationalization, and will therefore be used except where it might cause confusion.

TRANSNATIONALIZATION OF PRODUCTION

The economic restructuring process was introduced in Mexico after Import Substitution Industrialization (ISI) stopped producing the successes it had scored during the period of 1940-70. The introduction of ISI had marked the end of Mexico's phase of revolution and the start of a phase dominated by the interests of the bourgeoisie. The ISI model was the Latin American version of Keynesianism, and could be categorized as state-led capitalism, mixed economy or nationalist capitalism. As the spearhead of the ISI model, industry was seen to have the largest growth potential. The first economic objective of the Mexican state was to stimulate and protect a national industrial sector that produced for the internal market. As a result, industry's share of total output rose from 21.5 per cent in 1950 to 29.4 per cent in 1970 (Lustig 1992: 14).

Although the aim of ISI was development through replacing the import of manufactured goods by national products, Mexico remained pragmatic about transnational production. While having an extensive system of tariff and non-tariff barriers, and strict regulations regarding foreign capital in companies, Mexico was already for years a host country to several Transnational Companies (TNCs).[5] The main reason for TNCs to enter Mexico during the ISI years was production for the domestic market. Like the national industry, TNCs profited from the protected internal market and government support (also in the form of controlled wages). Especially in the small but powerful sector of intermediate, durable and capital goods that depends on the use of modern technology, foreign investment was important. At the end of the 1970s, around 50 per cent of total manufacturing production and about 65 per cent of intermediate and durable goods production was generated by Foreign Direct Investment (FDI) (Corro Barrientos 1991: 666-7; Weintraub 1990: 100-3).

---

5   For instance, in the 1950s the annual average of Foreign Direct Investment in Mexico accounted for $103.8 million (Weintraub 1990: 102). Mexico's foreign investment control laws, which restricted entry to economic sectors and limited foreign capital to a 49 per cent share, were *de facto* often lifted in the interest of TNCs because of the need for foreign investment in sectors of high priority to the government. More than the financial inflow, the technological input and international trade generated by such investments were considered important (Ortiz 1994: 158; Weintraub 1990: 100-2).

A major step towards transnational production was the creation of the *ma-quiladora* programme in 1965. The programme aimed to encourage export manufacturing in the border region with the US by taxing only the value added in Mexico of the export of assembled imported parts. Direct incentives for this programme were the liberalization of US customs regulations in 1962 and the end of the US programme for temporary Mexican agricultural labour in 1964. Indirectly, the international trend starting in the late 1950s to transfer labour-intensive industries from developed to developing countries also inspired Mexico's policy change (Fernández Jilberto and Hogenboom 1996: 144; cf. Sklair 1989: 1-21).

Whereas until the 1970s private (direct) foreign investment in Mexico combined import substitution with exporting, the 1980s showed a decisive move of TNCs towards export-processing assembly production. The major share of this export production has taken place in the *maquiladora* industry along Mexico's northern border. Already between 1975 and 1985, the most dynamic industrial export sector in Mexico was that of goods based on advanced technology, such as computers, office machinery and automobile engines. The *maquiladora* sector has experienced spectacular growth rates since the middle of the 1980s, and the increase of Mexico's manufacturing exports has been closely linked to the activities of TNCs. In fact, they have been responsible for about half of Mexico's manufacturing export such as automobiles and computers (Alba Vega 1993: 226-7; Pastor and Wise 1994: 464; Sklair 1992: 91).

The predominantly US-owned *maquiladoras* have been of great importance for Mexico-US economic integration. Through the *maquiladora* sector, transnational production-sharing arrangements gained momentum. In its traditional form, this industry is based on the comparative advantage of cheap Mexican labour. Since the late 1980s also new types of *maquiladoras* that are more capital and technology intensive have been created. Between 1985 and 1989, the share of the *maquiladoras* in Mexico's export to the US went up from 29 to 45 per cent, reflecting their increased economic significance as well as the growth of intra-industry trade (Eden and Appel Molot 1993: 23-47).

Mexico increasingly liberalized foreign direct investment, revealing the growing expectations of the role of this capital for economic growth through technological innovation and international competitiveness.[6] The US share of FDI

---

6 Figures on the extent of penetration of Mexican production by foreign capital as a whole differ widely. The 1989 liberalization decree aimed to increase the share of foreign direct investments in total investment from 10 to 20 per cent (Ros 1992: 60). Figures provided by Ortiz (1994: 169), show that 1991 FDI in services and in industry accounted for respectively 37.4 and 54.2 per cent of total investment, whereas in agriculture and

in Mexico has always been large, but as a percentage of total FDI in Mexico it has slowly but steadily gone down from 70.1 per cent in 1975 to 61.7 per cent in 1992. These data show that US direct investment in Mexico has expanded less than FDI as a whole. Interestingly, the relatively small share of Canada in FDI in Mexico also went down during the period 1975-93 from 2.9 to 1.5 per cent. Although NAFTA is likely to reverse this trend and strengthen the regionalization of Mexico's economy, prior to the agreement Mexico's liberalization gave way to somewhat less regional dependency (Ortiz 1994: 165-9).

Mexico's trade liberalization initiatives were extended in 1985, the reasons for which will be explained further on. In a few years, a rapid deregulation of imports occurred. Tariff levels were halved, the maximum tariff level was reduced from 100 per cent to 20 per cent (while Mexico's protocol for joining the GATT allowed for a 50 per cent maximum level), and in 1990 only 19 per cent of domestic production was covered by import licensing as compared to 92 per cent in 1985 (Lustig 1992: 177-20). At this stage, fossil fuels, transportation equipment and agriculture were largely excluded from liberalization. With respect to exports, many direct export subsidies were cancelled or lowered. As Mexico's former minister of finance, Jesús Silva-Herzog F. (1991: 33), has put it: from being a relatively protective area, Mexico became "one of the most open economies of the world".

Mexico's entry to the GATT in 1986 and to the NAFTA in 1994 have been crucial for embedding economic liberalization. Mexico's chief negotiator on NAFTA, Herminio Blanco Mendoza (1994: 20), argues that the two external reasons for the position of Mexico towards international trade agreements are the globalization of the world economy through block formation and the intensive competition for capital. These two tendencies were indeed the major point of argument for defending the policy change; trade liberalization was presented as more or less inevitable. Moreover, by Mexico's membership of GATT and NAFTA its political elite has been able to give its trade liberalization programme a structural character. Reversing this programme is likely to violate these agreements, and annulling Mexico's membership would be strongly resisted by external and internal actors with free trade interests. In this respect, free trade agreements can be perceived as a conditioning framework, as Grinspun and Kreklewich (1993) have argued.

---

cattle this figure was 0.4 per cent. Kehoe (1994: 22-3), maintains that "Mexico still has a long way to go in terms of receiving foreign investment before it becomes a major recipient by international standards".

Both the transnationalization of production and of finance concern capital movements. The major difference lies in that the former has to do with productive capital which implies a direct link with production, while financial capital takes the shape of financial services such as banking, insurance and stockbroking. The liberalization of capital flows by many countries has produced an increasing mobility of financial capital. As a result of its more indirect link to production and its increased mobility, financial capital can react more rapidly to changing government policies than productive capital can (Gill and Law 1993: 106-7).

In the 1970s, financial capital was pouring into Mexico. The reason for this was Mexico's stagnating industrial growth and the knowledge of its large oil reserves. The Mexican government contracted massive foreign loans and increased its petrol sales. In 1971 public foreign debt accounted for $6.7 billion, rising to $15.7 billion in 1975 and $33.8 in 1980, whereas private foreign debt between 1978 and 1980 increased from $7.2 billion to $16.9 billion (Lustig 1992: 19, 23, 32). As Barkin (1990: 95) explains, "[a]lready an attractive borrower and a favorite of the official multilateral financial agencies ..., in the mid-1970s Mexico became a magnet for international lending as a result of the announcement of vast petroleum reserves".

Because of rising interest rates[7] and falling oil prices world-wide during the early 1980s, Mexico's increased external debt only intensified its economic problems, and in 1982 the Mexican government could no longer pay its debt services. As individuals and companies feared for hyperinflation, Mexico experienced a massive capital flight. This debt crisis was followed by years of debt renegotiations in combination with economic adjustment and additional lending, in all of which the IMF played a central role. On the one hand, the IMF and the US government had to exert a lot of pressure to get the private banks to provide credits. On the other hand, insisting that the debt be serviced "has favored the financial institutions at the expense of the productive sector" (Weintraub 1990: 152). Moreover, the international management of the debt crisis favoured commercial banks and creditor governments which had provided loans without adequate supervision.[8] All in all, between 1980 and 1990 Mexico's

---

7   The increase of international interest rates was the result of a restrictive monetary policy by the US, and the gradual transformation of the US from the leading international creditor into the largest debtor country (Weintraub 1990: 135).

8   The peso crisis demonstrated that international and transnational banks as well as foreign shareholders had rapidly forgotten the lesson of 1982.

total external debt nearly doubled, its public sector external debt more than doubled, whereas its debt burden as a percentage of GDP went up from 26.0 to 41.7 per cent (Lustig 1992: 32-3, 60; Weintraub 1990: 135, 140, 147, 152).

Commercial banks have held a large share of Mexico's public foreign debt. Between 1985 and 1988, about three-quarters of the public sector's foreign debt were to commercial banks (Weintraub 1990: 137). In general, private bank lending is characterized by higher interest rates and shorter terms than official lending (i.e. from the World Bank), and less concern with political and social considerations. The most important foreign commercial creditors were US banks. Because of US government pressure and the banks' interest in protecting their portfolios, US private banks have had a leadership role for new bank lending to Mexico (Weintraub 1990: 138-41).[9]

Finally, portfolio investment (i.e. in shares and bonds) in Mexico is very popular among foreigners. Foreign portfolio investment was allowed in 1989 and since then its value has passed foreign direct investment. In the third year after this policy change, foreign portfolio investment accounted for 60 per cent of total foreign investment in Mexico. The problem with portfolio investments is their volatile character, reacting strongly to political changes, the behaviour of global stock markets, and investment opportunities elsewhere. As in most other areas, portfolio investment in Mexico is dominated by the US (Vidal 1992: 31; Vidal 1993: 10-1).

Reviewing the above figures of Mexico's FDI, the *maquiladora* industry, foreign portfolio investment, and foreign credits, we may conclude that trans-nationalization of production and finance in Mexico predominantly concerns US involvement. Indeed, even before NAFTA "practically every sector of the Mexican economy [was] already highly integrated with the US economy" (Székely 1991: 221). This integration has been most visible in manufacturing and services, such as food processing, chemicals, machinery, and electrical, electronic and transportation equipment. However, by further strengthening its economic dependency on the US through NAFTA, Mexico has become more vulnerable to US recessions and financial crises (Correa 1994: 28; Ortiz 1994: 168-70; Weintraub 1990: 105).

---

9 With NAFTA, the tendency towards transnationalization of Mexico's financial sector in which the US dominates is only to be extended. Small and local financial intermediaries are unlikely to survive regional competition, whereas even those that are linked to major economic groups in Mexico may have to struggle for survival (Correa 1994: 22, 25).

TRANSNATIONALIZATION OF THE STATE

Transnationalization of production and finance implies an increasing sensitivity of states to external developments. Independent national economic policies lose effectiveness as TNCs and transnational financial flows move more freely, while the national economic space loses its role as the starting point for growth and development. It may be argued that "as states lose control over the national economy as an object of economic management, they get involved in managing the process of internationalization itself and thereby further undermine national economic autonomy" (Jessop 1992: 6). However, the state is not a passive actor; on the contrary it plays an important role in the process of economic liberalization. Moreover, as the peso crisis showed, transnationalization also produces greater external sensitivity to domestic events. The transnationalization of the state thus not only involves a state increasingly internalizing the external, but to some extent also externalizing the internal.

More than TNCs, the transnational financial markets are the principal external constraint on governments in designing their policies. This has to do with the greater 'fluidity' (mobility and instability) of financial capital as compared to productive capital. Governments depend on the financial markets to finance their policies, and a fundamental policy change may result in a huge selling of public and private (short-term) portfolios. The global economic recession and the growth of both the mobility and scale of transnational capital in the late twentieth century have contributed to the competition between states for capital by providing an attractive investment climate. Helped by the increasing global acceptance of the view that liberalization is the best means for economic growth and development, transnational (private) and international (governmental) capital demands a policy of economic openness from indebted governments. Commercial banks have strong links among themselves and with international banks like the IMF and the World Bank, forming well-developed transnational financial networks which are powerful vis-à-vis individual governments (Cox 1991: 347; Gill 1993: 261-2; Gill and Law 1993: 101, 103, 106-7).

In the case of Mexico, the transnational financial community had to wait until 1985 before ideas of structural change seemed to gain sufficient support among domestic policy-makers. From 1982 to 1985, the Mexican government had no choice but to discipline its budget. The early cutting of subsidies and the selling of some state-owned companies, known as parastatals, combined with a loosening of the restrictive import and export regime, implied a dismantling of ISI structures. Mexico's debt management provided Mexico with the image of a model debtor.[10] However, it took a few years before there was genuine internal support for neoliberal restructuring, while the mounted external pressure remained necessary to 'convince' groups that resisted such policy (see also sections 3 and 4).[11]

The shift in the government stand came after the economic problems that hit Mexico in early 1985. The World Bank—like the IMF—started pushing Mexico, and posed trade liberalization as a condition of a $500 million loan. This combination of a problematic situation, external pressure by the World Bank and IMF, expectations of private foreign creditors, and the debate on the issue within de la Madrid's cabinet resulted in a policy change. In July 1985, de la Madrid announced an acceleration of structural change, including a significant liberalization of trade regulations by replacing trade permits with tariffs. Also accession to GATT was prepared in 1985 and formalized in 1986. Both in 1985 and in 1987, the World Bank provided Mexico with a $500 million loan (Cronin 1994: 20-5; Heredia and Purcell 1994: 5).

There is considerable scholarly disagreement with respect to the role of domestic and foreign actors in Mexico's liberalization process. On the one hand, there are studies claiming an important external influence (Cronin 1994; Heredia and Purcell 1994; Roett 1991). Conversely, Centeno (1994: 72) rejects instrumental links between international capital and the Mexican political elite as the basis of the adjustment policies, and rather sees the crisis and the elite's perception of it as the reason for change. Although the influence of external actors should not be exaggerated, it is likely that their pressure and support did contribute to the gradual dominance of proponents of restructuring within Mexico's political elite.

The process of the transnationalization of a state can also be deducted from the balance of government institutions. Transnationalization implies an increasing domination of institutions dealing with international economic affairs, such as ministries of finance, agencies of foreign trade and investment, and offices of presidents, at the cost of agencies dealing with internal affairs

---

10 Under de la Madrid, Mexico increased its debt service, which in 1988 accounted for 60 per cent of the public sector's budget (Centeno 1994: 198).

11 The World Bank considered trade liberalization the central element of structural adjustment, but during de la Madrid's first year liberalization was not even considered. The Bank of Mexico was at that time the only governmental agency in favour of neoliberal restructuring, and started advocating a more open trade strategy from 1984 onwards, while being in close contact with the World Bank. The Ministries of Agriculture, of Trade and Industry, and of Mines and Parastatal Industry opposed such a policy change. The Treasury and the Ministry of Planning and Budget took up a middle position, while the President himself was in doubt. As a result of this division, there was a consensus for a slow and selective liberalization process (Cronin 1994: 11-20).

(Cox 1991: 337; 1987: 228). In Mexico, institutional restructuring as performed by de la Madrid and Salinas strongly resembles this characterization of the transnationalization of the state. The banking and planning ministries that were dominated by the new political elite of so-called *tecnoburócratas* or technocrats gained influence at the cost of 'protectionist' ministries such as of industry, agriculture, and labour. Especially the planning ministry's authority over expenditure provided its top officials with command over Mexico's economic policy. Economic management became a highly presidential field of policy under Salinas, which enabled further control by technocrats with their predominantly economist qualifications (Centeno 1994: 91, 95; Centeno and Maxfield: 72-81; Cronin 1994: 24; Pastor and Wise 1994: 478).

The transnationalization of the Mexican state has affected its regional position. Mexico's entry to the GATT; its relatively good performance under Salinas in the eyes of the World Bank and IMF; as well as its entry to NAFTA and to the prestigious OECD as the first developing country all show the genuine wish of Mexico's new political elite to become part of the transnational network for capitalist development and liberalized production and finance. While Mexico's integration with the US is of high priority in this respect, the importance of Mexico to the US is also enormous and combines the interest of political and social stability south of the 2,000 mile border with the economic interests of US business in the Mexican market. The improvement in Mexico-US relations from the early 1980s onwards is linked to Mexico's Latin American relations in several ways. Whitehead (1991: 256) has rightly argued that Mexico's post-1985 economic policy involves a move away from a Latin American posture and towards a North American solution to its development problems. Simultaneously, Mexico became an example (again) for other Latin American countries. In particular since its NAFTA entry, Mexico seems to be viewed as a stepping stone for Latin America to the US.

TRANSNATIONAL IDEOLOGY AND ACTORS

Processes of transnationalization of finance and the state have been linked to two other phenomena: the increasing acceptance of liberal economic values, and the formation of a loose network of actors that promote these values. Based on liberal economic thought, the belief has grown world-wide from the 1970s onwards that progress above all requires market efficiency; free trade and investment; innovation; flexible production, labour and exchange rates; and controlled inflation and public expenditure. According to this view, the state's principal economic functions need reorientation from welfare to flexibility, international competitiveness and supply-side economics. It also implies a stronger role for the private sector vis-à-vis the public sector (Gill 1993: 262-3; Jessop 1992: 6).

World-wide, there is a large number of people connected to processes of transnationalization through their intellectual, political and/or economic roles, activities and interests. Among them are: top owners and key managers of TNCs; central and international bankers; leading politicians, academics, (government and international) officials, and businessmen; and people affiliated to trans-national production and finance, such as consultants and lawyers. Persons linked to international financial management have especially become more important transnationally. This group consists not only of leaders of transnational com-mercial and international official banks, central banks, and linked ministries (i.e. of economics and finance), but also encompasses intellectuals who support a liberalization of finance who are part of think-tanks and prestigious universities (Cox 1987: 359-60; Gill 1993: 261, 265-6; Sklair 1991: 62; Sklair 1992: 95).

Although there are evidently strong transnational links between these per-sons promoting globalization, economic liberalization and consumerism, de-fining their relations is problematic. Others have labelled them: transnational capitalist class (Gill 1990; Sklair 1991); transnational managerial class (Cox 1987); and an emerging neoliberal transnational historic bloc (Gill 1993). Sklair (1992: 95) argues that "[t]he concept of the transnational capitalist class implies that there is one central transnational capitalist class that makes system-wide decisions, and that it connects with the TCC in each locality, region and country". Despite clear indications of the growing importance of transnational politics, Sklair's conceptualization seems to exaggerate this tendency at the cost of undervaluing intergovernmental and domestic political processes. In addi-tion, the definition of a transnational class, and to a lesser extent the neo-Gramscian concept of a transnational historic bloc, lends too much consistency to these transnational relations. Notwithstanding the fact that these persons have played central roles in the growing global acceptance of neoliberal values and practices, as well as economic and political transnationalization, their unity is neither self-evident nor automatic. What has come into being is an inter-linked set of alliances among institutions and persons with similar views and interests, who meet at meetings of international organizations, business meet-ings, negotiations, et cetera. Although economic liberalization is the binding ideology among these persons, they are also bound by other, distinct loyalties, so that their ideas about the materialization of desired changes are likely to diverge.

In Mexico, the neoliberal agenda of economic integration has been pushed by so-called technocrats, who are internationally oriented and often trained in the US in economics and administration. This new political elite within the state-party system gained considerable influence during the *sexenios* of de la Madrid and Salinas. The technocrats' rise was the outcome of a fierce struggle within the PRI against the former dominant *políticos* who opposed neoliberal restructuring. While co-existing in the PRI, these two fractions have been strongly fighting each other for Mexico's development model and for power (see also section 4).

The rise of technocrats was partly the result of a strong external insistence on neoliberal economic restructuring, predominantly after Mexico's 1982 debt crisis. Initially primarily concentrated in the Bank of Mexico, technocrats seemed the most capable of dealing with the economic crisis that followed the stagnation of growth and debt problems. Mexico was in great need of capital, and as domestic savings were insufficient foreign creditors won ground. Private foreign banks laid down that additional funding could only come on the basis of structural policy adjustment. Most directly, the World Bank was actively and ceaselessly pushing Mexico towards a policy of liberalization by conditioning new loans. In addition, since the mid-1980s there has been an ongoing dialogue and strong working relation between the World Bank and the Bank of Mexico.[12] Technocrats have been concentrated in planning and banking agencies and the presidential office, which increasingly dominated Mexico's policy and from whose ranks de la Madrid and Salinas originated (Centeno 1994: 64, 71-7, 96, 199; Centeno and Maxfield 1992: 78; Cronin 1994: 13, 18-25).

Realism and ideological homogeneity have been central elements of the functioning of Mexico's technocratic elite. Within the government as well as towards society, the neoliberal programme has been presented as the only option possible to overcome the crisis, referring to the exigencies of the international economy. By claiming the inevitability of economic restructuring, the new elite produced an ideological homogeneity inhibiting internal criticism. This homogeneity can also be traced back to the educational background of its members. A majority received their training in US universities and Mexican private schools, especially in economics and administration, and were educated in the liberal and neo-classical traditions (Centeno and Maxfield 1992: 68, 84; Centeno 1994: 219-20; Cronin 1994: 26; Pastor and Wise 1994: 482).[13]

---

12 According to the World Bank (1994b), since 1982 relations with the "core of the country's intellectual/technocratic elite" have been positive, and the Bank estimates that through its analytical support it has "at times influenced directly or indirectly the course of Mexican policymaking".

13 Interestingly, several of the new elite's members have combined their political career with teaching in private Mexican universities, which has provided them with a continuous stream of young, like-thinking economists (Centeno and Maxfield 1992: 68).

In sum, the economic and political transformation taking place in Mexico since the early 1980s has been linked to various processes of transnationalization. Transnationalization of Mexico's production has a long history, whereas the transnationalization of Mexico's finance speeded up from the 1970s onwards. Linked to the economic crises that Mexico experienced in the 1980s, these processes contributed to a gradual transnationalization of the Mexican state. External pressure for neoliberal restructuring helped the upcoming technocrats in their fight for political influence. In the following sections we will further examine Mexico's neoliberal restructuring, and the political changes within the state-party system and between state and civil society taking place under Salinas.

— 1.3 Mexico's neoliberal development model —

The Import Substitution Industrialization model that was the basis of Mexico's development between the 1940s and the 1970s implied a strong state that interfered in key economic sectors and activities. The thrust of the model was to develop a national industry by active government support and protection against external threats, especially through reserving the domestic market for national producers. The Mexican government directed the economy by means of import controls, parastatal companies, limits to foreign investment, price controls and domination over banking. This powerful state control was supposed to produce economic growth that would benefit society as a whole.

While ISI, the Latin American version of Keynesianism, advanced development in Latin America as a whole, especially in the case of Mexico it proved a successful model. With the achievement of an average annual growth of 7.0 per cent during the 1950s and 8.6 per cent during the 1960s, these years were considered as the period of stable growth and stabilizing development (Lustig 1992: 15). Other Latin American countries were anxious to learn from the 'Mexican miracle'.

The debt crisis of 1982 marked the definitive end of the ISI period in Mexico. According to some analyses, the crisis was attributable to the ISI model that had supported inefficient production and irrational allocation of resources. Therefore, it was argued, ISI had to be abandoned and replaced by a model in which market forces, instead of the state, determine economic activities. In addition, liberalization was to solve the ISI problems of a limited internal market and rising costs of imported capital goods. Conversely, others maintain that not the development model of ISI but macroeconomic mismanagement during the 1970s caused the crisis. According to this view, the combination of Mexico's short-sighted domestic policy and unfavourable international tendencies was the main reason for Mexico's problems (cf. Lustig 1992: 3).[14] Even if ISI had been the primary cause of the 1982 crisis, a simultaneous abandoning of state protection and state intervention runs a risk of throwing out the baby with the bath water. As the 'Asian tigers' have demonstrated, the combination of an economic orientation towards the world market and active state intervention can lay the foundation for the successful industrialization of a (previously) developing country.

DE LA MADRID'S INITIATIVES

The 1982 debt crisis contributed to the victory of the supporters of a fundamental restructuring of Mexico's economy based on neoliberal principles. The economic restructuring initiated under President de la Madrid (1982-88) and consolidated by President Salinas (1988-94) meant a new role for the Mexican state in the economy. In the beginning, de la Madrid's proposals were still rather moderate and were permeated by old-style nationalist populist discourse. He initially attempted to make a gradual move from the old to the new model, because a sudden shift in economic control away from the state would entail wide-scale popular suffering. Moreover, economic restructuring was still heavily resisted by strong fractions within the PRI. De la Madrid started out by privatizing smaller parastatals, but restructuring at other levels only moved slowly. Halfway through de la Madrid's *sexenio*, however, a new economic crisis set in and internal and external pressures forced him to go ahead with an unambiguous introduction of neoliberal policy.

From 1985 onwards, Mexico's economic policy consisted predominantly of deregulation and liberalization, partly in relation to GATT entry in 1986. GATT membership implied more openness for imports, and protection in the form of tariffs rather than quantitative restrictions. De la Madrid's export promotion programme, which directly supported some 100 large exporting companies,

---

14 Although the ISI model may not have been the predominant cause of the 1982 crisis, ISI nevertheless had several deficiencies. Velasco Arregui, for instance, describes how the domestic industrial elite, promoted during the era of ISI by the Mexican state with the help of transnational capital, has been responsible for an inefficient and unbalanced manufacturing sector. The step from consumer goods to capital goods production was never taken, leaving Mexico dependent on imports of machinery and equipment. Moreover, despite the impressive growth rates, the industrial sector proved unable to absorb the large numbers of workers leaving rural Mexico (Velasco Arregui 1994: 164).

was abolished because of GATT regulations and World Bank demands. Mexico's entry into GATT equally put an end to many populist and nationalist regulations. Subsidies were cut back, import restrictions limited, and banking deregulated. In addition, opportunities for foreign direct investment were extended to more sectors, and larger shares of FDI were allowed (Cypher 1990: 181-9; Lustig 1992: 78-82, 96-132; Weintraub 1990: 89-90).

Finally, in 1987 de la Madrid opted for an unorthodox approach of shock treatments to stabilize the economy.[15] The Pact of Economic Solidarity between the state, the business and agricultural sectors and labour was an important element of this unorthodox programme. The signatories agreed on trade liberalization, wage control, and an ongoing correction of fiscal and monetary policy. Shortly after Salinas came into office, de la Madrid's pact was replaced by the comparable Pact for Stability and Economic Growth, which aimed to achieve economic growth through private investment, export of manufactured goods, public investment in infrastructure, and an expansion of the domestic market (Alvarez Béjar and Mendoza Pichardo 1993: 34-6; Aspe 1993: 22-4; Lustig 1992: 51).

RESTRUCTURING UNDER SALINAS

President Salinas aimed to complete the restructuring process initiated by his predecessor.[16] Important external support for Salinas' policy came in the form

---

15 According to Pedro Aspe, Minister of Finance and Public Credit under Salinas, it was a deliberate strategy to first have the orthodox fiscal adjustment programme and next the unorthodox shock treatments (Aspe 1993: 20). Others, on the contrary, argue that the failure of the early policies of de la Madrid prepared the way for more fundamental restructuring (Alvarez Béjar and Mendoz Pichardo 1993: 34). Another explanation is that for a long time de la Madrid lacked confidence for incomes policy, and required legitimacy vis-à-vis the private sector for a price freeze (Lustig 1992: 52). Given that there was still considerable opposition to neoliberal policy within the Mexican state, it is plausible that the first five years of de la Madrid's *sexenio* were also an intermediate period in which the new model of development could simmer politically.

16 Compared to de la Madrid, Salinas' National Development Plan was far more explicit with respect to the neoliberal character of his modernization project. The Plan maintains that ISI is exhausted and that the new economic strategy is to make use of opportunities offered by the external market in order to compensate for the lost dynamic of the internal market. Furthermore, the aim is to decrease the economic role of the state. It is worth noting that the Plan states that both extreme liberalism and statism are rejected, and that the path of modernization is presented as politically neutral (Poder Ejecutivo Federal 1989: 7, 15-6).

of the renegotiation of Mexico's debt under the Brady Plan, which was enabled by US government pressure on the banks involved. The deal involved extra credits in return for which Mexico had to encourage foreign investment, sell inefficient parastatal enterprises, reduce import protection, and liberalize its capital market. The main financial infusion was provided by the World Bank, IMF, Japan, and commercial banks. Through reduced interest payments and increased state income resulting from higher international oil prices, higher prices for public goods, increased taxes, and privatization, Mexico's public finances improved (Alvarez Béjar and Mendoza Pichardo 1993: 38-40).

The privatization programme was an important element of the neoliberal restructuring of the Mexican economy.[17] The privatization executed by de la Madrid had involved the sale of smaller enterprises, and the financial disentanglement of the rest. Under Salinas, major transfers of parastatals to the economic sector took place, with a value of about $20 billion (Guillen 1994: 33). The companies were not sold on the open market but through a state-controlled system of selection, and 93 per cent of the former parastatals were sold to large Mexican enterprises and economic groups (Guillen 1994: 32).[18] By transferring a considerable share of the state's economic power to large national enterprises, the privatization process strengthened them as the pioneers of the new economic model, although in the most important cases the Mexican buyers were associated with foreign consortia (Teichman 1993: 187; Garrido 1994: 167).[19]

It comes as no surprise, then, that throughout 1987-92 large national private enterprises were more successful than transnational enterprises and parastatals. Among Mexican private companies there is a tendency towards concentration

---

17 At the start of the de la Madrid *sexenio*, by the end of 1982, the parastatal sector consisted of 1,155 companies and accounted for some 10 per cent of total employment (Aspe 1993: 180). The majority of these enterprises had been set up between 1970 and 1982, in the context of stagnating growth and the abundance of oil revenues and credits for the Mexican government. According to Castañeda (1993: 61), the state was more or less forced to take up this role since the Mexican private sector, known for not being committed to long-term planning and investment, was reluctant to do so.

18 This transfer process lacked transparency, and many companies were sold cheaply. Teléfonos de México (Telmex), for instance, was sold to the powerful Grupo Carso for $443 million, whereas its official value was estimated at over $700 million (*Proceso* 996 4/XII/95: 19).

19 The acquisitions of former parastatal firms entailed an increasing dependency on outside capital of the major Mexican corporate groups. The privatization of banking in combination with the selling of industrial parastatals has given way to a number of economic financing groups in which Mexican companies cooperate with foreign counterparts and increasingly depend on foreign capital (Garrido 1994: 167-8, 174; Vidal 1993: 16).

of economic power, with the top ten of private economic groups each consisting of a number of the Mexican largest firms. The role of foreign companies was not straightforward. On the one hand, their number on the list of the 500 largest firms in Mexico fell. On the other hand, there is evidence that their participation and importance in the Mexican economy actually increased in the process of restructuring, especially in export-oriented and internationally competitive sectors (Alvarez Béjar and Mendoza Pichardo 1993: 42; Bielschowsky and Stumpo 1995: 156; Garrido 1994: 160-1, 165).

Several reforms of legislation initiated by Salinas served to strengthen financial intermediaries. Commercial banking was reprivatized in 1990, which greatly improved the business elite's confidence in Mexico's economy and the government. Foreign investment in banks, production and portfolio was liberalized. A new act also encouraged the integration of financial groups, predominantly by allowing the establishment of financial holding companies. Finally, Salinas' economic modernization programme included a repeal of regulations restricting private investment, and the abolition of most price controls (Aspe 1993: 85-90; Blanco Mendoza 1994: 59).

For the agricultural sector, a crucial measure was the reform of Article 27 of the Mexican Constitution in 1992. Since the revolution, the main contents of this law had been the promotion of land reforms, the protection of communal land ownership (*ejidos*), a restriction of outside investments and a prohibition of foreign direct investments in the ejidos. With the constitutional reform, these regulations were abolished, thereby giving up an essential element of post-revolution Mexico and opening up agriculture to free trade. Chapters 2 and 3 will further discuss the liberalization of Mexico's agriculture and its environmental effects.

Salinas' eagerness to strengthen Mexico's external economic ties and embedding trade liberalization had a higher purpose than securing trade flows. To ensure a continuous flow of foreign investment, Mexico had to become a trusted and esteemed member of the world economy. Salinas pragmatically opted for multiple negotiations. As global trade liberalization proved to move slowly and the threat of protectionism persevered, GATT membership was only perceived as a first step. The most important decision was to negotiate the NAFTA. With the US as Mexico's foremost trade partner, strengthening these regional ties could produce immediate economic benefits. Moreover, like Mexico's membership of the OECD, the US and Canadian acceptance of Mexico as a fully-fledged trading partner would serve as a global 'hallmark' for continuity and confidence. Mexico's entry to NAFTA showed the outside world the structural character of Salinas' reform policy, since a return to protectionist policy is impossible as long as Mexico participates in NAFTA. Mexico also liberalized trade with many Latin American countries, although only representing a few per cent of its trade relations.[20] Other attempts at trade encouragement involved discussing liberalization and cooperation with the European Union, and membership of the Asia Pacific Economic Cooperation (APEC). Like many other countries in Latin America and world-wide, open regionalism became Mexico's strategy for economic integration (Blanco Mendoza 1994: 82-3, 115-149; Fernández Jilberto and Hogenboom 1998; Teichman 1993: 178).

ECONOMIC POLARIZATION

What were the economic effects of Salinas' restructuring policy? As noted above in the analysis of the peso crisis, the neoliberal measures did not produce the expected economic growth during the Salinas *sexenio*. Economic productivity hardly increased, because the overvalued peso harmed the industry's chances both on the national market and abroad. Simultaneously, dependence on external capital remained strong. Whereas public sector indebtedness diminished, the private sector came to depend more on foreign portfolio investment.

The overall economic impact of de la Madrid's and Salinas' restructuring programmes may be characterized as polarization. Although the government succeeded in reducing the public sector and calling a halt to inflation, living standards of both the poor and the middle-class decreased while the economic elite grew richer. Between the start of Salinas' *sexenio* and the first six months of 1993, the purchasing power of the minimum salary had fallen by close to 50 per cent. A reduction of real wages was presented as the mechanism necessary to attract more external capital and prevent massive unemployment. Research indicates that over 40 per cent of the Mexican population continues to live in poverty. There was some expansion of employment in growth sectors, but in other sectors jobs were lost. In total, close to 600,000 jobs were created between 1988 and 1992, but such an increase is insufficient to keep up with the one million young workers entering the job market each year. In addition, the star performers of Mexico's industry laid off 6.3 per cent of their workers in 1994 (Alvarez Béjar and Mendoza Pichardo 1993: 38-42; Dresser 1995: 16; Heredia and Purcell 1993: 3, 7-8; *Mexico & NAFTA Report* 23/11/95: 4; Toledo Patino 1994: 57, 62-3).[21]

---

20 Mexico for instance joined the Latin American Integration Association (ALADI), the Group of Three (Colombia, Mexico and Venezuela), and the Mexico-Chile agreement.
21 These polarization tendencies were already visible under de la Madrid. Between 1984 and 1989, the poorest 10 per cent of the Mexican population saw their share of total household income decrease from 1.72 to 1.58 per cent, whereas the richest 10 per cent's

Polarization also occurred in the private sector. As a result of Salinas' focus on the macro level, the micro level was harmed by the restructuring policy. Only a small group of large and advanced industrial companies, both of national and transnational origin, that are internationally competitive and have access to foreign technologies, have been able to modernize. Large national firms were encouraged by the state, while TNCs had the capacity to adjust to the new policy because they are relatively dynamic, advanced and internationally integrated, and because they produce in sectors that in general benefit from liberalization. The majority of small and medium-sized industrial firms and service and agricultural companies stayed behind (Barkin 1993: 533; Bielschowsky and Stumpo 1995: 157).

— 1.4 The new role of the state —

The economic restructuring programme initiated under President de la Madrid and consolidated during the Salinas *sexenio* was linked to state reform and fundamental changes in Mexico's state-party system. As explained above, the rise of the technocrats within the political elite caused a change in the development model, which fundamentally changed the state functions with respect to the economy. In addition, the restructuring programme contributed to political instability. The clearest demonstration of such change was the increasing lack of political support for the PRI. In the presidential elections of 1988 Salinas officially won with only 50 per cent of the votes, despite the huge resource base and media coverage of the 'official' party as compared with opposition parties. This was the lowest victory in the history of the PRI, and there is little doubt that considerable fraud was applied to adjust the ballot-box results in favour of the ruling party. Whether or not the left-wing leader Cuauthémoc Cárdenas would have won in the event of fair elections, as was claimed by the opposition, may never be known. Still, the near defeat of Salinas demonstrated that economic restructuring was undermining the state-party system.

Despite major citizen disapproval of neoliberal restructuring, Salinas decided to intensify his predecessor's policy. The economic crises of the 1980s and the policies of de la Madrid had produced severe popular suffering. The government's budget cuts also entailed a significant decrease of resources to sustain

---

share increased from 32.77 to 37.93 per cent. In fact, the latter was the only group whose income as a percentage of total household income had augmented (*Proceso* 835 02/11/92: 13; Lustig 1992: 92).

clientelist relations between the government and corporate organizations. Consequently, the traditionally strong links of the PRI with the electorate had been weakened. Under Salinas, then, the Mexican state was greatly reformed. This state reform was technocratic, in other words initiated from above.[22] The main instrument was bureaucratic control over economic and political resources. The changes were profound; Centeno (1994: 3-4) describes the Salinas *sexenio* as a revolution.

THE NEW DISCOURSE

One of the indications of the changing role of the state is the discourse used during the Salinas administration. Modernization, new nationalism and social liberalism were the dominant concepts. Interestingly, each of these concepts is characterized by ambivalence, incorporating symbols of the Mexican Revolution as well as opposing values. The concepts can be perceived as attempts to smoothen the tensions in both the state-party system and civil society stemming from the restructuring of the state (Rousseau 1992: 29-35).[23]

Modernization was the key word for the role of the state in Salinas' campaign and his National Development Plan. Modernization was presented as a strategy of change, in order to limit and reduce the state for the sake of more social justice. As such, modernization was pictured as both a continuation of the past and a breach with it. The historic role of the state was said to be continued but this was to happen through a reformed state form (Centeno 1994: 175; Poder Ejecutivo Federal 1989: 16-21; Rousseau 1992: 33-4).

At the end of his third year in office, in 1991, Salinas came up with the concept of new nationalism. The adjective 'new' is important here as it enables combining old values with new ones. New nationalism was explained as a new economic direction—internationally integrating the Mexican economy, especially with the rest of North America through NAFTA—for the old political purpose of development and solidarity. New nationalism complemented the concept of modernization and equally served to legitimize economic restructuring and state reform (Centeno 1994: 200-1; Rousseau 1992: 34-5).

---

22 According to Salinas's private secretary Rebolledo (1993: 29), the federal government had to take the initiative for state reform since Mexico was in the situation of a relatively weak civil society versus a wide and influential state.

23 Mouzelis (1995: 240) rightly points out that "what is most striking in the national and political culture of semi-peripheral societies is the huge gulf between ideological rhetoric ... and actual practices".

In 1992, at the official celebration of the PRI's 63rd birthday, Salinas introduced the concept of *liberalismo social* to describe his political ideology. According to Salinas, social liberalism implied liberalism with a human face. It aimed to prevent an excess of statism and liberalism by finding an equilibrium. The concept of social liberalism forms the synthesis of two seemingly opposite ideological concepts: neoliberalism and neopopulism. As such, it was a powerful political initiative to secure support from two clashing political sides within and outside the party (Latapí 1992: 41; Rousseau 1992: 29-33, 35-6).

New state-society relations

At the time Salinas came to office, state-society relations were under pressure for three reasons. First, corporatist relations could not cover the increasing number of citizens outside the formal farmers, labour and middle-class structures: people earning their living in the informal sector; migrants living in illegal slums in vastly expanding cities; workers who frequently cross the border with the US in order to support their families in Mexico. The state-party system was not in contact with these people who had the right to vote, and who started to become well organized in popular movements.

Second, neoliberal restructuring had damaged Mexico's system of state corporatism. Stabilization and adjustment gave way to a lack of state resources to sustain corporatist relations. In addition, economic liberalization harmed the political compromise between the state, business circles and the working class. Like labour, businessmen with protectionist interests were strong opponents of neoliberal restructuring. While co-optation continued to be applied, the old inclusive representation system could not sufficiently perform the task of channelling and sustaining social discontent. In order to carry out the economic restructuring programme and stay in power, the new political elite needed to establish new ties with civil society (Bizberg 1993b: 299, 305; Bizberg 1990: 695, 698, 709, 720).

Third, the new political elite was involved in a struggle with the opponents of neoliberal reform within the state-party system. New ties with groups in civil society could also serve as a means to weaken these opponents. The old elite of *políticos* involved in corporatist relations lost its prominent position as these relations were of declining political importance. At the same time, políticos who were willing to could join the modernization programme through jobs in the new clientelist institutions, thereby linking their faith to the success of the new elite's plans (Dresser 1994a: 152; Rebolledo 1993: 19-21).

New state-society relations were thus to establish political stability in the context of structural economic changes. Salinas' extensive National Solidarity Programme (PRONASOL, or simply Solidarity) was an important initiative for renewing relations between the state and civil society. The programme's budget was relatively high, for instance $65 million in 1989, and $1.7 billion in 1990 (Poitras and Robinson 1994: 11). PRONASOL provided for (a share of the) materials needed by local communities for welfare and development projects. Many projects involved direct support for groups that were affected by the restructuring policy, such as farmers, labourers and the poor. By somewhat alleviating the situation of those most hard hit, PRONASOL helped to sustain neoliberal restructuring. In a similar way, the Direct-Support Programme for the Farm Sector (PROCAMPO) gave support to farmers producing basic grains (Bailey 1994: 97, 99; Dresser 1994a: 144).[24]

Compared to corporatist representation, PRONASOL was based on more active popular participation with far less bureaucracy, and a more direct relation between the source and beneficiaries of funding. Instead of building on the model of the paternalistic state, local committees were to propose such projects themselves and the community had to take responsibility for most of the work involved. As a result, the programme proved to operate relatively efficiently.[25] With PRONASOL, Salinas claimed that he opted for partnership with civil society. Among other things, the programme was a channel that provided the government with a good overview of the needs of social groups, while the activation of grass-roots remained controlled (Bailey 1994: 100, 117; Fox and Hernández 1992: 191-2; Moguel 1994: 168; Molinar Horcasitas and Weldon 1994: 140-1).

Despite a greater emphasis on popular participation, PRONASOL cannot be characterized as a democratizing programme. Instead, the programme bore a clear anti-opposition element. Although denied by the PRI, and despite formal regulations that Solidarity funding should not be linked to the PRI, in reality this was often the case at the local level, thereby continuing the clientelist tendencies of Mexico's political system.[26] Still, more than a PRI project, Solidarity

---

24 Comprehensive analyses of the politics of PRONASOL can be found in Cornelius, Craig and Fox 1994 and Dresser 1991.

25 Interestingly, the Solidarity concept had much in common with the ways many nongovernmental organizations (NGOs) operate: small, local committees representing the community's interests; self-activity supported by some external funding; pragmatism and co-responsibility. In several cases, key staff members from local NGOs were drawn into the Solidarity program, but more autonomous organizations were largely ignored. Generally, groups that criticize the government are often excluded from official social spending.

served to relegitimize and modernize presidentialism by strengthening the power of the *Presidencia* over the PRI, both at the federal and the local level. Requests for funding had to be directed to Salinas' office instead of going through the usual local, state and federal bureaucracy. Therefore, the president was able to circumvent both local politics and a corrupt state apparatus, and could use Solidarity to force local PRI politicians to reform their practices. In some cases of strong local PRI resistance to presidential influence, the programme even favoured opposition parties. In short, PRONASOL predominantly increased Salinas' popularity and his control over the party (Bailey 1994: 100, 117; Cornelius, Craig and Fox 1994: 12-4; cf. Haber 1994a).

POLITICAL PARTICIPATION

The group that was invited to become more involved in policy preparation was the private sector, especially organizations representing large companies. This initiative may be viewed as a political necessity. With a middle class demanding price stability and a favourable exchange rate, and the poor wanting work and higher income, Salinas had to make his economic programme work. Confidence and participation of the private sector were essential ingredients, especially since this sector was to replace the state and the parastatal sector as the motor for growth. A factor that has been of help in establishing these relations is the existence of the relatively closer links of technocrats with the private sector (Centeno and Maxfield 1992: 72; Castañeda 1993: 60).

Labour and farmers, on the other hand, experienced a declining political role. At the height of corporatist intermediacy, the largest representation organizations had had a double role. On the one hand, they channelled the main demands of their constituency towards decision-makers. On the other hand, they were effective mechanisms of state control over these groups. Whereas this

---

26 Molinar Horcasitas and Weldon (1994: 139) show that more Solidarity money was directed to regions where Cárdenas received strong support at the 1988 presidential elections. Their data indicate that next to poverty alleviation, the programme also served a political agenda. Part of the recovery of the PRI during state and local elections in 1991, for instance, can be explained by PRONASOL spending. Compared to the effects on party politics, Solidarity's impact on NGOs is less clear. Sometimes projects supported the activities of existing organizations or were complementary, but there have also been cases of competition and long-term NGO efforts being overruled by quick Solidarity results (Demmers and Hogenboom 1991: 43-4; Dresser 1994a: 155, 161; Haber 1994b: 293).

first, clientelist element was severely weakened, the latter remained virtually intact. This was demonstrated most clearly by the social pacts for lower inflation and a stable economy. The official labour organization proved willing to accept deals that attributed a large share of the burden to its own constituency, and until 1994 these deals hardly met organized popular resistance. Salinas was disliked by leading labour bosses, but they had little room to manoeuvre as Salinas took a tough stand against labour resistance. In addition, the tight economic situation and repression of left-wing opposition and independent unions further discouraged labour and farmer protests (Centeno and Maxfield 1992: 70; Centeno 1994: 12, 64; Teichman 1995: 13).

ELECTORAL POLICY

With respect to elections, the Salinas *sexenio* resulted in fragmented liberalization. The thrust of this change was a set of reforms enabling more electoral competition at the level of municipalities and states, which resulted in a more open political system due to more chances for local opposition government and more uncertainty for the PRI as a whole. However, in a centralist political system in which local governments have little authority and resources, the room to manoeuvre for a winning opposition party remains very limited. Moreover, electoral liberalization is not an equivalent of democratization as long as certain groups of people are still able to change outcomes by ignoring formal rule, and government authorities retain a considerable margin of arbitrariness (Loaeza 1994: 106, 113).

Moreover, both at the sub-federal and the federal level political liberalization was far from unbiased. The right-wing PAN was tolerated at the local level as an acceptable rival of the PRI and won several state and municipal elections. At the federal level, Salinas' policy of diminishing the economic role of the state and liberalizing the role of the Catholic church mirrored two important issues on the PAN agenda. This policy weakened the PAN's federal electoral position, but also turned the PAN into an acceptable ally in the Mexican Congress. The left-wing PRD, on the other hand, experienced strong repression. After the near victory of the PRD leader Cuauthémoc Cárdenas in 1988, the PRI clearly felt threatened. Especially in state and municipal elections, the PRD was often hampered, and fraud occurred in numerous cases. Political violence was also severe and 250 local PRD activists were killed during this 'bloody *sexenio*' (*Proceso* 935, 3/x/1994: 6-15).

Simultaneously, the PRI itself was faced with a number of fundamental conflicts. Despite the fact that Cuauthémoc Cárdenas and other vociferous left-wing critics had left the PRI prior to the 1988 elections to join the opposition, the party still had trouble in finding a consensus between its various groups. Apart from economic issues, a major issue in the PRI during the presidency of Salinas was the representation structures of the party. After the serious electoral competition at the presidential elections of 1988, it was clear that the party's social representation structures were insufficient to win the elections and that the PRI's electoral legitimation needed to be improved. In addition, the elections showed that the PRI had moved away from society and closer towards the state, which performed an unpopular economic policy. Especially the relation with the expanding urban population was at stake (Gómez and Bailey 1990: 57; Hernández Rodríguez 1991: 223-4).

The PRI leadership proposed to base representation more on territorial than on sectorial grounds. This was clearly an attack on the corporatist influence structures in the PRI, but also an attempt to obtain support from the middle class and urban movements. In addition, Salinas' party reform was to serve his economic reform, turning the party more into a governmental institution than a political party. However, the opposition to this proposal was strong, especially from the labour sector. Although only some of the proposed reforms were adopted, sectorial influence was still harmed. The resistance to the new leaders was also reflected in the adoption of a new party principle during the 1990 PRI Assembly which holds that the party should watch the government to prevent the application of a liberal economic policy. Mexico's entry to NAFTA, however, shows that this principle did not have much effect (Dresser 1994b: 141; Hernández Rodríguez 1991: 229-242).

The pace of political reforms is another indication of the difficulties experienced by the state-party system. The possibility of instability was often used as an excuse to slow down the pace of political reforms. To Salinas, economic liberalization mattered more than political liberalization, and he was not willing to put the first at risk for the sake of the latter. Traditional forms of PRI control partly ceased to govern Mexican society, but real democratization would entail strong criticism of Mexico's economic policy. This would be undesirable for the political elite that fostered this policy, as well as for the US government (Centeno 1994: 224-5; Harvey 1993: 7-11).

STATE AUTONOMY

Presidential centralism has traditionally been a key element of Mexico's authoritarian system. This system is based on the principle of executive control over the legislative and judicial powers. Most legislation comes from the president's office, and the until recently two-thirds majority of the PRI (and affiliated parties) in Congress rendered the legislative process a decorative act. As a result of the 1988 elections, however, Salinas needed to work with a coalition with the opposition in order to get enough votes for constitutional reforms. On several occasions he found the PAN willing to cooperate. The President's power also lies in appointing officials and politicians at various levels, as well as the next presidential candidate for the PRI. Therefore, an incoming President can bring in his own clique of supporters (a so-called *camarilla*). By hand-picking them for high positions, he produces a solid team that will perform his policy. In addition, by personally appointing the new PRI's new presidential candidate, a President strongly directs the country's course after the end of his own term (Cornelius and Craig 1991: 29-33).

Under Salinas, within the state-party system access to decision-making tightened, and technocrats dominated the cabinet, as has been explained in section 2. Technocrats have no corporatist experience, few links to the PRI patronage system (official unions, etc.), and little experience in grassroots organizations or local politics. Both in the administration of de la Madrid and Salinas, the political background of technocrats was far more often the PRI think-tank (iepes, now Cambio XXI) than an elected post or a position in a PRI-related political institution (Centeno 1994: 142; Centeno and Maxfield 1992: 69, 71-2, 84).[27]

Summing up the findings of this section, Salinas' political reforms were basically a combination of two, seemingly contrasting, processes: decentralization and centralization. On the one hand, the undermined corporatist model that had secured sufficient popular support for the state-party system since the Mexican Revolution was partly replaced by direct linkages with local communities. Simultaneously, local and state elections were less controlled from above. On the other hand, Salinas' team consisted of a relatively homogenous group of technocrats who further strengthened the presidential power and decreased the interference of the PRI in state affairs. By doing so, Salinas intensified presidentialist centralism, which has been a major pillar of authoritarian rule in Mexico, while starting to weaken the PRI's role in the state-party partnership.

Both changes, namely political decentralization and centralization, fitted the goal of a more autonomous state. Rather than letting the PRI recreate state-society linkages that were lost through the decline of corporatist mechanisms,

---

27 The background of technocrats also indicates a homogenizing tendency towards centralism and elitism. Increasingly, members of the political elite tend to come from Mexico City and its surroundings, and belong to professional and private industrialist fractions of the middle class instead of farmers and working class (Centeno and Maxfield 1992: 65-7).

the *Presidencia* initiated the renewing of these linkages. The new linkages, however, were rather *ad hoc* and flexible when compared with corporatist structures. Like the economic restructuring process, the political reforms were headed by technocrats in the presidency and federal top institutions, which could more easily distance themselves from traditional practices and populist forces. The increased autonomy of the state thus took the form of decreased party influence and less structural forms of state-society links.

At the end of Salinas' *sexenio*, not democratization but political uncertainty could be added to the overall continuity of centralism, presidentialism and state-party connections. From the Mexican revolution onwards, the PRI has been the alliance that provided a minimum of political coherence. As Loaeza (1994: 105-13) explains correctly, the combination of an economic crisis, numerous unresolved political tensions (between and within federal and sub-federal levels; between and within the state and the PRI; between and within civil society and the state-party system), and the availability of some new ways to express discontent are gnawing at the foundation of Mexico's stability.

— 1.5 The state, civil society and the private sector —

Whereas the nature and stability of Mexico's political system have often been described as exceptional, state-society relations in Mexico share basic characteristics with other late-developing nations. Mouzelis (1995) argues that authoritarian corporatism entails a weak civil society. This is indeed the case in Mexico. Within an authoritarian and corporatist system "the majority of civil organizations operate not so much as safeguards against state despotism, than as administrative extensions of the state's highly corrupt and particulistic apparatuses" (Mouzelis 1995: 232-3). This section analyses how during the Salinas *sexenio* various groups did try to change government policy and political structures. It describes the background of the participation of Mexico's private sector in the NAFTA debate, and of the obstacles to environmental activism.

POLITICAL REPRESENTATION OF THE PRIVATE SECTOR

Since the introduction of the economic restructuring programme, Mexico's private sector has experienced a process of economic polarization. Large national companies have in general profited from the reforms. Though the least vulnerable to foreign competition, they received the most governmental support in the form of financial assistance and a first choice of privatized firms.

Consequently, large Mexican companies easily adjusted to the new opportunities. Increasingly, major Mexican firms become part of production and
capital networks or pyramid structures of national and transnational companies. A concentration of wealth and the predominance of a few powerful
business groups are now fundamental elements of Mexico's economy (Garrido
1994: 165, 174; Garrido Noguera and Quintana López 1987: 117-8; Salas-Porras
and Vidal Bonifaz 1992: 122, 125; Valdés Ugalde 1994: 332).[28]

During the Salinas *sexenio,* a political cleavage occurred within representation organizations of the private sector. One reason for this cleavage was
the marginalization of small industry and government encouragement of large
companies. Especially the links between the political elite of technocrats and
the business elite expanded. The main organizations that represent the interests
of financial capital, export manufacturing and multinational companies were
already politically successful under de la Madrid. From that time onwards,
major business elite organizations found that the state was favourable to their
agenda (Harvey 1993: 12-3).[29]

Mexico's business elite was to some extent involved in the economic restructuring project and in the preparation of NAFTA (see chapter 5). Cooperation
intensified as the new political elite turned out to be far more receptive to the
demands of the business elite than its predecessors. Especially the Coordinating
Business Council (CCE) and the Mexican Council of Businessmen (CMHN)
were very close to the Salinas administration. Although organizations representing major companies did play an influential role, the nature of genuine
interaction might have been primarily informal. Teichman (1993: 178, 188)
claims that instead of building on extensive formal consultation with the private sector, Mexico's policy reorientation has been a state-led affair. The main
route to business participation, she argues, has been close personal contacts between the trade ministry and key individuals in the private sector.

---

28 The top ten of Mexican economic groups represent over half of total sales, assets and
employment. The businessmen who control these companies are heavily involved in
brokerage houses and insurance firms, have considerable international influence, and
have profited from the privatization programme (Valdés Ugalde 1994: 233).

29 Important organizations were the Coordinating Business Council (CCE), the Confederation of Chambers of Industry (CONCAMIN), the Confederation of National
Chambers of Commerce (CONCANACO), the Mexican Employers Confederation (CO-
PARMEX), and the Mexican Council of Businessmen (CMHN). The nucleus of the business elite holds the key functions in major private sector organizations. Valdés Ugalde
(1994: 234) estimates that approximately 120 individuals are in control of the principal
representation channels.

The political polarization of the business sector is well exemplified by the relations within the heterogenous CCE, which was the state's principal interlocutor with corporate Mexico during the NAFTA debate.[30] The CCE's leaders can roughly be divided into two groups. The first group consists of persons from big companies and elitist economic organizations who tend to support the PRI and have a pragmatic attitude in their relations with the government. The second group is formed by PAN supporters from somewhat less important medium-sized companies, and from organizations with numerous members. The first group has dominated CCE's leadership since 1985, even though big companies are a minority in the total group of companies represented by CCE.[31] The post-1985 situation not only reflects stronger elitist and PRI tendencies in the organization, but the new CCE leaders also have stronger links through their business or background with large capital and new financial dynasties (Tirado 1992; Valdés Ugalde 1994: 228).

Small national industry experienced a loss of political power. In 1980, small and medium-sized industrialists, represented by the National Chamber of Transformation Industry (CANACINTRA), had been influential opponents of Mexico's entry into GATT. In 1985, when GATT entry was discussed again, CANACINTRA maintained its anti-free trade position. With respect to NAFTA, a large share of small and medium-sized companies still wanted commercial protection. However, their political representation and their linkage to the state had diminished due to their decreased importance for the new development model. CANACINTRA had gradually shifted from defending small industrialists in favour of more powerful sectors such as the chemical and refreshments industries, and simultaneously its position on free trade had changed. This reflects two other tendencies in the Mexican private sector, namely a greater attention to macroeconomic instead of microeconomic problems, and a growing consensus on liberalization as the solution for economic instability (Davis 1992; Pastor and Wise 1994: 467, 482; Puga 1992: 127).[32]

---

30 The CCE represents a heterogenous group of economic organizations, with a large (such as the National Agricultural and Livestock Council (CNA) with 250,000 members) or a powerful membership (such as the CMHN, with 37 members who control 70 of Mexico's main companies). In addition, CCE's heterogeneity stems from the various sectors, regions and sizes of companies it accommodates. The CCE is also divided at an ideological level, especially between protectionist and liberal forces (Luna 1992).

31 This domination has been facilitated by the asymmetric representation of the CCE, which gives each member organization an equal say notwithstanding the fact that they represent very unequal numbers of companies.

32 In a reaction to the marginalization of small industry's representation, new organi-

Corporate involvement in electoral politics

Under Salinas, the relations of Mexico's business elite with the PRI improved significantly. During most of de la Madrid's *sexenio* the business elite was critical to the incomplete privatization and deregulation programme, as well as the lack of credits and the height of interest rates. In effect, they demanded consultation on Mexico's economic policy. In December 1987, the relation between the government and the private sector was stabilized by de la Madrid's Social Pact. The business elite was the main beneficiary of this pact, which formed an informal arrangement for negotiation between the government and the private sector. One way in which the PRI strengthened the bond with the business elite was the Commission for Financing and Consolidation of Resources of the PRI. This commission raised funds for the presidential campaign of Salinas and encouraged owners of major firms to contribute millions of US dollars, which guaranteed their future participation in the party. When Salinas came to power, a quick recovery of the business elite's confidence in the state-party system and its policy occurred as a result of reinforced restructuring. In early 1993, some twenty-five wealthy businessmen were approached by a PRI fund to contribute $25 million each. When this became known it turned into a small scandal, but nonetheless many such contributions were made (Montesinos 1992: 113; Morris 1995: 82; Teichman 1992: 98-9; 1993: 188; Valdés Ugalde 1994: 230-2).

While owners of large companies tended to support the PRI, PRI links with owners of medium-sized companies are problematic. The group of medium-sized companies is relatively new and largely located in the north of Mexico. Previously, Mexico's private sector had mainly consisted of either small or large firms. The medium-sized newcomers disputed the political domination of large enterprises and at first tried to strengthen their formal representation. As this did not improve their actual policy influence, they changed their strategy and started to fight state control through an electoral struggle against the PRI, which involved building a strong popular base. They have become important supporters of the PAN (Cypher 1990: 181; Heredia 1992: 290-1; Teichman 1992: 99).

The growing involvement of the Mexican private sector in electoral politics is an interesting phenomenon. Earlier on, private sector interest representation

---

zations were created such as the National Confederation of Micro, Small and Medium-Sized Industry (CONAMIN) and the National Association of Industrials of the Transformation (ANIT). These organizations expressed small industry's disagreement with Mexico's economic policy but had little influence on its contents (Puga 1992: 127-9).

through official chambers was the only formal route. The increasing political influence of electoral processes and opposition parties entailed both new threats and possibilities. The popularity of Cuauthémoc Cárdenas during the presidential elections of 1988 worried the private sector. Medium-sized and large companies were united in their fear of this left-wing candidate who attracted many dissatisfied voters. Simultaneously, the PAN became a viable alternative to those businessmen who felt that their interests were neglected by the PRI and who were fed up with its political practices (Valdés Ugalde 1994: 229).

POLITICAL AND ECONOMIC MARGINALIZATION

With the new political elite and the new development model, the relation between the state and civil society has changed. The technocrats have not simply copied the *políticos'* corporatist and patronage relations with civil groups, and they have operated more independently of the structures of the PRI.

The traditional consultation and participation of official unions in policy-making came to an end under Salinas. As a result of Salinas' attitude towards these unions (see section 4), they were faced with a decrease in control over issues that had previously legitimated their prominent role: wage policy, minimum wage, subcontracting, social security, housing programmes and pensions. Salinas attempted to resolve the tensions that arose as a result of this new situation by offering some compromises. This give-and-take approach proved successful in the sense that the weakened labour-government relation did not break altogether (De la Garza Toledo 1994: 203; Morris 1995: 84, 88).

The ways in which the new economic and political logic affected the position of labour varied per sector. Within the export-oriented *maquiladora* industry, labour representation was deregulated to a point of virtual disappearance of influence. This was a fundamental break with the past. While labour in the car industry was in general less affected, geographical relocation, internal flexibilization and annulment of collective contracts also weakened the labour position in this and other sectors. In addition, the economic crisis and the restructuring policy left numerous workers without a regular job, many of whom ended up in the informal sector. As a result, official unions have come to represent a smaller share of Mexico's total work force (Bizberg 1993a: 177-80).

Small farmers also saw their traditional relation with the government melt down. Corporatist linkages were weakened, and Salinas' agricultural reforms strongly affected the interests of subsistence farmers, who had traditionally been the most loyal PRI voters. Government support for basic foodstuffs was dismantled, price guarantees abolished, and subsidies for small farmers reduced.

In addition, Salinas reformed law 27 of the Mexican Constitution, which had created and protected *ejidos* (agricultural cooperations of small farmers). All in all, Mexico's small farmers were faced with economic and political marginalization which left many with little choice but to leave their land and search for work in Mexican cities or in the US.

The trend of economic and political polarization has brought severe hardship on the half of the Mexican population living in poverty. Evidently, these are the citizens that are hit the most by the halving of both the purchasing power of real wages and public expenditure on health care and education since 1980. This is especially the case for the one-fifth of Mexicans living in conditions of extreme poverty, predominantly in rural areas. The four poorest states of Mexico, namely Chiapas, Hidalgo, Guerrero and Oaxaca, combine high levels of poverty (70 per cent), illiteracy (50 per cent), unemployment, malnutrition and infant mortality with relatively low access to government resources. But workers in manufacturing industries also experienced a 36 per cent loss of purchasing power between 1982 and 1991. At the other end of the scale, a little over 2 per cent of Mexicans accounted for more than three-quarters of the national income in 1990 (Coote 1995: 12; Fernández Jilberto and Hogenboom 1996: 155; Moguel 1995: 210).

POPULAR ORGANIZATIONS, NGOS AND OPPOSITION PARTIES

The combined economic and political marginalization of a large share of the Mexican population formed a strong incentive for citizens to organize themselves, and since the early 1980s numerous formal and informal groups have been set up. Although the existence of political organizations outside the official channels has a long history in Mexico, recent developments are unprecedented. Independent unions and farmers organizations have attempted to improve their members' political representation vis-à-vis government agencies. Besides such 'replacements' of official interest organizations, many groups were set up to represent interests that had previously not been channelled by such organizations. Environmental organizations, urban movements, indigenous organizations, and women groups reflect new social situations, concerns and identities that do not fit into the old structures.

Although formally independent of the government, non-governmental organizations (NGOs) can of course not circumvent the realities of Mexico, especially the political and economic domination of the state-party system. NGOs, just like other organizations and institutions, need to get some of their supporters' demands met in order to survive. As a consequence, while they are often critical of the state, most Mexican NGOs approach the state for resources. As they seek to remain autonomous while simultaneously accepting governmental support, Mexican NGOs often operate with the government in an ambivalent way. As a result of their pragmatism, organizations may accept deals with institutions, despite their fear of dependency and their disinclination of such practices. Incorporation of critical organizations or co-optation of some of their leaders into government agencies happen frequently (Cook, Middlebrook and Molinar Horcasitas 1994: 36; Demmers and Hogenboom 1992: 16, 21; Fox and Hernández 1992: 192).

During the *sexenios* of de la Madrid and Salinas structural cooperation among NGOs was not frequent. One of the reasons for this is the issue-specific focus of organizations. Other explanations are a lack of experience and energy, and limited ties of NGOs with intellectuals and social movements. Finally, Mexico's political system limits the creation of strong networks. Repression of critical organizations is not uncommon, but far more frequently NGOs are limited in their activities by a lack of access to government institutions and the media. In addition, Salinas attempted to introduce a law that would treat *Asociaciones Civiles* (the legal NGO construction) as corporations and tax them accordingly, but it was withdrawn after severe criticism. Although the 1985 earthquake in Mexico City and the 1988 presidential elections enhanced alliances among groups with various interests, such as housing, rural development, environment, women and human rights, effective multi-sectoral networks only came into being at the local level (Demmers and Hogenboom 1992: 18; Fox and Hernández 1992: 180, 185).

Like the upcoming NGOs, the expanding political role of opposition parties under de la Madrid and Salinas could be called a success as well as a failure. The nation-wide support for Cuauthémoc Cárdenas in 1988, as well as the series of opposition (especially PAN) victories in municipal and state elections were unprecedented in Mexico's post-revolution history. On the other hand, the opposition was not able to break the PRI's omnipotence. Within a centralist and presidentialist system, local and even state level influence is only of limited importance as long as the federal authority can make financial shifts away from opposition rulers towards loyal institutions.

Apart from the obstacles presented by the system, the role of opposition parties was limited by the weakness of linkages to other organizations. Fox and Hernández (1992: 172), for instance, speak of a "frustrated construction of citizenship" due to a gap between social movements and political-electoral participation. The background for this gap is state pressure and repression, and the general distrust of political parties among independent organizations. Since cooperation with an opposition party is a direct condemnation of the PRI, NGOs can expect to lose important 'entrances' in governmental institutions which cannot be replaced by the opposition. The distrust of political parties is partly based on the gap between the issue-specific focus of NGOs and the parties' broad aims. Moreover, several organizations found that opposition parties, just like the PRI, are characterized by populist and clientelist structures. From this perspective, Cuauthémoc Cárdenas' democratization initiative prior to the presidential elections of 1988 was remarkable. Cárdenas not only brought together several left-wing political parties, but also built on an alliance of independent organizations. However, after the 1988 uphill battle was lost, state repression and internal political discord again severely weakened this alliance (Demmers and Hogenboom 1992: 17; Fox and Hernández 1992: 172, 188-9).

— 1.6 Conclusions —

In 1994, the year that NAFTA became operative, Mexico went through a number of shocks, which may be used as a guide for assessing the major political and economic tendencies of the Salinas *sexenio*. First, the political assassinations and the electoral tensions revealed the intensity of the struggles taking place within the political system. Mexico's historical image of political stability no longer holds. Second, the peso crisis showed the fundamental economic problems the country still faces. Third, the *Zapatistas* attracted attention to the devastating effects of economic restructuring on the poorer half of the Mexican population, and to the authoritarian character of the state-party system. Each of these events led to world-wide media coverage of the continuity of Mexico's authoritarian system, but this was hardly criticized by governments and international organizations. From the perspective of the early 1990s, the international acceptance of the state-party system in Mexico was exceptional and remarkable.

Mexico's entry to NAFTA was the culmination of the process of its transnationalization, which contributed to more international acceptance of Mexico. While Mexico's production has been transnationalizing for a long time, transnationalization of public and private financial capital only became strong in the 1970s. At the time of the 1982 debt crisis, this new dependence had produced an increased openness to external demands, especially from the US and other creditors. Although these demands were not immediately accepted, they contributed to the rise of technocrats in Mexico's state-party system. Under Salinas, technocrats came to dominate the policy-making process and performed an extensive neoliberal restructuring programme. Through membership of major regional and international agreements, predominantly NAFTA, economic restructuring has been further linked to external interests and has thereby been consolidated.

The consolidation of the neoliberal development model during Salinas' presidency has brought about two major changes. Economic leadership was partly shifted from the state to the group of large companies producing for the world market. These companies are supposed to play the key role in economic growth, helped by the acquisition of large privatized firms. So far, however, the success of these companies has not trickled down to the Mexican economy as a whole. This brings us to the second major change, namely economic polarization. While a few companies and families have been able to extend their affluence since the start of the restructuring process, many sectors and people have been marginalized. Small companies producing for the national market have been hit by the crisis and the new policy. Equally, millions of Mexicans have less work and a lower income than 15 years ago. Despite all the promises of international institutions and the Mexican technocratic elite, economic restructuring has not resulted in progress for the majority of Mexicans so far.

Politically, the new role of the Mexican state may be characterized as a double-edged sword. On the one hand, a decentralization and diversification of the state's relation with civil society has occurred. Salinas' Solidarity Programme and the restricted electoral liberalization opened some ways for political participation. On the other hand, increasing autonomy of the state bureaucracy and the persistence of authoritarian control were also significant tendencies. Presidentialism was reinforced under Salinas, and the homogeneous technocratic elite managed to strengthen its political role. Moreover, the new opportunities for popular participation may be less controlled than the corporatist structures, but do not represent progress in the direction of democratization. New avenues for political participation served only certain groups. Economic and political polarization produced a cleavage within the private sector. Meanwhile, a lack of unity, economic marginalization and repression of the left-wing opposition and critical NGOs and independent unions limited the possibilities for strong popular resistance to the policies of the state-party system.

What lessons can be learned from the above for the following chapter on Mexico's environmental politics? First, Mexico's environmental policy-making has taken place in the context of an authoritarian political system, and under Salinas the authority of the president and the state bureaucracy intensified. This can be expected to form an obstacle to environmental organizations who attempt to press for improvements in environmental policy. Second, growing concern for environmental deterioration coincided with processes of economic and political transnationalization. This implied the growing importance of external actors, interests, and values, including the environment, in Mexico. Third, Mexico's environmental policy-making has taken place at a time of economic and crises and neoliberal restructuring. These circumstances limited not only the government resources for environmental policy, but to a certain degree also the popular priority of the issue. Chapter 2 describes the evolution of environmental politics and policy-making in Mexico, with a focus on the post-1982 period.

This chapter has also presented the Mexican perspective of NAFTA's creation. Entry into a free trade agreement with the US was very important to Mexico's technocrats and President Salinas, not only for the trade and investment benefits but primarily as a consolidation of their neoliberal restructuring programme. In chapter 3, the NAFTA interests of other North American proponents of regional integration will be addressed, and the preparation of NAFTA as well as the reactions of NAFTA proponents to environmental criticism will be analysed.

CHAPTER 2

Evolution of Mexico's Environmental Politics and Policy

From the very start, long before the NAFTA environment debate, Mexico's environmental politics has been influenced by external information, prestige, cooperation and funding. Foreign studies and the 1972 environmental conference of the UN in Stockholm raised consciousness among Mexican academics and government officials. This stimulated early initiatives in Mexico, while the Mexican government wanted to build up the image of a responsible industrializing country. The transnational input became more diverse in the 1980s, when environmental contacts with the US government, NGOs and the World Bank were established by the Mexican government and groups in civil society. In the late 1980s and the early 1990s, Mexico increased its international efforts and received growing amounts of foreign funding for environmental programmes. In other words, transnationalization has been inherent in Mexico's environmental politics.

Looking back on the first twenty years of Mexico's environmental politics and policy, from the early 1970s until the early 1990s, several continuities come to the fore. Despite changes of presidents, government institutions, laws, development model, economic situation, international integration, and state-society relations, six characteristic elements of environmental policy in Mexico have persisted.

1 As already mentioned, developments in international environmental politics and external actors have contributed to the evolution of Mexico's environmental politics and policy, while a positive environmental image has always been important for the Mexican government.

2 The political role and policy input of actors outside the state apparatus, such as non-governmental organizations and the private sector, has been limited. Consultation by government agencies remained ad hoc and restricted, while the mobilization capacity of environmental groups was in most cases small.

3 Environmental degradation has been an issue of low priority to the Mexican government. Only problems of pollution in large cities have increasingly become a cause for concern, especially since the late 1980s.

4 Resources for Mexico's environmental policy have been insufficient, reflecting not only the low priority of this policy but also the government's budgetary limitation as a result of economic crises.

5 The government agencies responsible for Mexico's environmental policy have been relatively weak. Besides limited resources, a lack of experienced personnel and the virtual absence of authority over other government agencies have contributed to this weakness.

6 Finally, and as a result of the above, the environmental policy of the Mexican government has been typified by long-term fragmentedness and non-enforcement of legislation. In practice, Mexico's environmental policy has thus always fallen short of formal intentions and commitments.

The major issue in the transnational NAFTA debate on the environment that started in 1990 was Mexico's poor record of policy enforcement. From a Latin American perspective the performance of the Mexican government was probably above average, but the difference with the US and Canada was large. While some differences could be traced back to economic inequalities, Mexico's habit of not enforcing considerable parts of its formal policy contrasted with the two other North American countries. For a good understanding of the nature of Mexico's environmental politics and policy, this chapter examines their evolution until the time of the debate. The focus lies on the *sexenio* of President de la Madrid (1982-1988), when the environment became a real political issue in Mexico, and on the first years of Salinas' presidency (1988-1991). After early 1991, the NAFTA debate on the environment started to affect politics and policy in Mexico, and this process will be discussed in chapter 6.

Although important for this study, the actual gap between Mexico's formal policy and implementation is hard to estimate due to the general lack of transparency with respect to activities and results of Mexican government agencies. Government information is incomplete and unreliable, and there are few real policy evaluations, which reflects the lack of democratic control of Mexican government institutions. Apart from the major political and practical implications of this situation, it poses a problem for scholars analysing Mexico's policy. With respect to the environmental policy of the Mexican government, its fragmented nature over the long term is reproduced in official documentation and academic literature. In some instances of insufficient or contrasting sources, then, information obtained in interviews has been cautiously used to support the analysis. Moreover, rather than assessing this incoherent policy in great detail, the aim of this chapter is to analyse the political processes that contributed to the environment's becoming an issue in Mexico, and the background of limited government policy.

This chapter starts with an overview of the ways in which Mexico's major economic sectors (agriculture, oil and industry) and the urbanization process have contributed to the current state of the environment. Next, the evolution of Mexico's environmental policy and related politics will be described chronologically. Section 2 deals with the early phase of this policy during the 1970s. Significant progress in environmental policy-making took place during the presidency of Miguel de la Madrid Hurtado (1982-88). Interestingly, this policy progress also met with strong criticism and opposition from environmental organizations, as section 3 shows. The reaction of President Carlos Salinas de Gortari (1988-94) to this criticism and opposition, and his environmental policy until transnational criticism mounted in early 1991, are analysed in section 4. At the end of this chapter, conclusions will be drawn on the weaknesses that still remained after twenty years of environmental policy in Mexico, as well as on the political processes that contributed to this.

— 2.1 Economic development and environmental degradation —

From a geographical point of view, Mexico is fascinatingly diverse. Heading southward from the long border with the US, one first passes a hot desert area with at the east the Gulf of Mexico and at the west the Gulf of California. The higher and cooler mountain chains of the West and East Sierra Madre contrast sharply with these vast and empty stretches of land. Following the eastward curve of the country, one can see a mixture of desert and dry tropical climates, and more removed from the coast even mild climate areas where the steeps of old volcanoes are freshly green. On the side of the Pacific Ocean the hills and mountains are warmer and drier, but heading more south and eastward humidity increases. Here begins the humid tropical area with its great variety of flora and fauna, and many of Mexico's rivers. The eastern limits of the country are partly covered by the rainforest on the border with Guatemala, while the Yucatán Peninsula with its low vegetation stretches to the Caribbean sea.

It is only natural that a large country with such a diversity of climate, altitude and soil types should have many plant and animal species. Mexico is famous for its high biodiversity, ranking fourth on the world list, with approximately 10 per cent of the species known to humans (SEDESOL 1992a: 18). The diversity of soil types allows for a variety of crops, while the seas and gulfs surrounding Mexico have many fish. Underground, there are large oil wells (both on land and under water), as well as mines with copper, silver, gold and other minerals.

While Mexico's natural resources are abundant, its environmental problems are large and diverse. The water supply has always been limited, in particular in the vast desert and dry tropical areas, and increasing human use for agriculture, industry and households has added to its scarcity. Loss of fertile top soil through erosion, caused by deforestation, bad farming methods, and a natural tendency, is another major issue. High levels of deforestation, primarily for pasture and agriculture, also threaten the habitat of large numbers of plant and animal species. Other major environmental problems of Mexico are soil, water and air pollution, which also cause damage to ecosystems and species. A lack of treatment of solid waste (households and industry) and especially hazardous and toxic waste (industry) is causing major soil pollution, as well as affecting groundwater and rivers. Similarly, rivers and coastal areas experience serious pollution due to the far from sufficient sewerage and waste water treatment system. Last but not least is air pollution caused by vehicles and industrial production. In fact, air pollution ranks the highest for Mexicans living in large cities, where daily smog is a very serious health threat. Most of these problems are in some way intensified because of population growth.[1]

It is well-known that industrial development and extreme poverty are the two major sources of environmental degradation world-wide. For the Latin American region, a historical pattern of uneven capitalist development both at global and national level has had a great effect on the environment. Soil fertility has suffered from unsustainable agricultural activities; deforestation rates have been high; fossil fuels and mineral resources have been rapidly exploited; and industrialization has gone hand in hand with mass pollution (Faber 1992: 6-10).

The state plays a crucial role in capitalist development and its damage to the environment. In Mexico, one of the continuities in government activities has been the prevalence of economic development over social and environmental concerns. The Mexican state has been faced with competing demands on its limited resources to support the expansion of private investment opportunities, and this has been at the cost of popular demands for nature protection and social improvement. Even at times of growing environmental awareness, new industrial projects have been designed without considering ecological consequences (e.g. the Gulf Coast petrochemical complex). Despite the evidently worsening environmental conditions in the Valley of Mexico (Mexico City), new companies were allowed to establish production there. Also government programmes for productive investments have been known for their immense environmental effects (Barkin 1991: 95, 99).

---

1 According to the SEDESOL (1993: 5), the Mexican population increased from about 23 million in 1950 to 44 million in 1970 and 81 million in 1990. While population growth was about 3.2 per cent a year between 1950 and 1970, this growth slowed down to an annual 2.6 per cent between 1970 and 1990.

Mexican development over the past fifty years was based on three different models, but despite the changing nature of environmental destruction, degradation has remained. First, ISI had several destructive effects. State-supported development of heavy industry has caused many pollution problems. The policy of low prices for energy and natural resources such as water entailed waste instead of efficient use. Moreover, the agricultural sector was paying for ISI, and was deprived of funding for long-term development. Next, the short period in the 1970s of state-led development that was highly dependent on the oil sector again gave way to the expansion of polluting industries, especially oil and fertilizers. Moreover, direct state participation in key economic sectors inhibited the state's executive task of environmental protection.[2] Finally, the neoliberal model that has dominated since then has encouraged international competitiveness without much consideration for the ecological implications in certain sectors and regions. For a basic understanding of Mexico's most important environmental problems in the context of its economic development, we will give brief consideration to the problems linked to agriculture, oil drilling, industry and urbanization.

AGRICULTURE

After a period in which employment, poverty relief and food self-sufficiency were central to Mexico's agricultural policy, during the 1960s the policy goal slowly shifted towards integration into the world market. Under the development model of ISI, Mexico's agricultural sector had a crucial role as a provider of cheap food for the working class, and of foreign exchange[3] necessary to obtain capital goods. The agricultural sector increasingly became an adjunct of industrialization. As part of this process, the role of national and international agribusiness expanded and the use of labour per unit of capita investment declined. Agricultural production increasingly involved the use of improved seeds, pesticides, fertilizers, farm machinery, and modern processing techniques (Sanderson 1986: 36-9, 241-8).

---

2 In general, the state has the ambivalent task of promoting the national economy and protecting the environment. In the case of state domination in certain economic sectors and major financial revenues of the state stemming from this situation, the tendency of states to pursue economic growth at the cost of the environment tends to be even stronger.

3 According to Calva (1993: 17), the agricultural sector generated more than half of Mexico's foreign exchange between 1946 and 1965.

Governmental encouragement of commercial agricultural production has resulted in "the reemergence of a polarized agricultural structure" (Barkin 1990: 77). The economic integration of the agricultural sector, for which the opening of US markets was of particular importance, enhanced new opportunities for large and rich farmers. Government support in the form of irrigation works, credits and technical services mainly went to large agribusiness companies and helped them to make use of these opportunities. But as the governmental programmes and subsidies were directed at farmers that could be part of the modernization and internationalization trend, the majority of small farmers were not able to turn their plots into modern productive units. Simultaneously, small farmers that were primarily producing basic grains for the national market were affected by the policy of low set prices for these products (Barkin 1990: 32-3).

The industrialization of Mexican agriculture has had detrimental effects on the environment. The most severe problems are degradation of soil (predominantly erosion[4]) and water, water scarcity, and deforestation. Increased application of agrochemicals, as well as some of the farm machinery that is inherently linked to monoculture, have damaged Mexican soil and water resources. The growing number of irrigation works lower groundwater levels and make the soil salty. Deforestation is partly the result of expanding cattle-ranging for export by large farmers. The other side of the coin pictures poor farmers having few options but to exploit their land and illegally squatted plots in order to survive. In the state of Chiapas, for instance, this tendency is another major source of deforestation. Finally, the bad living conditions and perspectives for the majority of the rural population have made many men and families move to cities (see below for the environmental problems of uncontrolled urbanization).

OIL DRILLING

Despite evolving environmental legislation, the ecological impact of oil drilling has increased with the sector's expansion. After the nationalization of the oil industry in 1938 by President Lázaro, Mexican oil supplies were primarily to serve the emerging domestic industries. Although the Mexican Oil Company (PEMEX) produced with little environmental consideration, damage was limited as long as production was not very extensive. When in 1971 Mexico's

---

4   In a rough but conservative calculation of the economic costs of Mexico's environmental problems soil erosion ranked highest, approximately costing an annual $1.20 billion due to a loss of agricultural output (Margulis 1991: 2).

first environmental law came into force, PEMEX created an environmental protection commission, but this turned out to be merely a symbolic agency. In the second half of the 1970s, oil exploitation accelerated rapidly in an attempt to solve the economic problems Mexico was facing. Under President López Portillo, oil-dependent development prevailed: through cheap energy Mexican industry was to expand more rapidly, and Mexico started to sell oil on the international market to raise government revenues. Exploitation increased and the number of locations grew, especially in the south-east, to keep up with demand.[5] Due to the great importance of the oil industry (and the petrochemical industry, see below), it met with few administrative obstacles for locating facilities (Márquez and López 1988: 468-70).

Geographical expansion and increased production of the oil drilling sector have severely worsened its environmental impact. Problems range from contamination of land by the salts used for drilling, to the pollution of rivers, lagoons and the sea with chemicals and oil. The expropriation of farming land for drilling and the creation of industrial zones have resulted in rapid urbanization. Another environmental threat is the occurrence of serious accidents such as leaks and explosions. With the expansion of the Mexican oil industry, exploitation has increased significantly, more areas have been affected, and more accidents have occurred (Márquez and López 1988: 472, 476-81).

As a consequence, from the mid-1970s onwards PEMEX was more and more criticized for its polluting production, but this was of little effect as long as economic growth was based on the oil sector. Farmers in the south-east of Mexico started to protest against environmental degradation as well as expropriation procedures by PEMEX, thereby linking ecological and social problems. In 1979, the worst accident in the history of Mexican oil took place in the Campeche Basin, where the Ixtoc 1 well spilled crude oil into the ocean for almost ten months. Although the environmental impact of oil drilling became the issue of a public debate in Mexico, these growing concerns with the ecologically and socially detrimental effects did not bring much of a change to the attitude of the government to this industry. As oil had been given such a central role to Mexico's economy, the need for environmental programmes was largely overlooked. While environmental standards and measures were already created, a lack of institutional support inhibited implementation (Márquez and López 1988: 470-80).

---

5   The increasing number of oil complexes in rural areas was also the result of the government policy of economic decentralization.

Next to the environmental damage of oil drilling itself, PEMEX has indirectly contributed heavily to atmospheric pollution via the poor quality of combustibles. Vehicles are the single main source of air pollution in Mexico, and contamination of the air is increasingly a problem in urban areas. A substantial share of atmospheric pollution from industries is derived from combustibles. Lead in petrol, and sulphur in diesel and combustible oil have been the most contaminating elements.

INDUSTRY

The prevalence of economic growth over environmental protection for the Mexican government was also evident from its conduct toward other industries. Since the 1940s, the manufacturing industry has been Mexico's most dynamic sector: in 1940, the industrial sector accounted for 20 per cent of GDP, while in 1980 its share had risen to 39 per cent (Brañes 1994: 491). This process was accompanied by higher levels of contamination. Between 1950 and 1970, the pollution intensity of Mexican manufacturing industry increased by 50 per cent, and between 1970 and 1990 by another 25 per cent. Industry thus moved towards more polluting sectors, and especially the sector of intermediaries increased its share in pollution intensity from two-thirds in 1970 to four-fifths in 1989. In fact, the increase in pollution intensity during this period was almost exclusively caused by the petrochemical and fertilizer sectors (between 1950 and 1970 they were already responsible for half the increase of pollution intensity).[6] Public sector participation in industry, then, has been negative for the environment since it was concentrated in heavily polluting activities (Ten Kate 1993: 11-3).

Another way in which the Mexican government contributed to environmental degradation by the industrial sector was through energy pricing. Especially between 1976 and 1982 prices of hydrocarbons for intermediate use were kept low compared to international prices. This implicit subsidization[7] has contributed to the energy-intensity of Mexico's industries, which is the most important source of industrial air pollution. While during the 1970s and 1980s OECD countries were able to reduce the energy intensity of manufacturing industry, Mexican industry experienced an average annual increase of 4.8 per

---

6 Like PEMEX's predominance in the petrochemical sector, the fertilizer industry was also dominated by a public sector company (FERTIMEX).

7 Implicit subsidies for energy products accounted for 4 to 7 per cent of GDP between 1980 and 1985 (Ten Kate 1993: 44).

cent. This increase was mainly caused by an increase in energy use per unit of output rather than growing output (Ten Kate 1993: 31-9).[8]

A lack of environmental infrastructure and lax enforcement of environmental legislation tempted industrialists to reduce production costs by illegal releases of sewage water and emissions, illegal dumping of (hazardous) waste, and neglecting the protection of workers. Until recently, industrialists had little incentive to invest in security measures except for economic reasons (Alfie 1991: 58; Kelly and Kamp 1991: 22-3). With sewerage and waste disposal services being far from sufficient and in a poor state, soil and water contamination have been widespread. In 1988, for instance, Mexico had only four recycling plants (London Environmental and Economics Centre 1992: 93). As a consequence, not only the health of workers in industry has been endangered, but also much wider areas and much larger numbers of people have been 'paying' for industrialization.

Apart from major cities like Mexico City, Guadalajara and Monterrey, industrial pollution has been caused by companies in the border region with the US. Despite poor physical conditions and little infrastructure at the border, foreign-owned assembly plants (*maquiladoras*) have emerged and expanded quickly to close to 2,000 plants employing nearly half a million Mexicans (Sánchez 1991a: 304; Texas Center for Policy Studies 1990). Environmental control has been weak and the lack of infrastructure is notorious, so that in many places the air, the soil, and the groundwater and rivers are heavily polluted by non-complying industry. This situation increasingly attracted US attention, and became very important in the transnational NAFTA debate on the environment.

URBANIZATION

Rural poverty and the lack of urban planning caused uncontrolled urbanization. As already mentioned, Mexico's industrialization was encouraged by subsidized energy, water and food for cities, directly or indirectly paid for by rural areas. While in 1940 20 per cent of the population lived in urban areas, this percentage had risen to 66 per cent by 1990, while Mexico's population more than quadrupled in this period (Coll-Hurtado 1993: 18). Although rapid and uncontrolled urbanization has been troubling a number of Mexican cities,[9] the

---

8 An assessment of the economic and environmental effects of the introduction of a fossil fuel tax in Mexico shows that a 20 per cent tax would result in a 13 per cent emission decrease at the cost of a 0.6 per cent decrease of GDP (Romero 1994: 120).

9 The border city Ciudad Juarez, for example, had in 1990 eight hundred thousand

problems of the Valley of Mexico (Mexico City or the Federal District and its surroundings) with its 20 to 25 million inhabitants have been most severe.

Mexico City is not only the world's largest city, it also has the highest population density and population growth. This is a direct result of the continuous high government investments in the Federal District (which covers a major share of Mexico City) at the cost of other municipalities. Combining over a quarter of the Mexican population with 35,000 industries in a relatively small area is bound to have enormous environmental effects. The current rate of the city's population growth is approximately 500,000 persons *annually*, concentrated in its peripheries (Legorreta 1994: 40-1). This growth is largely illegal and unplanned, and many households lack basic services such as running water, sewerage[10] and waste disposal. As the densely populated areas expand, city transport continues to grow, and environmental degradation becomes more and more severe.

Geographical circumstances only worsen Mexico City's environmental problems. At a height of 2,235 meters (7,400 feet) above sea level and surrounded by mountains, air pollution tends to form a constant blanket over the city, with health-threatening levels of particulates, ozone and lead.[11] The capacity of the enormous installations that are pumping up about a quarter of the city's drinking water[12] and pumping out sewage water to surrounding areas is structurally insufficient. As if this is not enough of a disaster, the swamp basis of this city and the exploitation of deep water reservoirs cause a constant sinking of buildings and infrastructure. As a consequence, the existing network of pipes for drinking water and sewerage is always in a state of damage and repair, and while drinking water is lost, sewage water pollutes both soil and (drinking) water. Evidently, these problems are a direct threat to the health of the city's inhabitants.

One possible solution for Mexico's problems with water would be higher prices for tap water. In contrast to the relatively expensive (and poor quality) water delivered by truck to families without running water, tap water is highly subsidized as consumer prices are below the real costs of water collection.

---

residents and no waste-water treatment facilities whatsoever (EPA and SEDUE 1991: III-8, III-24).

10 Nation-wide, only 16 per cent of Mexico's municipal and industrial waste water is treated (GAO 1991: 4).

11 Margulis (1991: 2) estimated that the economic costs of the health effects alone from Mexico City air pollution may be over $ 1 billion a year.

12 Water for urban areas is increasingly withdrawn from rural areas, which makes farmers pay for the expansion of cities.

Therefore, consumers and authorities have no incentive to save water (per capita use is very high) and to explore other sources of water besides groundwater and rivers (for instance rain water).[13] Water prices that would reflect real costs would motivate government agencies to maintain the system, while it would provide the resources to extend the supply system to more households. Moreover, higher fresh water prices could also improve the waste water situation for two reasons. First, some of the additional resources could be used to change the current situation in which half of the Mexicans have no sewerage while only 15 per cent of all municipal and industrial waste water in Mexico receives treatment (Hernández Lezama 1994: 198). Second, higher prices would motivate industry to start treating its own waste water (London Environmental and Economics Centre 1992: 90-1). However, apart from industrial interests, higher prices for tap water are likely to be resisted by poor citizens (at least those with running water in their homes).

Decentralization policies developed from the 1960s onwards have never been effective in the sense of structurally slowing down the pace of urbanization. The major reason for this lies in the fact that centralization has been economically beneficial. In the case of Mexico City, a century-long history of being a major and expanding economic and political centre is not easily reversed. Although there seems to be a tendency of slowed down industrial expansion in the Valley of Mexico, urbanization figures are still rising and the processes of concentration and territorial expansion therefore continue (Legorreta 1994: 17-9).[14]

— 2.2 Emerging attention for the environment —

The concept of conservation of natural resources has a long history in Mexico's policy as in the rest of Latin America. The original text of the 1917 Mexican

---

13 This is stunning when seen in the light of water scarcity in Mexico. Currently, about twice as much water is extracted from rivers in the Valley of Mexico than can be naturally regenerated, resulting in very serious over-exploitation (Romero Lankao 1994: 240-1).

14 In the end, decentralization of Mexico City might occur. One scenario for change holds that the economic gains of major companies would be threatened by strongly increasing production costs (of services, transport, prime materials, soil and water). Another scenario envisions political conflicts over multiplying dissatisfaction due to the insufficiency of basic needs, to a situation of the government losing its capacity of political control (Legorreta 1994: 18).

Constitution already refers to the conservation of natural resources. This concept, however, did not have an environmental objective (as we know it now) but formed a rejection of the idea of private property of land and water that had dominated prior to the Mexican Revolution. Through the natural resources article, public interest goes beyond individual interests: the state may attribute the right of use or property to private persons but can equally disown them. The basis of conservation of natural resources, then, is social welfare through honest sharing, protection and rational use (Brañes 1994: 62-5, 73).[15]

The constitutional obligation to protect the natural resources did not prevent the environmental problems described above. In the late 1960s, these problems received some attention from academics and the Mexican government. International developments were very important in this respect. Between the late 1960s and 1982, the period described in this section, the environment gradually emerged as a political issue and a start was made with setting up Mexico's environmental policy.

FIRST INCENTIVES FOR ENVIRONMENTAL POLICY

In the 1950s, environmental degradation received some attention from a small group of Mexican academics who began studying issues like contamination and erosion. After a few years, in 1965, some of them established the Mexican Association against the Contamination of Water and the Air (AMCAA). The interdisciplinary Association aimed to offer its scientific knowledge to government agencies in order to develop the legal, administrative and technical foundations of a federal environmental law. However, this merely technical focus limited its political role. Generally, concerned academics had no links with popular movements and political parties, and there was no organized political activity on environmental degradation. Nevertheless, the environmental research activities of a few Mexican academic and official research institutions promoted government attention. Mexico City's rapid expansion during the 1960s added to this early concern (Godau Schucking 1985: 53-4, 79; Mumme, Bath and Assetto 1988: 11-2).

---

15 Individual laws were developed for each natural resource (water, soil, forests, and natural parks), economic sector (agrarian, industrial, urban, and the service sectors), and human activities affecting nature (hunting, fishing and cattle-ranging). As these laws did not consider the cross-cutting relations between natural elements or human activities, the holistic approach of conservation of natural resources as established in the Constitution remained merely formal (Carmona Lara 1991: 1667-8).

International developments were important in encouraging Mexican officials to include environmental protection in federal policy. First of all, academics and research institutions in Mexico that studied environmental degradation were very much influenced by international currents. Growing evidence of ways in which pollution affected human health through complex ecological processes made Mexican scientists study these effects at home, which provided indications of Mexico's degradation. The Mexican government was also directly activated by external developments, including foreign studies of pollution, the introduction of the National Environmental Protection Act in the US in 1969, and the plans for a UN International Conference on the Human Environment to be held in Stockholm in 1972. In addition, an element of political image-building was involved. Since stagnating economic development was bringing the Mexican miracle to an end, environmental policy was partly taken on as a means to improve the President's position and Mexico's international prestige. Among other things, the position of Mexico within the group of Third World countries could benefit from environmental initiatives (Godau Schucking 1985: 52-9, 79).

Although Mexico and the US already had a long history of conflicts and negotiations about their border's water resources,[16] these border affairs had little to do with Mexico's environmental policy initiatives. The use of groundwater, the use of river water and the salinity of river water remained the main issues in the border disputes until the middle of the 1970s. Already in 1944, the US-Mexico Water Treaty dealing with groundwater apportionment was signed, and the International Boundary and Water Commission was installed. However, groundwater continued to be an important bilateral issue. Moreover, other environmental problems in the border region persisted without receiving attention.[17]

There seems to be no point in trying to decide whether the internal or the external factors and actors dominated the initial phase of Mexico's environmental policy-making.[18] International developments encouraged Mexican academics and government officials to take up the issue, but were not enough by themselves. The fact that it would take much longer in several other Latin American countries for environmental legislation and agencies to be established supports this idea. The Mexican government was in no way pressed to act, but a combination of concern among some middle-range officials (in

---

16 According the Sánchez Rodríguez they go back as far as 1884 (1990: 27).

17 See Stephen Mumme's study (1988) of the border water disputes.

18 Godau Schucking (1985) argues that international input was the most important. Mumme, Bath and Assetto (1988) maintain the opposite.

which contacts with academics played a role) and the international window of opportunity for some high-level officials was reason enough to treat environmental protection as a governmental task.

Environmental degradation started to receive some governmental attention at the beginning of the *sexenio* of President Luis Echeverría (1970-1976). Already during his election campaign the issue was discussed at a meeting of the PRI on the possibility of an environmental law (Godau Schucking 1985: 55). After his inauguration as president at the end of 1970, Echeverría acted rapidly on environmental matters. In early 1971, the reform of article 73 of the Mexican Constitution involved the inclusion of prevention and control of environmental pollution. Linked to the constitutional reform, the Federal Law for the Prevention and Control of Environmental Pollution was passed. The Council of General Health, which functioned directly under the President, was given the responsibility for the implementation of Mexico's first environmental law, while the Ministry of Health and Assistance (SSA) was to coordinate Mexico's environmental policy. In 1972, the Sub-ministry of Improvement of the Environment (SMA) was created as part of the SSA to carry out both tasks.

While the list of environmental policy initiatives was impressive, practice was not. The reform of article 73 and the creation of the federal environmental law meant progress since it was the first time that the environment was mentioned in the Mexican Constitution and that an environmental law was established. On the other hand, the policy focus on contamination and human health implied a limited view of environmental degradation. Notwithstanding the negative effects of industrial expansion in several major cities and the border region with the US, industrial pollution was not the only urgent environmental problem in Mexico. Erosion, urbanization, desertification and deforestation were seriously affecting Mexico's environment, but the early policy neglected these issues. Turning environmental problems into a health issue, like campaigns against smoking or drinking, also minimized the issue (Carmona Lara 1991: 1669).

The limited focus of Mexico's first environmental legislation may be traced back to several tendencies. First, industrial pollution and its impact on human health were central to the international environmental concern that arose during the 1960s. Another factor is the Mexican government's haste for constitutional reform that was felt after the plans for the UN environmental conference in Stockholm. Finally, the focus was limited because the political willingness to deal with environmental issues was. Public health was the lowest common denominator for the environment: it formed a legitimate basis for change that could count on support from economic sectors and the bureaucracy (Godau Schucking 1985: 58, 79-80).

The administrative structures for environmental policy turned out to be weak and problematic. The Council of General Health that was responsible for implementation of the environmental law formally gained a lot of power over other institutions, and even seemed to have a monopoly on environmental pollution, but it never became effective. Instead, the government left the coordination and implementation task up to a weak ministry and sub-ministry. Coordination was very important since the environmental law involved responsibilities for a number of ministries (including those of Industry and Trade, Water Resources, and Agriculture) as well as parastatal firms like PEMEX. The question of how the inexperienced and small sub-ministry with a very limited budget was to coordinate and control such powerful institutions was not addressed (Brañes 1994: 77-8, 127; Carmona Lara 1991: 1669; Godau Schucking 1985: 58-62).

The prompt creation of Mexico's environmental policy should thus not be misunderstood as priority of the issues for the Mexican government. Having some basic environmental policy was perceived as urgent within the international arena, but the environment was of little importance under Echeverría and never received high-level attention. Besides the lack of pressure on the Mexican government, this was the result of a lack of common ground for this policy among officials. Simultaneously, it was clear that environmental regulation contained a potential conflict with not only specific economic sectors and established political interests, but also with the economic development model and international investors (Godau Schucking 1985: 57, 79-80; Mumme, Bath and Assetto 1988: 14).

Although the environmental sub-ministry was weak in developing regulation, some other activities were taken up, predominantly in large cities. Data were collected on the proportions of problems, the issue of degrees of pollution was tackled, there were a few meetings with representatives of polluting industries, and some technical specialists were trained. By educating school children and publishing a few environmental scandals, SMA had some success in consciousness-raising, but in general its tasks far exceeded its capacities (Godau Schucking 1985: 64-69; Mumme, Bath and Assetto 1998: 14).

EMERGING POLITICAL PRESSURE AND GOVERNMENT RESPONSE

In contrast to the virtual lack of public interest in Mexico's environment earlier on, attention for Mexico's environmental problems started to rise during the 1970s, which resulted in some instances of political pressure. In 1972, a first major political confrontation occurred over the plans for a large hydroelectric barrage in the south-east and the moving of several communities. Villagers, farmers organizations and a few environmentalists cooperated in their opposition against these plans, but had no success. In Mexico City, there was growing concern over the rapid expansion of the city and the worsening air quality. Between 1972 and 1974 there were protests against contamination caused by the Cromatos plant, and in 1978 popular groups protested against plans for new highways. In 1979 there were protests in the south-east of Mexico, where farmers demonstrated against the environmental degradation that was caused by PEMEX's drilling and refining of oil. In addition, the oil spill of the Ixtoc I well in the Campeche Basin attracted both domestic and foreign attention, especially in the US. Finally, plans for a nuclear testing plant on the shore of the Pátzcuaro lake in Michoacán produced strong controversy. Between 1979 and 1981, a coalition of villages, popular organizations, farmers and environmentalists launched a series of activities to thwart these plans, which in the end were dropped. The heterogeneous Pátzcuaro protests not only formed the basis for local initiatives for sustainable development in the area, but were a national example of how popular organizations and environmentalists can cooperate for a joint cause. These protests may be seen as the start of political pressure for environmental protection.

Within the context of emerging pressure on the Mexican government, a few initiatives were taken. Some governmental plans adopted environmental considerations, and SMA developed new initiatives and started to handle industry somewhat less gently than before. In 1978, the Interministerial Commission for Environmental Health was created, but it never became more than a place for discussion. In that same year, some efforts were made to regulate air pollution in Mexico City. However, fragmented institutionalization remained, and resources for policy implementation continued to be insufficient to meet the objectives. The lack of governmental efforts for environmental protection was partly caused by Mexico's increasing economic instability in the late 1970s and the early 1980s. Simultaneously, pressures for protection could still be neglected as only a small group of researchers, officials and organizations were working on the issue, while popular action remained ad hoc. Environmental policy could thus remain largely symbolic, and was directed more at international than national recognition (Godau Schucking 1985: 71-7; Mumme, Bath and Assetto 1988: 15-6, 26).

Mexico-US cooperation on environmental matters was taken up in the second part of the 1970s, but proved rather complicated. Beside federal meetings and cooperation, transfrontier contacts were somewhat extended between local institutions. The latter type of cooperation was formalized by a memorandum in 1978 which paid attention to border problems but lacked sufficient regulation. Vague wording and lack of clarity on responsibilities added to the memorandum's weakness. While on the US side the Environmental Protection Agency (EPA) signed the memorandum, on the Mexican side this was done by SMA: a sub-ministry. This was an unfortunate construction since not only did SMA lack authority vis-à-vis EPA, but the memorandum also received little support at higher levels in the Mexican bureaucracy and responsibilities were not clear (Sánchez Rodríguez 1990: 27).

While environmental protection became hardly more of a government priority under Echeverría's successor José López Portillo (1976-1982) there was one exception: the revision of Mexico's environmental law in the Federal Environmental Protection Law (LFPA) at the end of his presidency. During the second half of 1981 the new environmental law was prepared, and in early 1982 it came into force. The federal law meant a major improvement of Mexico's environmental legislation because it substantially reinforced the 1971 law. It covered more environmental problems, such as marine pollution, radioactive hazards and the contamination of air, soil and water. Options for penalties for violators of the law were extended. The new law also contained a procedure for filing public complaints and mandating the SMA to investigate violations, implying a formal expansion of the role of civil society in environmental protection (Mumme, Bath and Assetto 1988: 17). Implementation of the new environmental law became the responsibility of President Miguel de la Madrid Hurtado (1982-1988).

— 2.3 The de la Madrid *sexenio* —

During the presidency of de la Madrid, environmental problems seriously attracted the government's attention as a result of several developments. First, slowly but steadily public awareness of the environment was spreading and criticism of government policy increased. Emerging environmental activism demonstrated that rising environmental concerns could not be channelled by and responded to through existing structures and institutions. Second, international attention to environmental problems became of greater influence, partly because of the emerging tendency of foreign (governmental and nongovernmental) funding to include environmental prerequisites. Third, there were a few cases of severe pollution that the government had to respond to in order to prevent worse.

Right from the start, de la Madrid's team aimed to alter environmental policy, but the approach was ambiguous.[19] On the one hand, during his first years in office, de la Madrid created an environmental ministry, initiated a large public campaign, and adopted a number of new regulations. For the first time, environmental policy was included in the National Development Plan (1983-88), and a National Ecology Plan and a National Ecology Programme were presented. Reforms of the Constitution involved positive elements for environmental policy. At the end of his presidency, de la Madrid presented a substantially reformed environmental law. From this perspective, Brañes (1994: 157-8) may be right that of the four Mexican presidents between 1970 and 1994, de la Madrid contributed most to the advancement of Mexican environmental policy.

On the other hand, actual performance fell far short of expectations. While de la Madrid referred to environmental themes in his public statements more than any former president, and legislative and administrative advancements were considerable, budget cuts disproportionately hurt the environmental agencies. This supports the idea that, rather than a genuine attempt to improve environmental policy, the efforts of the De la Madrid administration were preemptive reforms that served to prevent uncontrolled mobilization (Mumme 1992: 127). This ability of the state-party system to incorporate a political issue before it becomes a source of wide-spread dissent has contributed to the PRI's domination of Mexican politics. The incorporation of an issue, however, does not necessarily imply that the issue is also given higher priority.

ADMINISTRATIVE RESTRUCTURING

In December 1982, shortly after de la Madrid took office, the institutional arrangement of environmental policy was changed. The Ministry of Urban Development and Ecology (SEDUE) was created out of the former Ministry of Urban Development and Housing (SAHOP), on the one hand, and SSA and ecology functions of the Ministry of Agriculture and Water Resources (SARH), on the other hand. Each policy area was represented by a sub-ministry: for

---

19 Environmental policy was already discussed by de la Madrid's team prior to the election campaign. At these internal discussions, the failures of the policy of predecessors were recognized (Godau Schucking 1985: 77).

environment the Sub-ministry of Ecology (SE) was created.[20] The six units functioning under the SE were: Prevention and Control of Environmental Pollution, Prevention and Control of Water Contamination, Ecological Law and Environmental Impact, Parks and Protected Ecological Zones, Ecological Protection and Restoration, and Wildlife. Apart from administrative change at federal level, de la Madrid aimed to decentralize certain environmental protection tasks to states and cities, resulting in states creating administrative units for environmental protection.[21]

The institutional reform that created SEDUE implied a new approach to environmental protection, reflecting the more comprehensive character of the 1981 environmental law. Environmental protection was no longer perceived as merely a health issue as it became linked to urban development, public works, and the use of natural resources. In an implicit manner, then, the idea of eco-development was adopted. However, the environmental law had a weak legal foundation, which limited SEDUE's ability to implement it. The federal character of the law also inhibited genuine involvement of lower authorities in environmental protection, despite formal aims and claims (Carmona Lara 1991: 1687-8). Moreover, the problem of the diffusion of tasks related to environmental protection (health, renewable and non-renewable natural resources) among government agencies was not solved.

---

20 There had also been an internal proposal to create a small but strong federal environmental body instead of a relatively large sub-ministry, as can be read in an undated report (*Programa de Ecología y Medio Ambiente, Documento de Síntesis*) by the Ecology and Environment Commission (probably a group of persons within and/or closely linked to the PRI and government agencies), written somewhere between de la Madrid's presidential campaign and his inauguration in December 1982. Ideas expressed at popular consultations during de la Madrid's campaign were points of departure for the report, that claims to be based on the views of more than 500 hundred persons. In the view of this commission, advantages of a federal environmental organism over a ministry would be: efficiency, flexibility, simplicity and transparency, which would contribute to a good image, decentralization, and continuity.

21 Decentralization was done through the 1983 reform of Article 115 of the Constitution that embodied a general extension of the authority of states and municipalities. With respect to ecological care, the reform allowed municipalities to establish environmental standards, and to become involved in urban planning and civil services (especially drinking water), involving control over the use of the soil, regulation of urban land property, provision of licenses for constructions, and participation in the creation of ecological reserves. In addition, the 1984 revision of the environmental law created the possibility of environmental control agreements between SEDUE and states or municipalities (Brañes 1994: 90-1; Mumme, Bath and Assetto 1988: 22; SEDUE 1983: 73).

The creation of SEDUE has often been misunderstood as the creation of a genuine environmental ministry. As Brañes (1994: 112, 133) explains, the installation of the ministry was largely a reinforcement of the existing legal and administrative structure of Mexico's environmental policy. First, SEDUE was not constructed as a super-ministry incorporating the environmental responsibilities of other ministries, with the exception of certain policy areas that had previously been the task of SARH. Second, SEDUE did not become a genuinely specialized ministry either, because it was not a merger of the environmental units of other ministries. Third, SEDUE could not be considered the coordinating ministry either. Although SEDUE was to coordinate other ministries on environmental matters, the National Ecology Commission (CONADE) created in 1985 was also charged with coordinating environmental policy.

The actual weakness of Mexico's first cabinet-level environmental agency vis-à-vis other ministries seriously limited its role. SEDUE depended on other agencies for policy implementation, partly because of SEDUE's limited resources. SEDUE's environmental budget, for instance, equalled only one sixth of PEMEX's budget for sewage and pollution control in 1984 (Mumme, Bath and Assetto 1988: 24, 28).[22] Due to its impotence, however, SEDUE could not influence the application of financial resources of other ministries and large parastatals. Moreover, non-compliance or even sabotage by other ministries and parastatal companies often impeded the implementation of SEDUE's tasks.

A short confidential office memorandum written in 1984 by an anonymous World Bank consultant illuminates the poor position of SEDUE within the government, and the notorious gap between formal administrative arrangements and their practice in Mexico (and Mexican policy in general).[23] The memorandum revealed wide-spread non-compliance with the official requirement that

---

22 Apart from its general image as a notorious polluter and the pile of information on the ecological damage of oil production and accidents, there is little information on PEMEX's environmental efforts. Stern (1993: 191-2) reports that PEMEX is conspicuously absent as a major buyer of environmental technologies and services, and that the company has only established small-scale environmental projects. On the other hand, the Trade Promotion Coordinating Committee mentions PEMEX as a large purchaser of remediation equipment, waste-water treatment equipment, and services (TPCC 1994: 6).
23 The assessment dated 24 January 1984 and based on a visit to Mexico confirms the widely known weakness of SEDUE vis-à-vis other secretariats and major parastatals. Although it describes the situation at the beginning of de la Madrid's *sexenio*, it is mentioned in this paragraph to give an idea of the depth of the problem. Despite various legal reforms that occurred after the World Bank assessment and did to a certain extent improve SEDUE's role, the structural weakness of the agency within the cabinet and the consequences for its functioning remained.

SEDUE should be notified beforehand of any individual, enterprise or government agency wishing to engage in activities that may modify the environment, after which a detailed impact assessment might be requested. SEDUE's environmental impact office was too small, under-financed and under-trained for this task (a professional staff of 22 was supposed to review 14,000 projects annually), leaving the executive agencies themselves responsible for carrying out the assessments. The Ministry of Programming and Budgeting (SPP) often ignored SEDUE's recommendations and allowed (funding for) major projects by ministries and parastatals without following the required procedures. In addition, governmental agencies did not provide SEDUE with their annual investment programme, so that SEDUE personnel often relied on informal contacts with persons working in other institutions for information on impending projects. Instead of being involved in project planning and design, SEDUE officials intervened in the implementation phase, as so-called firemen.[24]

Taken together, the evidence of SEDUE's weakness and failures shows that its mandate was insufficient for implementing Mexico's environmental legislation. SEDUE was presented as Mexico's first environmental ministry, and de la Madrid used its creation to improve the government's environmental image domestically and abroad. However, it is likely that SEDUE was conceived by the Mexican government to be less than effective in the implementation of the improving legislation.

LIMITS TO REGULATORY INITIATIVES

As a result of Lopéz Portillo's adoption of a new environmental law at the end of his *sexenio*, de la Madrid started with a set of new regulations to which he added a few more. With the 1983 reform of article 25, the Mexican Constitution

---

24 The case of the construction of a border highway (for military purposes) through the Lacandón jungle in Chiapas demonstrates to what this late intervention may lead. The World Bank memorandum describes how the Ministry of Roads and Transportation (SCT) was preparing this highway, which would encroach upon the Montes Azules Biosphere Reserve, without any consultation with SEDUE. When SEDUE required a preliminary environmental impact assessment, SCT had already advanced its plans considerably, and instead of rapidly producing an assessment it proposed that SEDUE contribute $4 million to reroute the highway away from the reserve. As SEDUE's 1983 budget for pollution control and ecology amounted to $7 million (Mumme, Bath and Assetto 1988: 24), this was impossible. Eventually, the whole highway project was cancelled by Salinas as a high environmental profile action (Barton Bray 1995: 186).

included not only the conservation of natural resources, but also care for the environment. This first explicit mention of the environment in the Constitution entails that the use of productive resources by social and private sectors be subject to environmental protection. While making a significant step ahead, the article is limited in that activities of the public sector (parastatals) are not included. Moreover, it is restricted by only mentioning the use of productive resources as a source of environmental degradation (Brañes 1994: 79-81).

De la Madrid's environmental policy focused on pollution and nature conservation, while natural resources and ecosystems hardly received attention. This is demonstrated by the subdivision of SEDUE's environmental budget between 1983 and 1988. While 44 per cent of this budget went to contamination control, and 25 per cent was used for conservation projects, only 18 per cent went to protection and restoration (Carabias and Provencio 1994: 401-4). Environmental regulations developed under de la Madrid were mainly directed at the industrial sector and urban areas. Particular attention was given to Mexico City, Guadalajara and Monterrey, the *maquiladoras* in the border area with the US, and the oil industry in the south-east of Mexico. In addition, some efforts were made to prevent pollution from injuring other economic sectors, like the fishing industry harming tourism. Air pollution in Mexico City, the most salient problem of failing environmental policy, was the largest single policy issue. An atmospheric monitoring system was already functioning in the capital in 1983 (Mumme, Bath and Assetto 1988: 24).[25]

Environmental policy continued to rely on planning, bargaining, education, data collection and incentives instead of sanctions, despite a revision of the environmental law of 1984 that somewhat extended the possibilities to impose sanctions and penalties on violators of the law. Besides the legal limitations on sanctions, high penalties for violations of environmental regulations were also unusual because of SEDUE's reluctance to impose them. Apart from a few cases in which SEDUE moved against contaminating industry, the ministry hardly forced private industries to clean up, pay for cleaning up, or cease production, as it did not want to police industries (Barkin 1991: 98; Mumme, Bath and Assetto 1988: 25; Mumme and Sánchez 1990: 49, 60).[26]

---

25 In 1986, a SEDUE report recognized the insufficiency of its policy measures. While protection measures in cities had been restricted to air pollution, sewerage and solid waste, protection in rural areas had focused on the "conservation of natural resources" (SEDUE 1986: 59). However, the report's clarification that the latter was done by means of national parks, ecological and biosphere reserves and hunting bans for certain plants and animals shows that nature conservation rather than natural resources had been its rural focus.

A major obstacle to implementing the new environmental regulatory system was the insufficiency of financial input, which was aggravated by the economic crisis of the early 1980s. Austerity and Structural Adjustment implied budget cuts that hurt SEDUE as a whole, but even more the ecological sub-ministry SE. Official figures are hard to obtain, but according to Günther (1989/90: 55-6) SE's budget as a percentage of the total government budget was reduced from 0.08 per cent to 0.04 per cent in the period 1984-1988. In other words, the government budget as a whole was under pressure and the environmental budget was disproportionally cut. This is confirmed by World Bank (1992: 7) figures showing that the operational budget of SE declined by 60 per cent in real terms between 1986 and 1989.[27] Consequently, the agency was not even able to plan for more than one year (Brañes 1994: 168, 598; Günther 1989/90: 58). Other ministries with environmental tasks were reported to spend little on protection too.[28] The Ministry of Agricultural and Water Resources, for instance, only allocated 0.6 per cent of its 1987 budget to soil conservation (London Economics and Environmental Centre 1992: 86). Brañes (1994: 168) therefore calls the 1980s a lost decade for the environment.

While the lack of resources can be partly explained by Mexico's economic hardship, the disproportional cutting of environment budgets supports the conclusion that the environment was low on the government's agenda. On paper, Mexico's environmental policy was considerably strengthened during the 1980s, but practice lagged far behind. In the unusually open and critical government report *Informe 1986*, SEDUE admits that between 1984 and 1986 little progress was made in executing the National Ecology Plan. The report acknowledges that protection efforts by the Mexican government had been insufficient, in part because of the discontinuity of SEDUE's work programmes

---

26 SEDUE's intention to sign understandings with private industries similar to those signed with major parastatals probably does not go beyond the discussion stage. This difference in attitude towards the parastatal sector and the private sector may be explained in two ways. First, according to a government publication, SEDUE perceived the parastatal sector as the sector contributing the most to ecological deterioration, and hoped that reforms in this sector would set an example to private firms (SEDUE 1983: 58). Second, de la Madrid was trying to win back private industries' confidence and encouraging this sector to take a lead in development, and being harsh on pollution matters went counter to these aims.

27 The report indicates that the salaries for higher level permanent staff decreased by 50 per cent, while the sub-ministry lost approximately 25 per cent of its permanent staff.

28 An early SEDUE report mentioned budgetary problems as a result of the fact that functions taken over from other state agencies have not been accompanied by a transfer of resources (SEDUE 1983: 57).

(SEDUE 1986: 59, 61). The threefold change of environmental ministers between 1982 and 1988 did not contribute to continuity either. In this context,
SEDUE's performance was strongly limited, and mainly consisted of planning,
bargaining, education, data collection and incentives, and promoting environmental values in and outside the government.

POPULAR MOBILIZATION[29]

While environmental policy remained weak, environmental degradation
rapidly became an important political issue in de la Madrid's *sexenio*. Increasingly, the environment became an issue of civil concern and popular mobilization, and environmental groups developed both at the elite level and at the level
of medium and low-income groups. During his first years in office, de la Madrid
actively encouraged popular mobilization on environmental issues. This initiative consisted of a 15-month national environment tour of public meetings and
forums at the municipal, state and federal level, launched in 1983. In 1984, this
tour ended with a national meeting that coincided with the United Nation's
World Ecology Day (June 5). The meeting was attended by a large pluralistic
group of representatives from ministries, agencies, the PRI, private sector organizations, environmental organizations and even an opposition party (Brañes
1994: 141; Mumme, Bath and Assetto 1988: 18-9).

   Environmental protests prior to 1982 had had limited political clout, so rather
than being a response to civil (independent) mobilization, the popular mobilization initiative of de la Madrid was to prevent the growing discontent from falling
outside the state-party structures of consultation and representation.[30] The few
regional environmental protests that had been witnessed before de la Madrid's
inauguration had not been of real concern to the federal government, but they
had shown the increasing uneasiness of Mexicans about environmental degradation and (the lack of) government policy. The environment was a new political
issue, and emerging environmental organizations did not fit into existing corporatist state-society linkages (unions, etc). De la Madrid's environment tour,
then, can be perceived as a means of establishing relations with environmental

---

29 Both this section on popular mobilization and the following section on environmental activism are substantially based on a previous study carried out with Jolle Demmers
(Demmers and Hogenboom 1992).

30 According to a US university source (19/IV/94), the idea for popular mobilization was
partly based on a trip by a team of Mexican government officials to Europe in the early
1980s to study the Green Movement.

groups and preventing uncontrolled mobilization. The tour lent the government an image of environmental concern: government discourse was stressing the need for action and the need for cooperation between state and civil society (Mumme 1992: 127; Mumme, Bath and Assetto 1988: 27).

After the conclusion of the environment tour in June 1984, environmental organizations were de facto granted a role as intermediary institutions between the Mexican government and civil society. Formally, the National Ecology Commission created in 1985 was the forum for popular consultation, but interaction between government agencies and environmental non-governmental organizations (ENGOs) tended to take place through direct contacts instead. Interestingly, even organizations that criticized Mexico's political system and the lack of public scrutiny found themselves being invited by government agencies to discuss policy, plans and projects, and they often responded positively. Although this interaction of the government with non-governmental groups had an ad hoc character, and government agencies made no commitments, it can be described as positive interaction.

There seem to have been at least three reasons for environmental government agencies to encourage, support and cooperate with ENGOs under de la Madrid, and they should be understood in the context in which these agencies attempted to improve Mexico's environmental policy: economic crisis, little priority of the issue within the government as a whole, and increasing protests from civil society. First, by being in constant contact with ENGOs, government agencies could remain informed of the concerns within civil society and the perception of governmental policy. Second, encouragement of environmental groups could provide needy government agencies with access to the qualities and capacities of these groups, such as knowledge, experience, local contacts, and helpful criticism. Third, cooperation could add to the government's legitimacy and prevent environmental organizations from openly expressing their criticism.

Inclusive and corporatist politics, which have been a major pillar of the continuity of the state-party dominance since the Mexican Revolution, affected the relation between ENGOs and the Mexican government. De la Madrid's environment tour fitted perfectly in the strategy of at least symbolically incorporating all political issues of (potential) importance, and taking the lead by adopting NGO terminology and models. The focus of NGOs on the government is partly the result of this limited room for independent activism. In addition, in many cases government agencies are the only available source of material or immaterial concessions.

The relation between the Mexican state and civil society has been strongly affected by the (threat of) co-optation of leaders (or organizations) that are

potentially successful. Co-optation not only takes the form of absorption into
official structures, but can also consist of persons or groups curtailing their criticism in exchange for government favours. NGOs have to choose between "two
uninviting alternatives": come to an agreement with the regime that comprises
their political independence but guarantees material concessions for their supporters, or remain independent and thereby risk losing popular support. Official encouragement of independent organizations is often used to weaken more
threatening groups. Even more serious is the threat of state repression of organizations that are successful and hard to co-opt (Adler Hellman 1991).[31]

Contrary to the tendency of increasing citizen participation in Mexico's environmental politics between 1982 and 1988, the involvement of economic sectors was in general low-key. The agreements that SEDUE signed with parastatal
companies were little more than statements of intent. Only in cases of public
pressure, such as pollution by PEMEX (air pollution due to poor combustibles),
AZUCAR (pollution of rivers and groundwater by industrial sugar refining), and
FERTIMEX (fertilizers) did SEDUE sign more effective agreements (Mumme,
Bath and Assetto 1988: 25; SEDUE 1986: 61). The involvement of private companies was also low. Apart from a list produced by SEDUE in 1987 that mentions
147 firms agreeing to environmental measures (Barkin 1991: 104), and some private sector activities in the border region with the US (see the section on expanding external influence), there are no accounts of efforts and results, even
though the private sector was to a certain degree participating in the popular
consultation forums at the beginning of the *sexenio* (SEDUE 1983: 57).

ENVIRONMENTAL ACTIVISM

Next to de la Madrid's environmental mobilization campaign, the emergence
of ENGOs was also part of a general surge of independent popular organization
in Mexico. The crisis of 1982 had grave economic repercussions for most Mexicans. In addition, the cuts in government budgets harmed the relations between the government and the corporatist representation organizations of labour, middle class and industry. Independent organizations, and later on also
opposition parties, became more numerous and larger in this context. In Mexico City, the major earthquake of 1985 added to this independent political mo-

---

31 A research among 40 Mexican ENGOs revealed that 31 worked with government
agencies, including 12 that received government funding. One out of four of the surveyed organizations had experienced state repression (Kürzinger et al. 1990: 37, 122,
Table 24).

bilization. The disaster not only brought the practice of massive corruption of government officials in urban development and construction projects into the open, it also demonstrated that in many instances non-governmental organizations were more effectively dealing with the emergency situation than government agencies were. Due to these changes, the pressure on the Mexican government for democratization was increasing. In fact, Mexican environmental organizations, like other NGOs, were perceived as democratizing forces that represented a part of civil society. As will become clear below, some ENGOs were indeed involved in the political struggle for democratization, and played an important role by channelling demands from civil society to the government, but political representation of civil society was beyond their capacities.

Meanwhile, several environmental incidents and processes contributed to the surge of environmental activism. Pollution caused by manufacturing industries and PEMEX became more and more known to the public. In Mexico City, air pollution increasingly reached alarming levels, especially in the winters of 1984 and 1985. And in December 1984, hundreds of people were killed when a government propane distribution centre in Mexico City's industrial suburb San Juan Ixhuatepec exploded.

Attempts were made to cooperate and coordinate activities among the growing number of environmental organizations. In 1984, the Alternative Network for Eco-Communication was established and joined by 130 organizations. The main success of this network was in bringing about contacts between many organizations. A year later, a large number of ENGOs were present at the First National Meeting of Ecologists in Mexico City. This time, a wide variety of groups established a joint agenda of action priorities, which ranged from defending tropical forests to stopping the nuclear plant that was built in Laguna Verde, Veracrúz. A side effect of the meeting was the foundation of the Pact of Ecologist Groups (PGE) by some 50 organizations in 1986.

The evolving environmental "community" in Mexico incorporated a wide variety of organizations. There are several classifications of Mexico's environmental NGOs in the literature.[32] They are based on either: the field of interest of organizations (e.g. nature conservation, ecology, eco-development); their socio-economic and geographical background (e.g. popular and intellectual groups; rural and Mexico City organizations); their main field of activity (such

---

32 Cf. Carruthers (1996); Kürzinger et al. (1991); Sándoval (1991); Quadri de la Torre (1989). Classifying Mexican environmental organizations is complicated as they are generally not open about their activities, strategies and funding. Unlike companies and political organizations, they do not have to account for their activities, except for externally funded projects (Barkin 1994: 345).

as political activist and research groups); or a mixture of these classifications. Building on the experience of the 1970s, cooperative relations have been not only extended among (different types of) environmental organizations but also between ENGOs and other groups such as indigenous social movements (cf. Carruthers 1996).[33] In addition, non-environmental organizations have been adopting environmental protection as part of their activities. There are, for instance, various peasant organizations in Mexico taking environmental responsibility, working on sustainable agriculture and forestry, and protesting against pollution (cf. Barton Bray 1995). These initiatives and new heterogeneous relations for sustainable development have largely emerged at the local level, and may be viewed as a counterweight to centralist government policy with its limited focus.

For a better understanding of Mexico's environmental politics at the national level, a short presentation of some of the more well-known ENGOs that have directed their activities towards influencing federal environmental policy follows. In particular, a number of environmental organizations in Mexico City with intellectual, upper-class (active) members have criticized the government and have proposed alternatives to existing legislation, programmes, and practice.

One of the older environmental organizations is the Mexican Ecologist Movement (MEM), founded in 1981 by Alfonso Ciprés Villareal and Jorge Gonzalez Torres, who had been active in the PRI for many years. The MEM claims to have many (10.000) members, but its president Ciprés controls everything and the MEM merely revolves around him. The Movement hardly has relations with other ENGOs. Many ecologist organizations do not trust the MEM and blame it for not taking a stand when really needed. The MEM appears often in the media; image building seems to be its main concern (Zagema 1991: 89-92).[34]

---

33 In his study of the alliances between environmental and indigenous social movements in Mexico, Carruthers (1996: 1018) finds that organic intellectuals play a key role as living bridges between the two, and that ENGOs predominantly have relations with grassroots support organizations. These support groups tend to play a double role. On the one hand, they emphasize autonomy from the state, and assist grassroots organizations in their activities so that these organizations can remain as independent from state interference as possible. On the other hand, support groups (or their individual members) also deal with the state through making policy recommendations, providing state agencies with information, and participating in political networks (Carruthers 1996: 1021; Demmers and Hogenboom 1992: 36).

34 In a study first published in 1987, Michael Redclift presents a very different picture of the MEM. In his view, the MEM is a very effective and independent pressure group, and highly critical of Mexico's official policy. Redclift mentions that several attempts have been made to infiltrate the organization, not only by the PRI but also by large industry

Jorge Gonzalez Torres left the MEM and initiated the National Ecologist Alliance (AEN). In 1987, the AEN evolved into the Ecologist Party of Mexico (PEM) that joined the coalition of opposition parties that supported Cuauthémoc Cárdenas' candidacy for the presidential elections of 1988. Although the PEM seems more open to other ENGOS than the MEM, many ecologist organizations distrust this party as well. This is not only the result of the suspicion of most ENGOS of party politics. The PRI past of Gonzalez and his behaviour as leader of the PEM have damaged his credibility. Probably Gonzalez has made deals with the PRI, and both in and outside Mexico the PEM is not perceived as a serious political party.[35]

A third organization is the Group of Hundred (*Grupo de los Cien*), which is well-known both inside and outside Mexico. A great number (more than one hundred) of famous artists and intellectuals have given their name to this group that is therefore able to easily attract media attention for its opinion on environmental matters. During the last few years, however, the poet and writer Homero Arídjis has often operated on his own initiative as representative of the Grupo.

Finally, after its creation in 1986, the PGE consisted of about 50 smaller ecologist NGOS, some radical, some moderate. The Pact functioned as a network and left considerable freedom to the opinions and activities of its member organizations. The PGE soon became an important forum for ecologist organizations, with the magazine *Ecología: Política/Cultura* serving as a platform. In addition, the Pact has been politically active and has sometimes worked with government agencies on environmental solutions and programmes.

Several weaknesses have inhibited the development of a genuine environmental movement in Mexico. Mexican ENGOS are generally small, and a disproportionate number of them are located in Mexico City, other major cities and the border region. Most groups lack resources and sometimes also knowledge and experience, which hinders the continuity of their activities. A fundamental lack of solidarity among the many and diverse organizations is also an obstacle to the development of a Mexican environmental movement. Personalism, a middle-class or elitist bias, and mutual distrust which is linked to the

---

and the Catholic Church (sic) (Redclift 1989: 164-6). Based on Zagema's research, my discussions with Mexican environmental activists as well as my attendance at a MEM meeting, I can only but conclude that Redclift's assessment is not (or perhaps no longer) accurate.

35 In an open letter published in *Proceso* (771, 12/VIII/91: 66), a large number of ENGOS and even candidates of the PEM itself accused the party of moral, environmental and electoral fraud during the 1991 elections. They especially denounced its leadership's way of doing politics.

culture of government co-optation are widespread among environmental organizations. At national meetings, organizations based in Mexico City tend to
dominate discussions. As a result, relations between ENGOs and other NGOs
often consist of exchange of information instead of effective means of political
strengthening. Similarly, relations of ENGOs with opposition parties have been
merely informal. Reasons for ENGOs to keep a distance from political parties
can be: a fear of losing identity within party structures; a fear of being caught
up in party politics and conflicts; a fear of (internal) conflicts within the organization; a fear of PRI repression in case of alignment to an opposition party; and
the expectation that there is little to gain from parties that are very vertically
structured and largely interested in gaining votes.

Linked to the lack of solidarity among environmental organizations is the
tendency among NGOs and social movements to sometimes reproduce negative
components of Mexico's political system. Despite their efforts at democratization of the political system, they often find themselves falling squarely into the
logic of clientelism (Adler Hellman 1991: 6). Especially ENGOs working at the
local level sometimes employ the same clientelist strategies (of giving and binding) as government agencies and the PRI, simply because it is a strategy to obtain popular support that works in Mexico. ENGOs may even compete with
government agencies or other NGOs for the favour of certain groups in civil
society. In addition, while critical ENGOs tend to reject a clientelist relation
with the government for the sake of independence, there are moderate and
pragmatic organizations for whom immediate support for their activities
weighs more heavily.

Mexican ENGOs have also been criticized for their restricted political views
and strategies. As noted before, Mexican NGOs including environmental
groups tend to focus on the government. Whereas ENGOs in other countries at
times choose to confront producers and consumers directly, Mexican groups
hardly use this strategy. Most environmental organizations focus on specific
local, regional and national problems, disregarding the more structural social,
economic or political causes of these problems (Alfie 1995: 18; Barkin 1991: 92-3).

Towards the end de la Madrid's presidency, discontent with his environmental policy was rising among ENGOs. After the first few promising years, it
became clear that his policy produced little results. The construction of Mexico's first nuclear plant in Laguna Verde (in the state of Veracrúz) articulated the
gap between formal policy and policy practice. It turned out to be a catalyst of
environmental protests against the government. After the disaster with the Rus-
sian nuclear reactor in Chernobil in 1986, groups protesting against the Mexican nuclear plant could count on widespread popular support. In 1988, local
groups, ENGOs and other non-governmental organizations created a network

to coordinate their protests. Large demonstrations and blockades attracted major media attention, and high-level government officials were willing to discuss with activists (Arías and Barquera 1988: 253-66, 341-58).

With the imminent presidential elections and the PRI's experiencing an unprecedented lack of popular support, the Laguna Verde protests even became a catalyst of strong criticism of the regime. The coalition of left-wing opposition parties headed by Cuauthémoc Cárdenas was increasingly favourite, and threatened the position of the state-party system. As opposition parties started to express support for the anti-nuclear movement, it became very problematic for the PRI and its candidate Salinas. The Laguna Verde protests addressed the need for democratization of Mexico's political system, presenting the nuclear plant as an example of the results of authoritarian rule. Critical environmental organizations joined the demands for political reform and became actively involved in this popular movement for democracy.

In Mexico City, people were very worried about pollution, ranking ecology just behind personal security as their principal noneconomic priority and pointing to air pollution as their number one concern (*Excelsior* 15/XII/87, 24/I/88). With one-quarter of the Mexican population living in the metropolis and the already declining support for the PRI in this city, these negative popular views of the government's environmental efforts became an electoral issue. In 1988 there were several demonstrations against government incompetence, and opposition parties adopted the environment as an issue of importance. Until the elections in July 1988 these open confrontations were largely tolerated, but afterwards critical groups were repressed (see 2.4).[36]

EXTERNAL INFLUENCE

Whereas Mexico's environmental policy politicized rapidly at the national level between 1982 and 1988, the involvement of external actors increased more slowly. Linked to a recognition of the border region's importance for Mexico's integration in North America, the border environment was taken more seriously by the Mexican government. In August 1983, de la Madrid visited the US to discuss the possibilities of an improved approach to tackle the bilateral environmental problems. Later that year, President Reagan and de la Madrid signed

---

36 Unless indicated otherwise, the above is based on a study carried out in 1992 (Demmers and Hogenboom 1992). Records of repression of environmentalists and other abuses of human rights with respect to environmental protests in Mexico can be found in Human Rights Watch and NRDC (1992).

the Agreement on Cooperation for the Protection and Improvement of the Environment in the Border Area in La Paz, Mexico.

The La Paz agreement created the first formal framework for combatting cross-border environmental pollution, primarily addressing pollution generated by the *maquiladoras* in Mexico and the copper industry in Mexico and the US.[37] Although the Mexico-US environmental activities with respect to the border were complicated by the economic inequality of the two countries, these pollution issues proved to enhance mutual efforts, to which some popular protests might have contributed. As it was signed at the presidential level and was the responsibility of SEDUE and EPA, the agreement had a stronger political and administrative basis while being more focused on communication and problem-solving than the 1978 memorandum had been. On the other hand, the new bilateral initiative was still limited since the La Paz agreement was not a treaty but an executive agreement, which is not binding or enforceable. Moreover, the annexes that were developed after 1983 showed that despite Mexican attempts to achieve a 'package-deal' agreement, environmental diplomacy remained largely based on the US case-to-case approach (Barry and Sims 1994: 74; Maihold 1989: 402-6, 409-10; Sánchez Rodríguez 1990: 7, 35, 54).[38]

From 1984 onwards, however, bilateral environmental efforts slowed down again. From the side of Mexico, the border remained a relatively high priority, as can bee seen from the amount of government spending for the border envi-

---

37 Among other things, the La Paz agreement established a zone of one hundred kilometres on each side of the border which was to be used on the basis of equality, reciprocity and mutual use. Next, a start was made with monitoring sources of pollution in both countries. The Reagan administration incorporated the principle that the polluter pays in the agreement, against Mexico's wish. Mexico claimed it had insufficient resources and hoped for financial support from the US. However, the US feared for a precedent, and turned Mexico's request down (Maihold 1989: 405-6; Sánchez Rodríguez 1990: 36).

38 The five annexes to the La Paz agreement addressed: (1) the construction of Tijuana-San Diego waste water facilities; (2) contingency planning and emergency actions for hazardous substance spills; (3) transboundary movement of hazardous waste; (43) emission limits for copper smelters; (5) programs on urban air pollution. While some annexes meant progress for bilateral environmental cooperation, annex 3 on the transboundary movement of hazardous waste remained problematic. The annex was supposed to deal with the trend of hazardous waste transport from the US to Mexico, and Mexico's problems with the waste from maquiladoras due to insufficient capacity for storage, processing and recycling. Illegal waste dumping in the Mexican desert demonstrated the failure of annex 3, and discredited the agreement as a whole (Maihold 1989: 406-10; Sánchez Rodríguez 1990: 42-51).

ronment between 1985 and 1988 (a total of $80 million), the year in which the federal environmental budget was substantially cut (Sánchez Rodríguez 1990: 20). The main reason for border cooperation to slow down, then, was the tough attitude of President Reagan towards Mexico in general. Between 1983 and 1986, environmental protection was in fact the only policy issue on which some results were obtained at the yearly presidential meetings, ironically lending an image of continuity to the tense bilateral relations at that time. Reagan's attitude, however, was the opposite of the increasing interest of the US Congress in the bilateral relations and the border environment. In contrast with the NAFTA debate, in the 1980s the Mexican government did not attempt to defend its interests by influencing the US Congress on bilateral environmental issues (Maihold 1989: 409; Sánchez Rodríguez 1990: 7, 20-2).[39]

The border environment relations involved more actors than only federal agencies. Besides SEDUE, EPA, and the International Boundary and Water Commission, states and municipalities were involved too. Especially in the US, these lower government levels contributed to environmental cooperation by means of interest representation and definition of the problems. Non-governmental organizations worked mainly on specific issues and played an important role in raising issues. Another input came from private sector groups such as Chambers of Commerce, representing their interests towards the authorities. Finally, the World Bank was involved via support for Mexico, such as the 1982 loan amounting to $450 million for improving the Cananea copper industry (Sánchez Rodríguez 1990: 16-7).

With respect to non-border concerns, international input was emerging from foreign ENGOs and development organizations. The support of these organizations contributed to the success of Mexican NGO initiatives. According to Barkin (1991: 103), "[t]he most effective nongovernmental efforts involved the collaboration of Mexican groups with interested parties from abroad". A research among 40 Mexican environmental organizations showed that half of them received resources from abroad. Both for funding and information, relations with US and European organizations were important, while Canadian

---

39 The recommendations of Sánchez Rodríguez (1990: 86-9, 114-7) in this respect are interesting, since they proved to be quite prophetic for the NAFTA politics, as chapter 5 will show. He argued that Mexico should change its negotiation strategy fundamentally in order to increase US financial input in the border environment and to improve the US perception of Mexico. As the US Congress seemed the most likely institution to bring about this change, he proposes several strategies: Mexico should aim for a more positive image in the US mass media; it should seek alliances with US environmental organizations; and the Mexican embassy should also directly lobby in Washington DC.

contacts were limited (Kürzinger et al. 1990: Table 18, 20). Also research by Barkin and Mumme (1992) shows that US organizations have had an influence, especially in the area of nature conservation. Another issue on which US and Mexican organizations started to work together during the late 1980s was the environmental record of World Bank projects.[40]

The final external actor that became interested in Mexico's environmental policy was the World Bank. However, of the six Bank loans to Mexico for projects with environmental components between 1981 and 1989 each had suffered from delays, while most were partially cancelled. The primary reason for these failures was weak government commitment (World Bank 1989: Annex 1). The above mentioned 1984 World Bank memorandum included a proposition to investigate the possibilities for World Bank support to Mexican environmental officials. Moreover, the memorandum proposed that the Bank use diplomatic pressure at the highest governmental levels in order to stop the permission for projects that had not been environmentally reviewed. This is a clear indication that pressurizing a government and providing direct support to a handicapped ministry were among the possible strategies of this institution. Nonetheless, the environment was largely absent in the Bank's loans to Mexico until 1988. Only in 1987 would the environment become a priority in the World Bank's overall policy (cf. Kolk 1996). In addition, until then Mexico's economic crisis and the structural adjustment policies prescribed by the World Bank had been the foremost issues for the Bank and the Mexican government. Apart from some environmental components in a few loans, and formal environmental impact assessments of loans and structural adjustment recommendations, the World Bank would only become genuinely involved in Mexico's environmental policy-making during the Salinas *sexenio* (see below).

---

40 In 1987 the National Wildlife Federation (NWF), for instance, contacted several persons and organizations in Mexico about the possible ecological impact of a World Bank financed agricultural project along the coast of Chiapas, and proposed that they contact World Bank staff. At the same time, the NWF provided the World Bank with the list of addresses of these Mexican persons and organizations and proposed that the World Bank contact them as well. This activity was part of a much larger campaign of the NWF (like other environmental organizations in the US and worldwide) to improve the environmental performance of international development banks (letter of Stewart Hudson, NWF, to Ramón Pérez Salcido of the Instituto de Historia Natural in Chiapas, 24/VI/87).

De la madrid's policy legacy

At the end of de la Madrid's term, several legislative changes created new possibilities for strengthening environmental policy. In 1987 article 27 of the Mexican Constitution was reformed, and since then it mentions the state's responsibility for maintaining and restoring ecological stability, while environment and development are linked. This reform can be seen as the first comprehensive approach of the environment in Mexican legislation. In the same year article 73 of the Constitution was reformed to include the participation of states and municipalities in environmental affairs, implying an important step towards decentralization of environmental policy (Brañes 1994: 83-7). The Constitutional reforms were the basis for the environmental law that was adopted shortly before Salinas took over in 1988. The General Law of Ecological Equilibrium ad Environmental Protection (LGEEPA) covers a wide range of environmental issues: pollution, natural resources conservation, environmental impact and risk assessment, and sanctions. The general law contains a more specific definition of environmental regulation and is clearer on the relations between the various government agencies involved in environmental policy than the previous law. Regulation on environmental impact assessment was strongly improved and strengthened; fines and closures for polluting industries were extended; and the law called for technical standards in several areas (Mumme 1992: 132).

The new environmental law no longer carried the adjective 'federal' because the executive forces were no longer only the federal government. Although the federal government remained the main authority in environmental issues, the decentralization effort meant a shift away from earlier legislation. Another new element of the 1988 law was the inclusion of social participation, including popular consultations. This law provided more opportunities for citizen participation in environmental policy-making. It also required the formal representation of 'principal sectors of society' on the National Ecology Commission, and formal agreements of cooperation between the government and private and public organizations. In theory, then, the new environmental law would mean a policy that would be less federative, abstract and general, with more transparency towards civil society and more authority within the government (Brañes 1994: 144-6).

All in all, de la Madrid's policy was characterized by impressive intentions and formal policy and a low level of achievements. Legislation was improved, but enforcement lagged far behind because of impotent institutions, little resources, and low government priority. The context of a range of economic crises can only partly explain these deficiencies. Almost until the end of the de la Madrid *sexenio*, the controlled political role of environmental organizations contributed considerably to the government's ability to combine major commitments with little progress. Only then did Mexico's environmental policy become really politicized and popular mobilization took on other forms than planned by de la Madrid's team, with the Laguna Verde protests even threatening the state-party system. The slowly increasing international attention to the environmental policy of the Mexican government in some cases supported protection efforts, but also implied the emergence of external pressure on Mexico's policy-makers.

— 2.4 The early Salinas years (1988-1991) —

The environment was already a sensitive issue for Salinas early in his election campaign. He included environmental protection in his speeches and stressed the need to continue de la Madrid's efforts. However, by stressing the importance of better regulation, improving policy performance and identifying policy priorities (instead of de la Madrid's comprehensive approach), Salinas attempted to build up his own environmental image subtly without explicitly criticizing de la Madrid. By presenting the Laguna Verde issue as the responsibility of de la Madrid, Salinas attempted to remain aloof from the controversy. A favourite topic in his election campaign was the need for consultation of civil society, especially environmental organizations and private sector organizations, on environmental policy. The near defeat of the PRI in the elections further stressed the need to improve the PRI's environmental image (Mumme and Sánchez 1990: 53-4).

When President Carlos Salinas de Gortari came to office in December 1988, he had to do something rapidly about his poor political legitimacy. Yet, as described in chapter 1, instead of softening the hardship of economic restructuring he went on to consolidate the neoliberal policy of his predecessor, which prevented him from restoring state-civil society relations by returning to traditional clientelist linkages. Salinas then sought ways to establish new relations with civil society while further strengthening presidentialism. The environment was one of the issues by which Salinas attempted to win back popular support.

In the first months of 1991 it became clear that environmental issues could not be neglected in the NAFTA negotiations. Major environmental organizations in the US criticized free trade with Mexico because of its bad record of environmental policy implementation. In order to obtain congressional approvement for more government authority in the NAFTA negotiations, in May

1991 President Bush announced that the US negotiating team would work with the principle of maintaining US environmental laws, regulations and standards, and that the administration would make a review of US-Mexico environmental issues (see 4.2). From then, the transnational NAFTA debate came to influence Mexico's environmental politics and policy, as chapter 6 will show. The analysis in this section therefore focuses on the period until early 1991.

SALINAS' ENVIRONMENTAL POLICY

Salinas' early environmental policy was largely a continuation of the policy of de la Madrid, although 1989 marked a temporary regression. The National Development Programme 1989-1994 mentions environmental protection as an element of one of the four central policy objectives (improving living standards), and social participation and international cooperation as strategies to achieve this (Poder Ejecutivo Federal 1989: 21, 125-6). In reality, Mexico's environmental policy was actually set back in 1989, when SEDUE's budget was further limited and little happened apart from efforts in Mexico City (see also below). In the National Programme for Environmental Protection 1990-94 (note that 1989 is not covered), Salinas' goal was formulated as harmonizing economic growth with a restoration of environmental quality (SEDUE 1989: 35). However, the programme did not contain a new policy strategy, while again neglecting important matters like natural resources and ecosystems. This continuity of actual policy is remarkable in the light of tendencies for improving protection efforts: popular mobilization on the issue in Mexico; international attention for the environment; knowledge of Mexico's environmental deterioration; and conceptual progress in the field (Brañes 1994: 163-5; Carabias and Provencio 1994: 405).

While the pollution of Mexico City was already the most important single issue on the environmental agenda of the Mexican government, during the first years of Salinas' presidency this focus even intensified. The PRI had lost a lot of votes in 1988 in the capital, and a substantial share of this loss was interpreted by the PRI as resulting from the rapid deterioration of health conditions. In addition, the fact that the most prominent environmental organizations were located in Mexico City contributed to the attention for Mexico City, and pollution in general. Salinas announced some new environmental plans for the capital, like regular mandatory emission tests for vehicles and a new water conservation programme. In addition, several initiatives of de la Madrid were extended, such as garbage collection and sanitation, reforestation, and more green space. Salinas also ordered the permanent closure of 65 industries, and he announced that the electric power plants and ten polluting industries in Mexico City would be converted from oil to natural gas. In 1989, then, Salinas largely only made progress in Mexico City (Mumme and Sánchez 1990: 59-62).

A very prestigious programme was added to these initiatives for the capital in November 1989, when a large four-year package of environmental measures to improve Mexico City's air quality was presented: the Integral Programme of Combat against Contamination. Among these measures was the Day without a Car programme that allowed car owners to use their car only four out of five working days. Other measures were the extension of the metro net, the introduction of lead-free petrol (promoted by price incentives), less lead in leaded petrol, new and cleaner taxis, minibuses and buses for public transport, as well as converters in all new vehicles, and a reforestation project (Every Family a Tree). According to official information, the whole four-year programme was to involve an unprecedented amount of $5.75 billion (SECOFI 1993: 73), for which the Mexican government counted on considerable international assistance (see below). These efforts did have some positive effects with respect to levels of lead, carbon monoxide and sulphur dioxide, but ozone levels proved harder to decrease. In late 1991 and early 1992, total air pollution was even higher than ever before.[41]

Outside Mexico City, SEDUE's programmes remained largely directed at pollution and conservation. The cities of Monterrey and Guadalajara and the issues of waste water and solid waste received special attention. Provisions in the 1988 environmental law enhanced the development of technical environmental standards that specify the limits and procedures for polluting emissions. By 1990, SEDUE had created 50 of these standards (SEDESOL 1992a: 11). Attention to the condition of rivers and lakes involved several research and sanitation programmes, and a treaty was signed with the US to protect the Río Bravo. In addition, some progress was made in the field of environmental impact assessments.[42] Most of the government resources for pollution measures, however, were spent on monitoring (Carabias and Provencio 1994: 406-7). Simultaneously, nature conservation was an important policy area for Salinas' national and international image. Various natural protected areas were created, measures for protected areas and endangered species improved, hunting regulations became stricter and especially the Lacandón jungle could count on

41 On 17 March 1992, the highest air pollution ever measured in the world was reached, and alarm phase II of the city's pollution emergency plan was set in motion.
42 Brañes (1994: 179, note 158) mentions official sources claiming an increase of assessments from 22 in 1988 to 799 in 1991. According to a SEDUE official, nearly 1500 projects were evaluated from 1988 to 1991, 20 of which were turned down (Rodarte 1992: 80).

presidential attention. Actions by US environmental organizations also forced Salinas to ban the hunting of marine turtles in 1990 (see below). Finally, the decentralization of Mexico's environmental policy was partly materialized. The states started to develop their own environmental laws, and at the end of 1991 27 of the 36 states had passed their law.

Apart from the above mentioned programmes, Salinas made very limited progress in overall environmental protection until early 1991. Low government priority for the environment resulted in ambivalent policy. Formally, care for the environment was pictured as an issue of the highest policy importance, but in many cases other issues turned out to be more pressing due to budget limitations and the need for economic growth. More fundamentally, neoliberal restructuring involved a deregulation of economic activities which countered environmental policy needs, especially with respect to natural resources. Industrial policy had been directed at internationalization, which implies a deepening of the industrial model. Legal arrangements on technology and on foreign investment had not contributed to more sustainable production either. In general, the integration of environmental considerations in non-environmental legislation remained marginal (Brañes 1994: 493, 508, 589-90).[43]

Reliable official information on government budgets is lacking, but other sources suggest that SEDUE's resources were cut back in 1989 while the budgetary increase in 1990 was insufficient to improve policy enforcement genuinely. According to Mumme and Sánchez (1990: 55), general budget cuts as part of the new austerity programme obstructed earlier plans for a 43 per cent expansion of SEDUE's environmental budget. A World Bank report (1992a: 7) refers to 1989 as the leanest year for the ecology sub-ministry SE, after a steady decline of resources since 1986. According to this report, the operational budget of 1990 was 30 per cent higher in real terms than the year before. Nevertheless, an enormous shortage of qualified inspectors remained, as low salary levels forced SE to hire persons with little relevant experience, who tended to leave the agency for better paid jobs in the private sector after they had received their training. Combining this information on the poor quality of SEDUE inspectors with the actual number employed helps to explain the enforcement problem of the environmental ministry. In 1990, SEDUE's industrial enforcement staff, responsible for inspection of over 30,000 industries in the Federal District, consisted

---

43 An example of this policy ambivalence was the Day without a Car programme in Mexico City. Parallel to the implementation of this programme to reduce air pollution, the government encouraged the production and consumption of motor vehicles. Moreover, the sale of cars went up after the start of the programme as many car owners simply bought a second car to circumvent government driving restrictions (Mumme 1992: 134).

of only 9 persons (Mumme 1992: 133). Nationwide the staff consisted of 140 persons. In 1991, there were 46 inspectors in the border region with the US (Rodarte 1992: 80).

Weak implementation of environmental regulations by industry had two other causes. First, SEDUE officials remained reluctant to issue fines against non-complying companies. Conflicts were largely handled through consultations and temporary (partial or total) closures and agreements.[44] In addition, SEDUE signed over 2,000 environmental agreements with private industries, representing nearly $600 million in "green investments" (Rodarte 1992: 81).[45] This touches on the second obstacle to environmentally sound production: funding for the Mexican private sector. In order to invest in modern equipment and environmental technologies companies require credits, but business loans are expensive in Mexico. While large companies can turn to the international market, small and medium-sized companies generally need smaller loans and cannot meet the minimum requirements of this market (loan guarantees, etc.). An attempt was made by the Mexican government to deal with these credit problems through an equity fund and a 50 per cent guarantee on environmental loans in the hands of NAFINSA (Mexico's state-backed lender). However, these options were not used much and far from solved the fundamental problems (Stern 1993: 190-1).

In short, in the first phase of his presidency Salinas largely continued de la Madrid's policy, focusing on pollution control and nature conservation. As improvement of the environmental situation was important for recapturing popular support, especially in Mexico City, a few new programmes were introduced. Three fundamental deficiencies of Mexico's environmental policy nevertheless remained: insufficient development of policy instruments, fragmented regulations, and weak enforcement. The lack of specified ecological standards for instance, was very problematic. Also policy instruments like inspection and control, safety regulation, and sanctions were weak. Next, fiscal encouragement of environmentally sound production was still scattered among various regulations and agencies. A similar fragmentedness limited financial mechanisms. Finally, due to the structurally low government budgets for envi-

---

44 Alonzo (1992) reports that in 1989 and 1990 5,405 inspections took place, which resulted in 3 permanent closures, 980 partial or temporary closures, 29 relocations, 1032 mandatory and 679 voluntary compliance agreements.

45 This "soft" approach to industries is labour-intensive, because a strict and sanctioning approach encourages companies not to wait until an inspection visit before making the compulsory changes. On the other hand, it has a positive side in that it is less sensitive to corruption than a system relying more on fines (Newman 1995: 40, 42).

ronmental protection and the administrative weaknesses with respect to this policy area, enforcement of laws and regulations remained poor (Brañes 1994: 170-173, 588, 598).

CHANGING INVOLVEMENT IN ENVIRONMENTAL POLITICS

As mentioned above, the popular mobilization for democratization preceding the 1988 presidential elections seriously challenged the PRI's political leadership, and the movement that attempted to stop the Laguna Verde nuclear power plant from starting production was an important element in the anti-system surge. Nonetheless, the presidential elections were won by the PRI candidate, and the Laguna Verde movement could not stop the nuclear plant from starting operation. Subsequently, the period of relatively open confrontation with the government was followed by repression of protest groups. While Salinas was presenting himself as an advocate of the environment, critical environmental organizations were attacked. Predominantly in the period between Salinas' election and his inauguration (from July to December 1988), after international attention for Mexico had faded, critical ENGOs were intentionally weakened by the government. The major strategies of control applied were co-optation (a few leading environmentalists were recruited into government agencies), divide and rule, violent attacks, and censorship. Main victims among ENGOs were organizations that had played a prominent role in the Laguna Verde, and groups that had strongly criticized Mexico's environmental policy and the political system that was responsible for it (Demmers and Hogenboom 1992: 70).[46]

To a limited extent, ties with more moderate environmental organizations were strengthened after Salinas' inauguration. The new president repeatedly stressed the importance of popular participation in environmental matters, and there were new legal facilities for this purpose. The 1988 environmental law and the National Development Plan 1989-1994 included several forms of popular consultation, but these proposals were bureaucratic, incoherent and hardly linked to one another (Brañes 1994: 142-4). Still, formal avenues for political participation by ENGOs were opened up, such as the creation of environmental committees in Mexico City. Critical groups were largely excluded from this consultation, while moderate groups were incorporated in the new frame-

---

46 Ironically, at the end of 1989 SEDUE officials stated that environmentalist pressure had subsided since the late de la Madrid years (Mumme 1992: 139).

works. Despite such consultations, actual NGO participation in policy-making was exceptional, but the role of ENGOS was again channelled and controlled by the government (Demmers and Hogenboom 1992: 70).

The excluded critical ENGOS had no way of fighting for their position: the PRI, after all, had increased possibilities for popular involvement, and nationally and internationally showed off with this 'political openness'. As their avenues for pressurizing the government had been restricted, critical environmental organizations attempted to enforce their position towards the PRI indirectly by improving their internal structures and international relations. The relations established with US and Canadian NGOS during the transnational NAFTA debate would become important in this respect, as chapters 4 and 6 will show.

Besides environmental organizations, other political actors adopted some environmental demands. Farmer and indigenous groups incorporated environmental concerns in their struggle for land and means of production. Through this process, environmental protection as a political issue became more intertwined with social and economic demands. This implied additional popular support for environmental protection, while enhancing the incorporation of environmental concerns in local initiatives for development (Leff 1994: 46-7). The Mexican private sector slowly began to recognize the importance of the environment and some corporate organizations started to discuss the issue. On the other hand, after the 1988 elections opposition parties largely neglected the environment, implying that they had primarily and temporarily adopted the issue in a response to protests that were silenced after the elections.[47]

Foreign NGO influence on Mexico's environmental politics increased, predominantly from US-based groups. Barkin and Mumme (1992: 4) found that between 1989 and 1991 at least twelve major US organizations attempted to influence Mexican environmental affairs by influencing the position of the US government towards Mexico (what Barkin and Mumme call indirect investment in Mexico). Of these twelve, the Natural Resources Defense Council, the National Wildlife Federation and the Environmental Defense Fund are among

---

47 The left-wing PRD granted a relatively small role to the environment in its 1991 programme, and its approach remained largely sectorial, focusing on agriculture. Environmental problems were perceived as resulting from a development model based on a predominant role for speculative capital. According to the PRD, the use and protection of natural resources should be the basis of a new economy. The right-wing PAN considered corruption and social irresponsibility as the major causes of environmental destruction, and viewed environmental education as an important tool for protection. The issue is only vaguely touched upon, however, and remains separated from development and social and economic dimensions (Quadri de la Torre and Provencio 1994: 74-9).

the most influential of environmental lobbying organizations in the US (Barkin and Mumme 1992: Table 8). With respect to marine turtle and dolphin preservation, Greenpeace and the Earth Island Institute successfully led an extensive campaign that attracted international attention and forced the Mexican government to substantial conservation commitments (in 1990 and 1991 respectively). However, this conservation focus was at the cost of costal communities that depended on the trade in turtles and dolphins (Barkin and Mumme 1992: 15).

After years of few advances, US-Mexico governmental cooperation on the border environment was rapidly extended after the announcement of the NAFTA plan in June 1990. In 1989, EPA and SEDUE had started a programme of joint *maquiladora* inspection, but apart from several temporary plant closures the approach remained largely voluntary and results were poor (Mumme and Sánchez 1990: 62). Immediately after the announcement of free trade negotiation, however, the two governments started working on the Integrated Border Environmental Plan. In November 1990 Salinas and Bush signed a communique that called for the development of the Border Plan, based on the 1983 La Paz agreement, and the plan was completed in February 1992 (see 6.1). Earlier on, criticism from environmental organizations and the border region's environmental problems in themselves had not been urgent enough to enhance government efforts, but the fact that trade liberalization would bring about more economic activities in a region that was already damaged by economic integration (*maquiladoras*) was a strong incentive. Although the governments were reluctant to link border environmental initiatives to the trade agreement, the NAFTA plan proved to contribute to environmental cooperation.

FOREIGN FINANCIAL SUPPORT

While Mexico's government resources for environmental protection decreased in 1989, Salinas turned out to be very successful in attracting foreign assistance for this purpose. Especially the Integral Programme on Mexico City's air pollution estimated at $5.75 billion received major international support of about $3.5 billion (Alonzo 1992: 7). Japan, Germany, Great Britain, France and the US, as well as the World Bank, provided funding for this programme. Japan was the first to give a multi-million loan for the air pollution programme.[48] US sup-

---

48 Peña Ramirez (1991: 12) mentions $2.2 billion, while Mumme (1992: 133) mentions $850 million. According to a Mexican government official, the Japanese loan amounted to $300 million (interview 10/x/95).

port was based on a 1989 agreement between EPA, SEDUE and the Federal District, which involved assisting policy development and enforcement, by means of the exchange of experts, training, and research. In 1990, the Mexican Petroleum Institute signed a Memorandum of Understanding with the US Department of Energy to jointly perform a $9 million research project on Mexico's air pollution (Alonzo 1992: 8).

Other environmental programmes of the Mexican government and industry could count on international financial support too. Japanese credits went to parastatal industries like PEMEX, FERTIMEX and the Federal Electricity Commission (CFE) to adapt to environmental restrictions, while the Interamerican Development Bank donated 700 million to the Mexican government, and Norway another 130,000 dollar to SEDUE (Peña Ramírez 1991: 12). The World Bank partly acted as a co-financier with Japan for projects in the energy and environmental sectors (World Bank 1993: 18-9). The Danish government supported the construction of a large waste treatment project in Mexico City. In addition, the US NGO Conservation International arranged a debt-for-nature swap by buying $4 million Mexican debt for $1.8 million. In return, the Mexican government distributed the proceeds to various governmental research institutes and NGOs for environmental protection programmes. Finally, Salinas had good ties with some other large US ENGOs, which were based on long-term projects of these groups in Mexico (US ENGO source 28/IX/95).

The role of the World Bank in Mexico's environmental policy increased significantly after 1988. According to a report of the World Bank (1989: 20) on Mexico, "the Bank will have to place environment as a priority item in discussions with government officials". Despite the history of problems with environmental funding of the Bank to Mexico, the Bank responded positively and rapidly after being approached by the Mexican government. The Bank considered water and air pollution in Mexico City, as well as soil erosion, the priority areas for Mexico's environmental policy, and various credits were provided for projects with environmental components.[49] In 1990, Mexico and the World Bank started preparing the first environmental loan (Mexico Environmental Project) that would be approved in 1992 (see 6.3). Another loan was prepared for a project to decrease air pollution caused by traffic in Mexico City. While in total the World Bank's funding only amounted to a very small part of

---

49 These projects were: the improvement of solid waste disposal in several cities; adequate and sustainable use of forest resources in various states; drinking water and sewage projects; environmental infrastructure of the Lazaro Cárdenas industrial port; decreasing urban transport emissions and agricultural environmental damage in Chiapas (SEDESOL 1992: 30).

Mexico's government budget, the Bank's loans were quite important for the environmental sub-ministry.[50]

Apart from the impact of financial support, World Bank loans affected Mexico's environmental policy in other ways as well. In general, World Bank funding is not very attractive for a government agency because it involves more demands, conditions and limitations than a project funded by government resources. On the other hand, the fact that a World Bank loan implies more vigilance can be positive too, and the agency can also benefit from the Bank's experience. After 1989, Mexico's Ministry of Finance realized that more had to be done for environmental protection. As this ministry did not have much confidence in the environmental sub-ministry, World Bank involvement was preferred (World Bank source 16/v/94). Although the execution of these projects and the reimbursement of the environmental loans turned out to be quite problematic (see 6.3), the preparation of the projects produced close links between World Bank officials and Mexico's environmental sub-ministry.[51] In fact, according to another World Bank source (8/iv/94), the Bank played a crucial role in the environmental policy efforts.[52]

In sum, within a very short period Salinas managed to attract major external resources for his environmental policy.[53] Evidently, Salinas managed internationally to create a reliable image as far as his environmental policy was concerned, which was also shown by several international awards, such as the Earth Prize for Salinas in 1991.[54] The World Bank and the US government were no

---

50 According to information from the Embassy of Mexico in Washington DC (1992: 15), the environmental expenditure of SEDUE between 1988 and 1990 was still completely financed by government resources. In 1991, in addition to the nearly $11 million government resources (less than the 1990 budget), $18 million was provided by the World Bank's Mexico Environmental Program, and nearly $10 million by other loans. However, these figures should be read as indications of the importance of external funding rather than as facts, as they were used for Mexico's NAFTA lobby and may be partly based on estimates and optimistic expectations. It is for instance curious that funding from the World Bank programme that was approved in 1992 was already part of SEDUE's 1991 environmental budget (see 6.3).

51 Prior to the approval of a World Bank loan, it generally takes two years of preparation by a World Bank team and a team of the government concerned.

52 One of the ways in which the World Bank attempted to change Mexico's environmental policy was by pushing the integration of economic instruments, such as market incentives, price tariff policies, tax policies, and tradeable emission permits, and the 'polluter pays' principle (see 6.3).

53 According to Mumme and Sánchez (1990: 56), the World Bank mentions Mexico as the first recipient in the world of credits to fight environmental contamination.

longer the only supporting actors involved, and especially the Japanese contributions were considerable. Unfortunately, the interest rates on the environmental credits are not known. So-called soft loans (with interest rates below commercial levels) imply political support, but some of the loans might have been merely commercial.[55]

While Salinas was already early on praised and supported by external actors, domestically this was hardly the case. Our analysis of Salinas' environmental policy until early 1991 has shown that 1989 was a meagre year, and the initiatives of 1990 involved only limited progress. Apart from a few prestigious projects, especially in Mexico City, Salinas largely continued de la Madrid's policy, including its deficiencies. Mexican environmental organizations who had succeeded in turning these policy weaknesses into a major political issue before the 1988 elections attracted much less attention after Salinas had come to office. Popular mobilization collapsed after the victory of the PRI and the start-up of the Laguna Verde nuclear power plant, and critical environmental organizations re weakened by state repression. These domestic tendencies, however, did not form an obstacle to Salinas' "green" image abroad.

— 2.5 Conclusions —

From its development in the early 1970s onwards, Mexico's environmental policy has been characterized by fragmentedness which reflected the low priority of the environment for the Mexican government. Environmental legislation improved over the years, but implementation of laws and enforcement of standards were largely neglected. The environmental agencies functioned with insufficient resources, especially after the more than average budget cuts in the second half of the 1980s. There was a structural lack of environmental concern

---

54 The prize was designed by the Nobel Organization, United Earth and the United Nations Environmental Programme (UNEP), and Salinas was the first to receive it. The awarding organizations stressed the creation of the Integral Programme on air pollution in Mexico City, the protection of marine turtles by the creation of reserves and prohibiting capture and trade, and the successes of the protection programme for the endangered grey whale.

55 The World Bank probably did not provide soft loans, because these are supplied to very poor countries. Governments might have provided soft loans, but perhaps even these were close to commercial rates. A Mexican government source (17/x/95), for instance, argued that the international support should not be exaggerated because most of the funding was in loans, not gifts.

and commitment from the other agencies which inhibited genuine integration of protection measures in other policy areas. The attempts of environmental agencies with little authority to execute their task of coordinating the environmental activities (and activities with environmental effects) of other government agencies and parastatals were bound to fail.

While relatively isolated within the government, the environmental agencies were also rather closed for non-governmental organizations, apart from a short phase of relative openness at the time of de la Madrid's popular mobilization campaign. On the one hand, the lack of policy influence of environmental NGOs might be explained by their inability to create a strong movement. On the other hand, the one-off emergence of a strong environmentalist and popular movement against the nuclear plant of Laguna Verde that damaged the legitimacy of the state-party system in 1988, caused the repression of critical environmental organizations. Moderate organizations benefited from new formal avenues for participation, but their role remained limited. Both with respect to government policy and democratization, environmental organizations thus remained largely marginal. They were more influential on environmental awareness and public opinion, although government agencies contributed to the spreading of information. Increasingly, local organizations and projects incorporated environmental concerns.

The low priority of the environment for Mexico's government and the weak enforcement of environmental policy can partly be explained by the nature of the Mexican political system. While Mexico's poor economic situation and the urge to achieve economic growth contributed to the policy subordination of the environment since the 1970s, the lack of options for non-governmental organizations and the electorate to influence government policy produced a large distance between demands from civil society and performance of the Mexican government on the environment from the 1980s onwards. Only popular discontent and pressure with respect to the air pollution in Mexico City had effect, but overall the issue obtained no priority under de la Madrid and Salinas. In a more democratic system, government policy would to a larger extent reflect concerns and preferences in civil society. In addition, in countries with genuine parliamentary control of government there is generally greater policy transparency, while the gap between official policy and enforcement is unlikely to be as wide as in Mexico. On the other hand, Mexican policy-makers were attuned to international tendencies in which industrial pollution and endangered species were major concerns. With a few impressive projects, especially in Mexico City and natural areas, the lack of actual policy priority was veiled.

Moreover, in contrast to the formal plans, Mexico's neoliberal development strategies hardly included care for the environment, while increasing environmental problems and domestic pressures, since protection efforts did not affect overall government policy. Even with air pollution in Mexico City, an extremely costly programme was started while industrial location policy remained untouched. Similarly, ecological destruction as a result of Mexico's policy with respect to the agricultural sector or the *maquiladoras* is evident, but has not been an incentive for change. However, this fits the neoliberal model of international integration as the recipe for economic growth and progress, which implies decreasing government interference in production processes. The prevalence of economic liberalization has come at the cost of the Mexican government's responsibility for environmental as well as social objectives, and thereby the prospects of sustainable development.

These conclusions and this chapter's evidence of the limits of Mexico's environmental policy are confirmed by Carabias (Carabias and Provencio 1992). Shortly before the unexpected appointment of Julia Carabias as Environmental Minister in late 1994, for she was not a member of the PRI and was a political "outsider", Carabias analysed and criticized Mexico's environmental policy in a book on this theme.[56] She argued that the environmental policy of Mexico consisted of partial focuses which did not form a whole, and that the legal integration of the environmental policy was limited, while the policy remained disconnected from Mexico's general development strategy. In her view, SEDUE did not achieve its goals because it focused too much on pollution and protected areas, while neglecting natural resources and ecosystems (Carabias and Provencio 1994: 401-2, 409).

The transnational involvement in Mexico's environmental politics and policy increased over time. In the early 1970s, developments in the US and worldwide encouraged the Mexican government to take up the issue, but this was a voluntary initiative that served Mexico's international image. With the US, the border region was for many years the only area for environmental cooperation, and these border efforts remained weak until the NAFTA plan. Apart from very limited Mexican resources, the preference of the US for a case-to-case approach, and the dependence of environmental efforts on the bilateral relations in general inhibited a comprehensive joint strategy for tackling border problems. This situation started to change in the late 1980s, when the US also began to support a Mexican programme against air pollution control in Mexico City. This programme was in fact receiving major international support and showed

---

56 At that time, she was known as a knowledgeable biologist whose research was to find ways of merging protection of ecosystems and natural resources with improving living conditions in rural areas.

Salinas' success in obtaining new resources for his environmental policy. Mexico's efforts towards economic liberalization and integration contributed to the willingness of international creditors to provide funding.

This chapter has analysed the reasons why environmental degradation did not become a policy priority for the Mexican government until early 1991, but was merely a political theme. This changed with the NAFTA debate on the environment, when Mexico's international environmental image was rapidly reversed from positive to negative. The weak enforcement of Mexico's environmental policy had been known and criticized by domestic environmental organizations for years, but the Mexican government had successfully diverted these pressures without having to change its policy fundamentally. External actors, however, would prove harder to manipulate by the Mexican government. However, as chapter 5 will demonstrate, the Mexican government did not stand alone in its efforts to convince external critics, and especially the US Congress, of its environmental credibility. In order to understand this transnational support for Mexico, in the following chapter we will analyse the interests involved in the creation of NAFTA.

CHAPTER 3

The NAFTA Plan:
Economic and Environmental Dimensions

While free trade and investment with the US would fit well into Mexico's neo-liberal restructuring, until 1989 the Mexican government expressed reluctance about a free trade zone with the US. A traditional anti-US attitude, and hesitancy about intensifying the unequal bilateral relation hampered further economic integration. However, the new Mexican elite of technocrats, who were familiar with the US through their educational background, realized that they needed US capital and the US market to make their development model work.

Various interests merged in the plan to create a North American free trade zone. Evidently, the governments of Mexico, the US and Canada considered pursuing NAFTA beneficial. In addition, in each country several economic sectors and certain types of companies were expected to gain from the agreement. In order to understand the support for the agreement, the first section of this chapter presents an overview of the interests, expectations and needs of the governments and of groups within the countries, focusing on Mexico and the US. Chapter 5 will then review the main representation institutions of these pro-NAFTA interests, and analyse their efforts and mutual relations in the NAFTA preparations.

In the second section, this chapter provides an overview of critical studies that assessed possible environmental risks of NAFTA at the time of the environment debate. They described problematic links between trade liberalization and environmental protection in general, and the negative effects that could be expected in the NAFTA countries. Critical environmental assessments available at the time NAFTA was negotiated were far from complete since the issue was rather new. Nevertheless, the studies pointed at serious environmental risks as a result of legal, economic and political changes that NAFTA was likely to produce. The overview of critical studies helps one to understand the ideas and concerns behind the issues that were raised by environmental organizations in Mexico, the US and Canada in the NAFTA environment debate (see 4.2). Critical assessments were very important for their position and activities. In fact, several assessments were made by persons working in environmental organizations, while several of the academic researches were performed by persons who had relations with environmental organizations, or were in some way affiliated to an organization, and contributed with their research as well as presentations or comments to the NAFTA environment debate. As we shall see in chapter 5, criticism of environmental organizations triggered a strong reaction by NAFTA proponents.

— 3.1 Economic interests linked to NAFTA —

In June 1990, President Carlos Salinas de Gortari and President George Bush signed a declaration advocating a free trade agreement. Plans for free trade between the two countries had been developing for at least a decade. As early as 1979, during a visit of President Jimmy Carter to Mexico, the US proposed a common market of Mexico, the US and Canada. The year after, incoming President Ronald Reagan proposed a US-Mexico free trade agreement in his presidential campaign. In 1982, the US Trade Representative initiated formal free trade talks with Mexico, without much success. On the other hand, Mexico's accession to the GATT in 1986 implied a fundamental change of attitude of the Mexican government towards trade liberalization. In 1987, a US law firm drafted a framework agreement that mainly covered the car and electronic industry, which was followed up two years later by the development of an understanding that contained new elements such as sector-specific technical standards. In late 1988, shortly before both came to office, Salinas and Bush discussed bilateral free trade, but Salinas rejected this at the start of his presidency.

The Mexican position finally became positive in 1989. According to José Córdoba Montoya, chief of Salinas' coordination office and possibly the second most powerful person during his presidency, this decision was taken after discussions by Salinas, Trade Minister Jaime Serra Puche, Minister of Finance Pedro Aspe and Córdoba himself in a hotel in Davos, Switzerland (*El Financiero* 6/VII/95: 1). In Davos, prominent businessmen, politicians and economists meet yearly at the World Economic Forum to informally discuss global issues. The fact that during this Forum Salinas' team decided to change its position on Mexico-US integration suggests that transnational discussions influenced this policy shift.

The private sector was also involved in the early preparations for Mexico-US free trade. After Reagan's proposal, the Mexico-US Business Committee discussed the issue at a plenary meeting in 1981. In 1984 and 1985, the Mexican Business Council for International Affairs (CEMAI), the US Chamber of Commerce, the American Chamber of Commerce in Mexico and the Council of the

Americas all announced their support for a bilateral free trade agreement. Some business organizations participated in drafting agreements in the late 1980s. Until 1990, however, US business organizations did not expect a free trade agreement to happen as the Mexican government had not been very cooperative and the framework agreement as well as the understanding had a limited scope (US private sector source 19/IV/94).

In 1990 it was not clear whether Canada would join the free trade plans of Mexico and the US. Salinas' proposal to Bush was an extension of the Canada-US Free Trade Agreement (CUFTA) between the US and Canada, but the declaration of June 1990 only concerned Mexico and the US. The CUFTA implemented in 1989 had been the first step in North American free trade and can be taken as the precursor of NAFTA. Although Canada had no strong economic incentive to participate in NAFTA as trade with Mexico was expanding but still marginal, it announced its willingness in January 1991, the reasons for which will be explained below.

NORTH AMERICAN REGIONALIZATION

According to free trade proponents, the creation of NAFTA would be good for each of the three countries' economies. First, with the removal of tariffs and non-tariff barriers (some immediately, some gradually within 10 or 15 years), trade among the three countries would increase and companies that were traditionally protected would have to compete and consequently modernize. Second, the enlarged internal market of 360 million consumers would provide the advantage of economies of scale. In addition, countries were expected to specialize and attain more market competitiveness and excel in products with comparative advantages. Due to all these changes, efficiency would increase, prices would fall, and economic growth would follow.

More important than trade, NAFTA was also to enable free investment among its partners through national treatment of NAFTA investors. Investment liberalization was expected to have a greater economic impact than the liberalization of trade flows. The effects of NAFTA on capital flows (a so-called dynamic effect) was estimated to be more significant than static effects stemming from the adjustment of prices and resources to the new situation (Kehoe 1994: 3-4). While trade liberalization in Mexico had been considerable prior to the NAFTA plan, liberalization of investment had been relatively slow. Therefore, Mexico's participation in NAFTA involved much more of a change for investment than for trade opportunities. Several interests merged in the liberalization of foreign investment in Mexico. First, this form of liberalization had been vigorously promoted by the World Bank and large Mexican and transnational companies. Second, the Mexican government expected investment liberalization to solve the problem of a lack of capital inflow for industry. Consequently, it appears that the NAFTA initiative "was motivated by the quest for a higher degree of capital mobility rather than by the pursuit of trade gains" (Ros 1992: 54).[1]

NAFTA's importance, however, went beyond short-term and long-term trade and investment flows. The agreement would confirm and consolidate three processes, which will be expanded on below: first, Mexico's adoption of a neoliberal development model; second, the integration of Mexico in the North American economy; and third, the economic regionalization of North America. Although North American trade was relatively liberal preceding NAFTA and the agreement would be restricted to free trade and the free movement of capital (unlike the European Union),[2] NAFTA's economic and political impact might be considerable. NAFTA's confirmation effect was of particular importance at the politico-ideological level as the agreement validated neoliberalism and regionalization, whereas its consolidation effect encompassed the strengthening of proponents of these tendencies.

To return to the first point, NAFTA would imply support for as well as a further strengthening of Mexico's neoliberal restructuring and the economic sectors that stood to gain from it. With the abolishment of both trade barriers and restrictions on foreign investment, NAFTA would involve further liberalization of the Mexican economy and guaranteed access to US markets, the largest importer of Mexican products. By means of this liberalization Mexico expected an increase in the politically indispensable funding from the US.[3] In this respect,

---

1 NAFTA was nonetheless always called and referred to as a *trade* agreement. A reason for this might be the negative connotation of 'free investment'. Whereas free trade can be pictured as being an affair of societies as a whole, free investment is more identified with the interests of large, transnational companies and banks.

2 NAFTA is more than a free trade zone since the agreement also incorporates free investment. It is, however, not a common market as common tariffs to other trade partners are not part of the agreement.

3 It has often been argued that Salinas had little choice but to propose NAFTA because of a disappointing trip to Europe, where Germany and France showed no interest in expanding trade with Mexico. According to Castañeda (1993: 61), on the contrary, "[t]he lack of European and Japanese funding was a false argument: the new Mexican team never really expected other areas to foot the bill for Mexico's recovery. The problem was that existing levels of funding from the United States were simply not substantial enough to finance higher levels of growth, infrastructure, trade and modernization, let alone Salinas' agenda for the poor".

the determination to enter NAFTA served as a clear sign by the Salinas administration to show the outside world the structural character of its reform policy. A return to protectionist policy would be impossible as long as Mexico participated in NAFTA. The fact that the US and Canadian governments considered Mexico to be a good partner for free trade gave external investors more confidence in the Mexican economy and political situation.

Second, the creation of NAFTA would similarly confirm and consolidate Mexico's economic integration into North America. In fact, it would be more correct to speak of Mexico's integration in the US economy since trade between Canada and Mexico was very limited, as Figure 3.1 illustrates. With respect to direct investment, the *maquiladoras* in the Mexican border region with the US had been of great importance for Mexico-US economic integration, whereas US direct investment in Mexico in general accounted for more than 60 per cent of FDI (see 1.2). With respect to trade, the US was traditionally been Mexico's largest partner, accounting for two-thirds of Mexican trade. For the US, Mexico was a rather small export market, accounting for about 7 per cent of its total exports, but nonetheless ranking third behind Canada and Japan. Mexico was the fastest-growing US trade partner, and in 1992 US-Mexican trade reached $73.2 billion (*The Economist* 13/11/93: 24). In particular, the potential of the Mexican consumer market, with the "average Mexican"[4] buying more US consumer products than any other foreign citizen, was of great interest to US producers.

Third, NAFTA would confirm and consolidate the regionalization of the North American economy as a whole. Between 1980 and 1989, intra-regional exports among the three North American countries went up from 27 per cent to 34 per cent of total exports (Krasner 1993: 93). North American regionalization partly followed from the block formation in Europe as well as the less formalized regionalization of the Asiatic market, which had helped the economic expansion of these regions. This regionalization tendency was only partly responsible for the dramatic decrease in the US share of global production and trade,[5] but it does explain the US focus on the region in its attempt to

---

4 One can hardly speak of the average Mexican because, despite a growing middle class, income is still very unequally distributed in Mexico. At a population of around 90 million, 13.5 million people are officially classified as living in extreme poverty and another 23.6 million as poor (*The Economist* 22/01/94: 19).

5 During the 1980s, the US share of world trade fell from 20 to 12 per cent, and its share in global production decreased from 30 to 20 per cent (Caballero U. 1991: 58). Between the 1960 and 1988, the share of US capital in FDI world-wide fell by more than half (Moody 1995: 97).

reverse this decrease. For the US, intensifying North American integration also seemed to be a political compromise between multilateralism and protectionism in the US. Another reason for the US to initiate regional trade agreements (next to its multilateral trade efforts) was the frustration with GATT and increasing US trade deficits in the early 1980s.

FIGURE 3.1 *North American Exports in 1992 (in billion US dollars, and as percentage of total exports)*

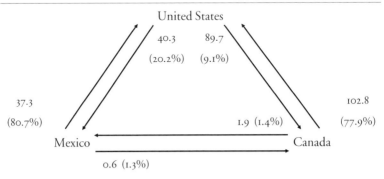

Source: United Nations 1996

Eventually, North American regionalization was expected to become American regionalization. Especially in the US, there were ideas of a free trade and investment area embracing the entire Western Hemisphere, for instance called the Free Trade Agreement of the Americas, and Latin American countries perceived Mexico as their example. However, it was clear that the timing of other countries' entering NAFTA would for a large part depend on the outcome of the struggle between liberalizing and protectionist forces in the US. On the one hand, in particular business organizations representing large and transnational corporations are strong proponents of a free trade agreement for the Americas (cf. Sherwood Truitt 1992). On the other hand, as the NAFTA debate would demonstrate, there are considerable pressures in the US that attempt to obstruct such free trade initiatives.

NATIONAL NAFTA PROGNOSES

The expected advantages of NAFTA varied for each country just as the impact between and within economic sectors would be different. Sectors and companies previously protected by trade barriers and special subsidies might be harmed by liberalization, while those with strong free trade interests were likely to profit from it. Studies of the possible economic impact of NAFTA largely focused on the effects at the national level. Here we will look into some of the prognoses for the sake of a general overview of how the trade agreement was expected to affect the national economies of its member countries. Despite the 'self-confidence' of various economic analyses that will be referred to below, it was impossible to predict what would happen after the integration of economies of such a different scale and level of development and technology, and how various economic processes would interact. For a better understanding of the politics behind NAFTA, expectations at the level of economic sectors will be assessed below.

Most studies of the possible effects of NAFTA predicted that the economic gain, as compared to the preceding situation, would be for the greater part for Mexico. Although the Mexican consumer market had great growth potential, Mexico's economy was too small (about 25 times smaller than the US economy) to have a large impact on its associates' overall economies. In 1991, only 7.9 per cent of US exports and 0.3 per cent of Canada's exports went to Mexico (Globerman 1994: 10). One study predicting a 5.0 per cent increase of GDP for Mexico, for instance, estimated that the gains for Canada and the US would be 0.7 per cent and 0.3 per cent respectively (Kehoe 1994: 11). For political reasons, however, proponents of NAFTA continuously presented the agreement as a "win-win-win situation".

A summary that Ros (1992: 69-71) made of various studies of the economic impact of NAFTA supports the idea that for Mexico the economic impact of investment liberalization would be far more substantial than the impact of free trade. The trade gains from resource re-allocation and specialization would probably be very small. The gains from economies of scale,[6] industrial rationalization and lower prices of investment goods might be small too. Macroeconomic adjustment effects were expected to be negative but again small. In short, free trade in itself would be of little profit to Mexico. Increased capital mobility, on the contrary, was expected to spur Mexico's economic growth. An analysis based on Applied General Equilibrium Simulations (an economic computer model) found that a NAFTA without free foreign investment would result in an increase in economic welfare of 1.6 per cent of Mexico's GDP. This would be up to 5.0 per cent with the inclusion of free investment (Kehoe 1994: 11).

---

6 Since Mexico's internal market is rather small, it is expected that Mexico will profit more than the other countries from NAFTA's economies of scale.

While NAFTA was generally expected to spur foreign investment in Mexico, its wider impact remained hard to foresee. The majority of studies of the possible impact of increasing FDI in Mexico estimated that the effect on Mexico's export would only become apparent on the medium term. Since the legalization of foreign portfolio investment (i.e. buying shares) by foreigners in 1989, it had been the dominant type of foreign investment, but portfolio investments have a volatile character and react strongly to national and international changes (Vidal 1992: 32). Although it was likely that NAFTA would contribute to economic growth in Mexico, it remained questionable how it would affect politics. Modernization theory, often applied by proponents of free trade, holds that economic liberalization automatically entails political liberalization. Indeed, political tensions within the PRI and the weakened linkages of the PRI with civil society had been partly caused by the shift towards the neoliberal development model, and might eventually result in the end of authoritarian rule. The opposite, however, can be argued too (cf. Smith 1993). As described in chapter 1, some electoral processes were liberalized under Salinas, but on the whole state autonomy increased.

While the prognoses of the national economic advantage of NAFTA for the US were very limited, there were considerable US interests at stake. As mentioned above, regional economic ties had gradually become more important for the US, and US free trade proponents considered Mexico's entry to the North American free trade area as the start of a project encompassing the complete Americas. As will be shown below, various powerful economic sectors in the US stood to gain considerably from access to Mexico's market with its natural resources, low labour costs, and about 90 million consumers. In addition, NAFTA had an important political agenda for the US in the sense that increased economic growth in Mexico was expected to contribute to Mexico's political stability, to reduce illegal migration to the US, and to help combat the drug trade. This concern with political stability, however, should not be taken for concern about democratization.[7]

As mentioned above, the direct economic gains for Canada of joining NAFTA also seemed limited. By being part of NAFTA negotiations, Canada rather wanted to safeguard its bilateral relations with the US and the arrangements made in the CUFTA. The likelihood that the US would want to expand NAFTA to other Latin American countries later on could not be neglected

---

7   According to Smith (1993: 372), US congressional approval of the fast track procedure (see below) for NAFTA in May 1991 already made a considerable political contribution by legitimizing Salinas's authority and neutralizing international criticism of Mexico's electoral fraud.

either. While Canada had been neglecting Latin American relations, the potential of this region was increasingly recognized, resulting in a changing attitude. Finally, Mexico was Canada's most important trade partner in Latin America (immediately followed by Brazil), although in 1991 Mexico accounted for only 0.3 per cent of Canada's exports (Globerman 1994: 10).

NAFTA INTERESTS WITHIN MEXICO

In order to understand the support for NAFTA in Mexico it should be underlined again that the most significant economic impact of NAFTA was expected to stem from its liberalization of foreign investment. This feature enabled the Mexican state to "convince" official labour unions that NAFTA would be in their interest, as new investments would create jobs and higher wages.[8] NAFTA was also presented as being in the interest of Mexican capital, because more foreign investment would broaden economic expansion and complement local capital initiatives instead of competing with them.

Most of the sectoral prognoses for Mexico were based on the results of Mexico's liberalization policy in the wake of NAFTA. In the manufacturing sector the winners were the growing export sector, dominated by large companies with rising productivity and wage levels. This was especially the case in machinery, electronic equipment and the transport industry. The losers were companies producing for the internal market, which were characterized by static productivity and wages such as textile producers. For other sectors the predictions varied. Whereas small companies in the food business, and metal and non-metal mineral industry had proven to be able to adjust to the economic openness, many other small and medium-sized companies were expected to be unable to compete with large US corporations. As a consequence, NAFTA could give way to an increasing rate of capital concentration in Mexico (Bizberg 1993a: 182-3; Russell 1992: 28).

Mexico's financial sector, which has been described as oligopolistic and inefficient (Ros 1992), worried about competing with external capital. Presidents of large Mexican banks had their doubts regarding NAFTA, and wondered whether they would be able to handle the number of new clients, whether the opening of Mexico's financial market would not be too sudden, and whether they

---

8 Besides the need of more funding, more jobs was exactly what Salinas needed, being faced with an "overheated economy" and insufficient legitimation (Castañeda 1993: 65-6). However, whether modernization indeed creates jobs remained to be seen.

would survive in the North American market. Studies indicated that like other economic sectors Mexico's financial sector would considerably transnationalize under NAFTA, and that especially small banks and financial firms were likely to be sold, merge, or go bankrupt as a result of intensifying competition. It was generally expected that foreign banks would concentrate on big corporate projects as they had done already since the 1970s. Mexican banks, on the other hand, had concentrated on lending to the dwindling market of the public sector, and therefore lacked experience with the exploding market of the private sector. In particular, they feared that foreign companies would take over their major market: Mexico's national oil company PEMEX (Correa 1993, 1994; *Proceso* 826, 31/VIII/92: 26-8; *Financial Times* 10/XI/93: 6).

At first sight, NAFTA's impact on labour in Mexico seemed promising. It was generally expected that in the short run the US would lose some employment to Mexico and that increased export and investment would create new Mexican jobs. Mexico's experience with economic liberalization had also demonstrated that employees in the export industry were better paid than their colleagues in other industries. However, this same experience had shown that modernization fed unemployment and average real wage decline. In addition, employees of large companies that dominate in the export sector (known to include a relatively high share of women) had low levels of labour organization and representation since these companies went through a process of flexibilization (Bizberg 1993a).

Unlike the US, little research was performed on possible employment effects of NAFTA in Mexico. For instance, what might be the overall impact of increasing competition, forcing companies to modernize production, which often means laying off personnel? How many small Mexican companies would not be able to compete under NAFTA and subsequently disappear (as happened widely in the 1980s)? Whether this kind of information was available to the Mexican government at the time of NAFTA preparations is unknown.[9] A study by the Office of Technology Assessment (OTA), an "analytical arm" of the US Congress, revealed that both in Mexico and the US active labour and industrial policies were indispensable as market forces alone would not produce the social and economic rewards promised by the heads of both states. According to the OTA, Mexico stood at a juncture between continuing 1980s policies of main-

---

9   In general, there was a lack of profound and comprehensive assessments of the possible economic effects of NAFTA on Mexico. An elite working group consisting of leading private sector representatives and key policy-makers of SECOFI commissioned approximately eighty sectoral NAFTA studies, but their results were not made public (Pastor & Wise 1994: 480).

taining low wages and eliminating foreign investment regulations, or a development policy like Asian Tigers, involving "strategic protectionism" and commitment to social justice (OTA 1992: 3, 20).

The impact of NAFTA on Mexico's agricultural sector was generally estimated to be large and dramatic (see also 3.2). In spite of certain new opportunities for export of fresh fruit and vegetables to the US and Canada, the overall prospect seemed negative. NAFTA was likely to produce many problems as Mexico's 20 million small agricultural producers would not be able to compete with US and Canadian farmers (*La Jornada* 12/VIII/93: 40). After the destruction of many support programmes for farmers, NAFTA's gradual abolition of agricultural import restrictions would particularly affect the large number of small Mexican farmers. Consequently, an OECD study concluded that "regardless of whether the adjustment is gradual or immediate, liberalization contracts substantially the size of the rural labour force" (Levy and Van Wijnbergen 1992: 62). Estimates ranged from several hundred thousand to eventually 15 million people.

Taken together, prognoses indicated that, with the exception of large export companies, NAFTA's impact within Mexico was likely to be mixed at best. Whereas Mexico's export sector was likely to flourish with free trade, it needed to be seen how other sectors would be affected by increased competition, on the one hand, and possibly cheaper credits and an expanding market, on the other hand. For small Mexican farmers, however, there could be no doubt that the outcome would be very negative.

NAFTA INTERESTS WITHIN THE US

In the US there was an obvious conflict on NAFTA between capital and labour. As capital mobility, which eases regional production-sharing arrangements, was a more important feature of NAFTA than trade liberalization, US labour was likely to lose from the agreement, while gains would flow mainly to capital (Ros 1992: 77). In addition, trade-dislocated workers in the US tended to be minorities, women and older workers for whom adjustment to such changes is relatively hard. Besides, compared to other industrialized countries, US labour market programmes were very limited, and public expenditure on unemployment insurance and training of workers was very low (Rosen 1994: 35, 43). Several studies, some commissioned by the pro-NAFTA lobby, nevertheless maintained that US labour would gain from free trade in the long run. In short, the information was very diffuse.[10] Salinas claimed that "the US is losing jobs to countries with the highest wages in the world, not the lowest" (*Time* 27/07/92).

Despite these and other optimistic notions, us trade unions opposed the agreement and developed a strong anti-NAFTA lobby.

The free investment element of NAFTA thus gave rise to a strong anti-NAFTA lobby among us labour, but it also meant an extension and strengthening of the pro-NAFTA alliance in the us. The traditional free trade proponents would be the us export-producing firms, notably capital and consumer goods industries, which had already seen their sales in Mexico double or triple since the introduction of Mexico's import liberalization. Due to investment liberalization they were joined in their support for NAFTA by the service sector[11] and us TNCs. Internationally competitive service companies include banks, insurance companies and investment brokers, as well as owners of financial capital. In other words, these sectors represented us and transnational capital and they were expected to become major beneficiaries of free foreign investment in Mexico. Their revenue might increase by some 15 per cent because of growing Mexican demand for capital (*Business Week* 30/VIII/93: 36). As feared by Mexican bankers, prognoses predicted that foreign banks would occupy the most profitable segments in the Mexican corporate and retail sector (*Financial Times* 10/XI/93: 6). This estimation was based on the fact that Mexico's recently reprivatized banking system was rather fragile. For that reason, the liberalization of the financial system under NAFTA was to be gradual, but it would nevertheless create new opportunities for us and Canadian banks on the Mexican market by allowing the purchase of Mexican banks and the establishment of Mexican subsidiaries.

us TNCs believed NAFTA could enhance their global operations and competitiveness, and considerable pro-NAFTA pressure came from sectors and companies that would benefit from expanding Mexico's *maquiladora* sector. With the agreement, their opportunities to reduce costs by moving production to lower cost areas or closer to their consumer markets would increase. Through easing production arrangements with Mexican plants, NAFTA would encourage TNCs to rationalize their regional activities and to invest more in Mexico

---

10 Hufbauer and Schott (1993) predicted a 170,000 net increase of us jobs, whereas the Economic Policy Institute estimated that because of NAFTA 500,000 us jobs would be lost. Over 20 studies of the effect of NAFTA on us employment all yielded different conclusions (*Financial Times* 12/05/92: 29). A Department of Commerce report, prepared and suppressed under Bush, concluded that NAFTA would cause a loss of us jobs for the rest of the decade (*Mexico & Nafta Report* 28/10/93: 4).

11 Numerous service firms started business in Mexico from the late 1980s on. FDI as part of total investment in services accounted increased from 12.7 per cent in 1986 to 40.1 per cent in 1992. From 1989 to 1992 17.2 per cent of foreign direct investment in Mexico went into financial services (Ortiz 1994: 168, 171).

(Gestrin and Rugman 1994). US TNCs had been very active in the Mexican export sector, and implementation of the agreement was also important for them because of growing protectionist forces in the US. Furthermore, economic growth stemming from NAFTA would be beneficial for TNCs, especially after the economic crises had caused Mexican consumption to stagnate.

US retailers were equally interested in Mexico's expanding consumer market. They expected that Mexico's economic restructuring would raise the purchasing power of their clients: the middle and lower classes. In the early 1990s, joint ventures were established between practically all the major US retailers and large Mexican store chains. US firms wanted to profit from the large market and profit margins twice those of the US, whereas their Mexican partners wanted to take advantage of US technology and distribution networks. However, as a consequence of this development, small stores and supermarkets in Mexico were losing business together with small Mexican suppliers who lacked capital to expand and modernize (*Financial Times* 19/1/93: 21).

Finally, for US companies involved in environmental technology, Mexico was a booming market. There was a great need for environmental infrastructure, equipment and services to deal with air and water pollution, and solid waste. Only few Mexican companies produced the goods and services required, and foreign competition was very limited so that imported environmental technologies used by Mexico's major industries largely came from the US (AMCHAM 1993: 17). In 1992, the Mexican market represented $1.5 billion, and it was estimated to grow to 2.6 billion in 1995 as a result of increasing government efforts for the enforcement of environmental legislation (TPCC 1994: 3). The Environmental Technology Export Council (ETEC) representing US companies played an active role with respect to NAFTA, and both Mexican business and the Mexican government encouraged ETEC to support NAFTA (US private sector source 22/IV/94).

In short, the interests of the following US sectors would be served by NAFTA:
- TNCs (especially the electronics and auto industry);
- financial services (banking and insurance);
- other service sectors (such as telecommunications, transport and construction);
- export-producing firms (notably capital and consumer goods industry);
- other industries with a growth potential on the Mexican market (including environmental technology, chemicals, energy, biotechnology, retailers and tourism).

Taken together, a broad range of US companies was expected to gain from NAFTA, whereas the effect on economic growth would be the largest in Mexico.

For Canada, on the other hand, NAFTA would primarily serve to safeguard its interests in the US and to be incorporated in future initiatives for trade and investment liberalization with the rest of Latin America. A range of other interests merged in the NAFTA plan, predominantly the concern of Mexican technocrats for external embedding of their neoliberal project, US concern about Mexico's political stability and the endless stream of Mexicans crossing the border to look for illegal jobs in the US, and joint interests in consolidating and extending Mexico-US economic integration. Finally, at the regional level NAFTA would consolidate and intensify North American integration, while laying the foundation of sustained economic integration of the Americas.

The proponents of NAFTA made major efforts to pass the agreement, and established numerous transnational relations among them, as will be shown in chapters 5 and 6. Government agencies of Mexico, the US and Canada negotiated the provisions of the agreement, and were supported in various ways by private sector organizations. Both government agencies and private sector organizations were also involved in dealing with criticism of and resistance to NAFTA. The rather broad US sectoral interests in NAFTA contrasted with the Mexican situation, where export-producing firms and a few Mexican TNCs seemed the potential winners. Another difference between Mexico and the US was the attitude of private sector organizations in the NAFTA debate. While Mexican organizations primarily followed their government, US organizations operated more independently and developed many initiatives on their own. Despite differences like these, private sector organizations and government agencies organized a transnational NAFTA lobby after opposition in the US turned out to be fierce. Chapter 5 describes the major actors behind the transnational NAFTA lobbies, and the ways in which these actors reacted to claims that the agreement would be detrimental to the environment in North America.

— 3.2 NAFTA, the environment and Mexico: the linkages —

After the Mexico-US announcement of their free trade plan, various critical studies of NAFTA's possible environmental effects were carried out. They pointed out that North American free trade might have damaging environmental side-effects due to economic, political and policy changes. However, whereas analyses of possible economic effects of NAFTA were already quite tentative, there were even less in-depth studies of and scenarios for the environmental impact of the agreement. Most studies were confined to a broad assessment of the changes NAFTA might produce with respect to the economy and politics, and subsequently to the environment. The possible development of specific economic sectors and their environmental performance under a free trade agreement was hardly the subject of thorough analysis. Since the trade and environment issue was rather new, there were few examples available. A lack of profound economic assessments also complicated such efforts.

Within the group of actors raising the issue of environmental protection with respect to NAFTA, we cannot easily distinguish between academics and environmental organizations, or the academic debate and the political debate. The lack of information forced environmental organizations to study how NAFTA would affect the environment. For many ENGOS, the NAFTA preparations were the first time that they dealt with the trade and environment link, which forced groups to encourage some of their office members to become specialists on the subject. At the same time, various scholars who studied possible environmental effects of NAFTA were also affiliated to non-governmental organizations. The critical academic and political debate thus became mixed.

Environmental impact assessment studies available at the time of the NAFTA debate can be divided into three groups. First, there were general studies on the interaction between trade liberalization and environmental legislation, often based on the experiences with the GATT and the CUFTA. Second, a number of analyses dealt specifically with the possible effect of NAFTA on Mexico's environment. Finally, there was a set of studies of the possible environmental effects of the agreement on the US. In this section we will look into each of these three types of studies, quite elaborately on Mexico and more summarily on the US.

FREE TRADE AND ENVIRONMENTAL LEGISLATION

The links between free trade and national environmental policy are complex. Free trade implies abolishing national rules that restrict import and export. Sometimes such rules function as a means of environmental protection or controlled exploitation of natural resources. Both export and import controls, as well as relatively stringent environmental and natural resources legislation, can be considered as a trade obstruction under a free trade agreement. Trade liberalization thus seems to require that participating nations have similar policies and standards in matters that are somehow trade-related, because exceptions can easily be regarded as either indirect subsidies or non-tariff trade barriers. Since negotiations of trade agreements as well as dispute settlement processes take place behind closed doors, and deviating national policies are discouraged, free trade agreements have been accused of undermining national democracy (Ritchie 1993: 184; Shrybman 1993: 282).[12]

National policy regulating the exploitation and use of finite natural resources, such as oil, gas and minerals, and slowly renewable resources such as
fishery and forestry, can be considered as obstructing free trade. As these resources are growing scarce, a government may want to require efficient exploitation, for instance by prescribing certain techniques or technologies. A restriction on the export of non-renewable resources might also be an option to
preserve the last reserves for national use, future generations or more efficient
exploitation by advanced technologies. Except when explicitly excluded from a
trade agreement, such export controls would be considered contrary to the objective of free trade of goods.

The conflict between free trade and national policies on natural resources
may be illustrated by the case of Canada's Fisheries Act under the CUFTA. The
Act required that fish caught in Canadian waters, before export, be landed in
Canada in order to be reported through biological sampling. This control on
catch reports was introduced for the conservation of herring and salmon after
inadequate fisheries management had resulted in severely depleted stocks. The
US challenged the Act on the grounds that it protected the fishing industry of
the Canadian province British Columbia, and a dispute panel subsequently
concluded that the Act was incompatible with the CUFTA. The panel argued
that a trade-restricting conservation measure could only be allowed when conservation was the sole aim of the measure and when no other means were available (Shrybman 1993: 276).[13]

Free trade also implies that import controls are regarded as non-tariff barriers to trade, but such controls may contribute to environmental protection
and sustainable development. Developing countries, for instance, apply import
controls for the protection of local small-scale farming and fishing. Without
import quotas or taxes, small farmers have to compete with cheap imports from
industrialized countries, and local agriculture and fisheries are likely to be intensified in an unsustainable way (Ritchie 1993: 180). With respect to environmental legislation, import controls can be applied to cancel out the advantage
of cheaper imports from countries with lower environmental norms. Removal
of such restrictions for the sake of free trade renders more stringent environ-

---

12 More in general, free trade is held to conflict with national policies of: getting prices
right; a more just income distribution; fostering local communities; controlling the
macro-economy; and respecting ecological limits (Daly 1993: 124).

13 The agreement's restrictions on export controls go beyond GATT regulation and Canada is obliged to share its resources with the US. One of the principal reasons why the
US government was interested in the CUFTA was to secure US access to Canadian energy
resources (Shrybman 1993: 274-6).

mental standards than those of the major trading partners economically malign to national producers. Moreover, companies may threaten to move production to countries with laxer environmental protection if the government preserves tougher rules, or they may actually do so.

The well-known dolphin/tuna case between Mexico and the US illustrates the treatment of import controls under free trade agreements. In 1991, a GATT dispute panel decided that the US was not allowed to boycott Mexican tuna. The US government, pushed by NGOs through a Federal District Court, defended its ban by stating that the number of dolphins and other sea animals accidentally killed by Mexican tuna fishers (through their use of driftnets) exceeded the standard established by the US Marine Mammal Protection Act. By applying the act to fish imports, the US equated the environmental costs of foreign fishers with those of US fishers. The GATT panel, however, ruled the embargo illegal and stated that the restriction of trade for the protection of the environment outside a country's borders contravened GATT regulations. The US denied informal charges of ecological imperialism, and argued that its only aim was to make the same demands on foreign fishers as on US fishers (Shrybman 1993: 278-9; Phillips 1993: 134-6).[14]

The dolphin/tuna case shows that production or process standards are considered non-tariff trade barriers under free trade agreements. In general, free trade agreements respect national legislation on product standards, which means that imported goods should comply with the national standards of the country where they are sold. These standards, among other things, prescribe to what extent certain toxins are allowed in products. However, governments cannot prescribe how imported goods should be produced beyond their national territory. In other words, free trade agreements do not permit production standards for imports, such as a ban on meat for which rainforest has been destroyed.

As shown in the above mentioned cases, there is a strong entanglement of environmental and economic matters in trade disputes on environmental issues. In general, a trade restriction for environmental reasons has an economic impact, and if an environmental restriction is economically advantageous for national producers, their foreign rivals can be expected to challenge the restriction. This environment-economy interlinkage also complicates the

---

14 Greenpeace and Earth Island Institute were the most important organizations behind the US boycot (see 2.4). Mexicans generally resisted unilaterally imposed norms of the US on Mexico, and felt that economic interests rather than ecological concern was behind the boycott. Even Mexico's environmentalists criticized the US on this matter. Nevertheless, the activities of US ENGOs contributed to Mexico improving its record.

creation of government subsidies or programmes for environmental protection. Market prices do not reflect the real production costs of a product, because a part of the costs is "externalized" to society as a whole via air and water contamination, waste disposal, unsustainable exploitation of natural resources, et cetera. The price of a commodity can be lower if weak environmental legislation enables producers to externalize a larger share of the costs. Government subsidies created to support national industry in countries with relatively high environmental standards (in other words, industries that internalize a larger share of the production costs in the commodity price) can be challenged under GATT when such subsidies affect the export or import of the commodity (Wallach 1993: 32).

In sum, free trade agreements may limit governments in setting their own policies with respect to environmental protection and natural resource use. If an environmental law harms free trade it may easily be challenged, and a dispute panel may force a country to abrogate the law. Subsequently, a government would have to find other ways of implementing its policy goal. Probably alternatives are more expensive or complicated, otherwise they would already have been preferred. In certain cases, these extra expenses and complications may produce political resistance to the extent that a government has to abandon its policy goal altogether.

Policy harmonization is sometimes proposed as a means to solve the difficulties of free trade among countries with different levels of environmental protection, and the European Union has taken some steps in this direction. Harmonization of environmental policy does, however, embody several bottlenecks. Politically, multilateral policy harmonization restricts local and national governments in setting their own environmental standards. In general, multilateral import standards have tended to neglect social, economic, and other concerns, accepting only "scientific evidence" for environmental regulation (Ritchie 1993: 182-4). Moreover, with international inequalities, some countries have far less influence in multilateral talks than others. Another objection against harmonization of environmental standards is that it discourages progressive policy initiatives. When several countries have to agree on environmental standards, it is less likely that they will adopt the standards of the country with the most stringent legislation than that they will settle for a compromise. Even if an agreement allows for higher national standards, the harmonized standard is likely to operate as a ceiling since free trade agreements limit a country's ability to compensate national producers for higher standards. Less countries are likely to set an international example (Shrybman 1993: 282). Taken together, multilateral harmonization of environmental standards may not be a useful way out of the trade-environment problem under free trade.

ASSESSING NAFTA'S ENVIRONMENTAL EFFECTS ON MEXICO

At the time of the NAFTA debate, several attempts were made to estimate the agreement's impact on Mexico's environment. Some critical studies are reviewed here in order to understand the ideas and concerns behind the position of environmental organizations in the debate. A few assessments were based on a politico-ideological approach to predict some general implications of the agreement for Mexico, and will be discussed briefly below. Other studies focused on the ways in which NAFTA-enhanced growth would affect Mexican sectors such as industry, agriculture and natural resources, and subsequently the environment. These sector studies often referred to the weak enforcement of environmental legislation in Mexico, and they will be reviewed more extensively.

Mexico's economic integration with the US and Canada was expected to run several risks stemming from basic national differences, including Mexico's far greater biodiversity and its distant social and cultural situation. A first risk, as argued by Toledo (1992: 348-51), lay in the adoption of US and Canadian technology. This technology intensively uses energy, natural resources and capital while economizing on labour, and would not "fit" a tropical ecology. Without a Mexican science and technology project, NAFTA might result in massive import of environmentally damaging capital goods and technology. According to Toledo (1992: 352), a second risk would be the dominant position of the market in the NAFTA project. The agreement was to improve the standard of living through increasing production and consumption. However, instead of satisfying local needs, free trade would probably direct economic activities increasingly towards foreign trade. These activities were likely to be environmentally damaging without proper government policy and with market prices that do not include the public value of biodiversity and natural resources.

The inequality between Mexico and the US was often mentioned as a reason for caution. There were concerns that in NAFTA negotiations, Mexico would yield to many US demands while Mexican demands would be brushed aside (Alfie 1991: 61). It was argued, then, that free trade between an industrialized and a developing country should be approached cautiously (Kelly and Kamp 1991: 3). In addition, because of the fact that Mexico-US integration was extended through a free trade agreement, it was expected that the development gap between the two countries would not be the subject of negotiations. The European Union, conversely, created programmes for the development of the most impoverished countries and regions within its territory. This form of including development issues in economic integration initiatives was raised as an example for NAFTA (Castañeda and Heredia 1993: 83).

INDUSTRY

NAFTA promised to spur Mexico-based industry through total access to the US market, national treatment of US and Canadian capital in Mexico, and later on an expanding national market. This expansion of industry and the location of new installations could have a major environmental impact. The border zone and large industrial cities such as Mexico City, Monterrey and Guadalajara (and their surroundings) were already suffering heavily from industrial pollution. Several of the industries that were likely to intensify investment in Mexico under NAFTA were known for their polluting production, most notably automotive products, cement and chemicals (Bath 1991: 11-3; Sánchez 1991a: 309-10). No matter whether this production would take place at the border or in Mexico's interior, it was likely to be environmentally damaging as long as a lack of resources, experience and political will would limit enforcement of Mexico's environmental legislation. In addition, to prevent the problems of the past, industrial expansion should have to be better planned and controlled, and new plants should be built in less stressed areas (cf. Barkin 1991; Mumme 1992; Mumme, Bath and Assetto 1988).

Several studies of the possible effects of NAFTA on Mexico's industry focused on the *maquiladoras*, since the border zone was expected to industrialize further. There were assessments that at least in the short run, Mexico's environmental policy would not keep up with renewed rapid economic expansion in the region, such as with respect to industrial waste. Formally, the *maquiladora* programme required companies to return all their production waste back to the country of origin, although in reality many companies circumvented this requirement and illegally dumped it.[15] NAFTA's rule of national treatment of each other's investors would, however, abolish this prerequisite. Instead, companies would have to dispose of their waste according to Mexico's environmental laws. Unfortunately, Mexico's waste installations and vigilance system would not suffice for an adequate processing of this waste. With more companies, and not even a share of the *maquiladoras* returning their waste to the country of origin, waste problems might increasingly worsen (Sánchez 1991b: 13-5).

Other concerns for the Mexico-US border were water and transport. A lack of water was the predominant restraint on further development of the border area, with its polluted rivers, unsustainable exploitation of ground water (from aquifers), and insufficient sewage treatment systems. While the latter already

---

15 In 1991, less than one-third of the *maquiladoras* sent their hazardous wastes back to the US for disposal as required (*Los Angeles Times* 19/11/91: A24).

had serious health implications, the other two problems were likely to become acute in the near future (Kelly and Kamp 1991: 19-20). In addition, the border transport growth was expected to continue under NAFTA. Previously, the establishment of *maquiladoras* had strongly increased transport between the two countries. Next to industrial expansion, increasing export of some Mexican fruits and vegetables would contribute to more transborder trucking. Especially Mexican trucks were a source of pollution, and this would probably inease with free trade, unless strictly controlled (Bath 1991: 14; Kelly and Kamp 1991: 31).

Whether and to what degree NAFTA would encourage polluting industry in the US and Canada to locate or relocate production to Mexico was unclear. Sánchez (1991a: 310) found that for 13 per cent of a group of surveyed *maquiladoras*, weaker environmental controls were the primary reason for relocating to Mexico, while it was an important reason for another 13 per cent. Factors like cheap labour and better access to the Mexican market were expected to attract US and Canadian companies even more. With weak policy enforcement, the environmental behaviour of these new industries would depend substantively on their good will. The question remained where new industrial installations would be located. On the one hand, it was argued that the bad situation in the border area would discourage new investments there; companies would tend to look for locations with more possibilities and less problems (Bath 1991). The same argument was made for some of Mexico's major industrial cities.[16] On the other hand, the border region was expected to remain attractive because of its proximity to the US (Sánchez 1991b: 17), whereas large cities might remain attractive as big consumer markets.

Some studies warned of forms of polarization due to NAFTA. Mexico's entry might intensify the process in which capital was the main beneficiary of economic growth while local communities had to bear "external" costs such as pollution (Sánchez 1991b: 12). If NAFTA involved immediate harmonization of North American environmental standards, this could give rise to a process of industrial polarization. If small Mexican companies were required to meet these standards instantly, they would not be able to produce competitively on the regional market (Kelly and Kamp 1991: 18). Obviously, with respect to en-

---

16 In addition, Mexico had a directional policy that required special permission for a 100 per cent foreign ownership in companies in Monterrey and Guadalajara. This requirement aimed at stimulating new foreign investors to establish companies in cities which were less overburdened. Under NAFTA, however, these and other government measures to direct development might be challenged as contravening a national treatment of foreign investment (Kelly & Kamp 1991: 6).

vironmentally-sound production, experience, and resources, Mexican firms had a large disadvantage compared to US and Canadian firms.

The assessments of the environmental impact of NAFTA-enhanced industrial expansion in Mexico, however, remained far from complete. A complicating factor for all the above mentioned studies was the very limited data on industrial emissions and resource use, on the environmental programmes of companies, and on the effectiveness of government regulations. In addition, at the time NAFTA was negotiated there was a general uncertainty as to how investors, producers and consumers would react to regional free trade. As a result, studies of NAFTA and industrial pollution in Mexico basically pointed out that there were serious risks, but they left many questions unanswered.

AGRICULTURE

As mentioned under 3.1, the impact of NAFTA on Mexico's agricultural sector was expected to be fundamental and dramatic. While its share of GDP had steadily decreased, agriculture was still important, and 30 per cent of the Mexican population was economically dependent on this sector (Calva 1991: 50). NAFTA would gradually abolish import restrictions for agricultural products. It was expected that Mexican export of certain fresh fruits and vegetables such as tomatoes would consequently expand, but free trade would damage the production of basic grains in Mexico. In combination with policies of lower subsidies for farmers, less and lower price guarantees for basic food supplements, and the privatization of communal land ownership (the reform of *ejidos*, see 1.3), NAFTA would bring about a new type of agricultural production in Mexico. Traditional agriculture, based on labour-intensive methods and consisting of small-scale and diversified production, still prevailed in Mexico's countryside. This traditional farming seemed unlikely to survive competition with modern North American methods that were labour-extensive and based on large-scale monoculture. The disparity in productivity per agricultural labourer was enormous. For example, in the 1980s the production of one ton of maize required 17.8 man-days in Mexico and only 1.2 man-hours in the US (Calva 1991: 15).

Apart from different agricultural methods, Mexico's low productivity was also the result of natural circumstances and government policy. The US, for instance, has relatively more plains, sun hours and rain than Mexico, whereas Mexico's quantity of natural resources (e.g. soil for cultivation, forest, irrigated land) per agricultural labourer is substantially lower (Calva 1991: 24-5). Another major difference was the level of state support, as government support for Mexican farmers was very low. In 1988, US and Canadian governmental subsidies accounted for respectively 35 per cent and 43 per cent of total agricultural production, while this was only 3 per cent in Mexico (Calva 1991: 27).[17] In this context, Barkin (1992: 377-8) warned that NAFTA would discourage the traditional production of basic grains because of cheap imports.[18] Only large-scale production seemed likely to be competitive with these imports, but modern producers would probably concentrate on the production of fruits and vegetables for the US and Canadian market, without compensation for decreasing small-scale production of basic grains. This would render Mexico more dependent on import of basic food supplements.[19]

Environmentally, increasing large-scale agricultural production in Mexico would have serious effects. First, the modern agromodel uses more energy, water and other resources than traditional production. Machines would take over a lot of work, automatic irrigation systems would be introduced and more fertilizers and chemicals would be applied.[20] Second, large-scale production of monocultures and the use of pesticides would substantially decrease biological diversity (Barkin 1992: 380-5; Ritchie 1993: 175-7). Third, the industrialization of agriculture would give rise to pollution, even more so since Mexico's infrastructure for waste water was insufficient (Sánchez 1991a: 306). Fourth, land would be abandoned because it is unsuitable for large-scale production or because farmers lack credits, and the abandoned plots would suffer from erosion.[21] Finally, many small farmers (possibly up to 15 million people) would

---

17 US and Canadian farmers were not only helped with price policies and subsidies, but also by state programs for research and technology, which partly explains the large technological gap with Mexico. As government budget cuts reduced productive investments and credits, Mexico actually experienced a process of agricultural de-modernization, as Calva calls it (1991: 15-22).

18 In the period 1987-89, the average production cost of a ton of maize was $259 in Mexico versus $93 in the US; Mexican beans $641 versus US beans $220; Mexican wheat $153 versus US wheat $144; Mexican rice $224 versus US rice $190 (Calva 1994: 33).

19 For the Mexican government, the import of basic grains would be lucrative as it would have to spend less on subsidies. Liberalization of Mexico's agriculture would also be lucrative for some large agroproducers, since costs of large-scale production in Mexico might sometimes be lower than in the other NAFTA countries because of cheap labour, soil and water, and weak enforcement of environmental regulation (Barkin 1992: 378-9).

20 Agricultural liberalization would also have side-effects on energy use. More trade implies more transport, while NAFTA might also lead to an increase in food processing and food packaging, rendering North American agriculture as a whole more energy-intensive (Ritchie 1993: 176).

21 Calva (1994: 35) estimated that complete free trade of grains under NAFTA would leave over 10 million hectares of agricultural land uncultivated.

eventually leave the interior and migrate to cities in Mexico or to the US (Calva 1994: 35). Urban environmental problems in Mexico would consequently grow even worse (see 2.1).[22]

NATURAL RESOURCES

The issue of NAFTA's possible effects on Mexico's natural resources was also the subject of study prior to the signing of the agreement. Of course, the use of natural resources is directly linked to the above mentioned and other economic activities. Nonetheless, the issue will be dealt with separately here, since it has important implications for Mexico and has its own trade peculiarities. Especially the liberalization of exports was a ground for concern as export restrictions can be a means to control or direct the exploitation of a country's natural resource base. If not explicitly mentioned otherwise in NAFTA, restrictions on the exploitation of slowly or non-renewable resources, such as fossil fuels, forests, water and fish, might be considered a non-tariff trade barrier (Alfie 1991: 61). It was argued that one of the interests of the US in free trade with Mexico, as with Canada, was access to its abundant natural resource base. With the average US citizen consuming more natural resources than citizens of any other country in the world, US resources have been depleting and have become insufficient to support the US lifestyle. In that context, NAFTA might strongly affect Mexico (Barkin 1992: 280-1; Shrybman 1993: 275).

Fossil fuels were a major US interest in the creation of the CUFTA and of NAFTA. In the US, the world's largest energy consumer, petroleum played a central role in economic growth. The resource base of its own territory, however, had become limited.[23] NAFTA would encompass deregulation of energy trade, implying that Mexico would allow the US access to its more abundant petroleum reserves. Furthermore, liberalization of Mexico's oil sector was of great interest to US and Canadian TNCs (Alexander and Stump 1992: 1-12; Dillon 1993: 326).[24]

---

22 An alternative development strategy to the liberalization versus low productivity situation of Mexico's agricultural sector is, for instance, Barkin's plan for a "war economy" (Barkin 1990).

23 In 1993, Dillon (1993: 315) claimed that US crude oil reserves were equivalent to only nine years of production.

24 Canada's relatively open energy sector has for long been dominated by foreign companies. In 1979, 72 per cent of Canada's petroleum industry was in the hands of TNCs, and 82 per cent of revenues were foreign-controlled (Dillon 1993: 318).

Liberalization of the Mexican oil industry was a sensitive issue in Mexico, and from the outset of the negotiations it was clear that despite US demands for total liberalization, Mexico's energy sector would only be partly included in NAFTA. Since the nationalization of the oil industry in 1938, oil had been a symbol of national independence in Mexico. The Constitution prohibited foreign firms from becoming involved in most oil activities, and direct investments were traditionally very restricted. In reality, however, since the late 1970s the share of foreign capital in Mexico's national petroleum company PEMEX was large.[25] The main reason behind Mexico's willingness to liberalize its oil policy from the 1970s onwards was the need for capital. PEMEX was to be further privatized to cover debt payments and to attract new investment and technologies to exploit offshore and deep wells. Through PEMEX's payment of high taxes, expanding sales also contributed to government resources (Dillon 1993: 322, 328). Under NAFTA, PEMEX would maintain its monopoly of oil exploration, but energy services would become more open to foreign investment.[26]

The environmental impact of NAFTA's energy deregulation could be serious. Like Canada, Mexico was likely to accelerate the exploitation of its fossil fuel reserves for export to the US.[27] Instead of conserving its energy resources for future generations and more efficient technologies, Mexico would be selling them cheaply. In addition, petroleum exploration is an environmentally damaging activity, and has been a source of major contamination in Mexico (see 2.1). With NAFTA, PEMEX was expected to expand its offshore oil drilling in the Gulf of Mexico. Foreign investment and technology would modernize exploration, but it remained to be seen whether enforcement of environmental legislation would be taken seriously. As long as the Mexican government was the main beneficiary of high levels of production, it seemed unlikely that this same government would demand costly measures (Alexander and Stump 1992: 1, 15; Márquez and López 1988: 472, 476-81).

---

25 In 1981, PEMEX's foreign loans amounted to $20 billion (Dillon 1993: 322).

26 However, the extra government income from further liberalization might be somewhat disappointing as Mexican subsidies for the oil industry were likely to increase as well. The US heavily supported its energy industry, and US investors would probably demand similar support in Mexico before investing in its energy sector. While subsidizing the depletion of its energy resources for export to the US, NAFTA would prohibit Mexico, as well as the other countries, from levying export taxes (Alexander & Stump 1992: 14, 17, 36).

27 Shrybman (1993: 275) states that one of the first effects of CUFTA was a new round of energy megaprojects in Canada for the US.

Water was another natural resource that was believed to be negatively affected by economic changes as a result of NAFTA. Mexico's water problems were closely linked to industrial and agricultural activities. Even though scarcity of water was a national problem, most attention had been paid to the border region, where water scarcity was hampering further development. On the US side of the border, the price of water is an extra problem besides its availability. Free trade and national treatment of US producers in Mexico were expected to stimulate production across the border. This would produce further competition for scarce water in Mexico, and expand the unsustainable extraction of water from ground water in deep aquifers (Sánchez 1991b: 20-1).

Mexico's tariff system for water consumption would probably not prevent a further polarization of access to this resource. Large companies, with a high profitability and with access to credit, would be able to use far more water than small landowners and *ejiditarios*. Poor Mexican farmers would thus suffer from competition from the North American water market (Sánchez 1991b: 21-2). Similarly, agriculture in the border region would stand to lose from increased competition for water. Demand of industries and cities was likely to dominate over demand of the agricultural sector. Hence farmers might have to move away from the border into Mexico's interior, thereby moving the water problem to new areas.

In sum, despite their weaknesses, critical assessments of NAFTA's environmental effects in Mexico showed that there were considerable risks involved. Combining information on previous environmental damage by major economic activities in Mexico, and the effects of liberalization and economic integration up to that time, with the expected economic changes that NAFTA would bring about suggested that NAFTA might contribute considerably to the degradation of Mexico's environment. The exploitation and use of natural resources as well as industrial activities were likely to be rapidly expanded. Theoretically, damage could be limited, and if major progress were made in environmental policy, economic expansion caused by NAFTA might even produce less damage than before. However, at the start of the NAFTA debate there were no real signs that the Mexican government was up to that task.

POSSIBLE ENVIRONMENTAL EFFECTS ON THE US

In the US, there was fear that under NAFTA Mexico's weak enforcement of environmental legislation would be detrimental for US economic and environmental interests. Economically, Mexico would derive unfair trade advantages from its low protection levels and might turn into a "pollution haven", at the cost of US industry and employment. Many environmental concerns had to do with the possibility of NAFTA legally and politically limiting the options for local, state and federal environmental protection. For several reasons, free trade with a country with less stringent environmental legislation, let alone enforcement, could harm progressive policy in the US.

First, stringent US environmental standards were expected to be challenged by Mexico-based producers as non-tariff barriers to trade. Especially tough standards for residues of pesticides on food seemed likely to be challenged by Mexican farmers as unfair regulations or protectionism if they found it hard or impossible to reach those standards. In addition, many US environmental laws provide states with the option of setting more stringent standards than the federal standards, but NAFTA could pre-empt that legal option. This would imply that the trade agreement would hamper the sovereignty of the US (Alfie 1991: 60; Kelly and Kamp 1991: 15-6; Wallach 1993: 28).[28]

Second, if not challenged, tougher US standards might be indirectly harmed by lax environmental policy enforcement in Mexico via political pressure for downward reform of US laws. Differences of environmental policy between Mexico and the US were most evident at the level of enforcement. As described in chapter 2, a combination of low government priority, few resources, and weak government agencies had resulted in lax enforcement of Mexico's environmental legislation. Unregulated competition between companies producing in Mexico and in the US would place US-based producers at a disadvantage, because the latter would have to apply higher standards, requiring higher investments. In other words, for producers in Mexico, the difference of environmental policy with the US would function as an indirect subsidy. This situation would probably give rise to stronger political pressure from business and farmers in the us for lower environmental standards, and some might use NAFTA to threaten to move to Mexico. (Alfie 1991: 61; Kelly and Kamp 1991: 18).[29]

Another issue of importance in the US was food safety. There were concerns that NAFTA would lead to harmonization of food standards. Given that some Mexican standards were less stringent, this might result in lower US standards for pesticides and food additives. In addition, NAFTA could require reduced inspection of agricultural products, increasing the chance of dangerous food

---

28 Similarly, with the CUFTA Canada's stringent regulation on pesticides had to be eased, while problems arose over the obligatory replant of forests (CNI 1991; Ritchie 1993: 170).

29 In theory, the problem of different levels of environmental protection could be solved by formulating process standards, but generally free trade agreements do not allow for such requirements (Kelly & Kamp 1991: 17; Wallach 1993: 28-9).

supplies entering the us.[30] Finally, NAFTA plans for energy deregulation would sustain the enormous energy consumption in the us and discourage energy alternatives in the three North American countries. Consumers would not have an economic incentive to save on energy as long as fossil fuels remained heavily subsidized, and the development of other, more sustainable energy resources would be postponed. The tendency to continue with excessive consumption of non-renewable resources which produce many environmental problems (acid rain, global warming, health damage) obviously clashed with sustainable development (Alexander and Stump 1992: 36; Shrybman 1993: 275). Taken together, however, us environmental concerns over NAFTA predominantly involved the possible limits to stringent laws and standards.

— 3.3 Conclusions —

The us government had been interested in free trade with Mexico as early as the late 1970s. From then, it had arranged several bilateral discussions on the matter, but for several years without success. In 1989, Mexico's government shifted from a negative to a positive position, as it estimated that free trade and investment with the us would be the means to secure the success of the economic restructuring programme. This opened the way for bilateral overtures. The Canadian announcement in early 1991 that it would join free trade negotiations implied the start of creating the world's largest trading zone. Although economic interests were important, political reasons too contributed to the decision of the three governments to pursue North American free trade and investment. In addition, while NAFTA would imply further economic liberalization, it would also have a consolidating effect on the ongoing processes of Mexico's neoliberal restructuring, its economic integration in the us, and regional integration in North America as a whole.

Early assessments of NAFTA's economic effects showed that the agreement's contribution to growth would be the largest in Mexico and would have relatively little effect in the us and Canada. Internationally competitive companies would regionally be the main winners of liberalization. In Mexico, this concerned a rather limited group of large companies, while the expectations for other companies were mixed or poor. Within the us, there were also some

---

30 In the case of the CUFTA, for instance, us inspections of Canadian meat had been identified as a trade barrier. After these inspections were largely abolished, tons of tainted Canadian meat were shipped to the us (CNI 1991).

smaller specialized firms that might profit from NAFTA, implying a somewhat more heterogenous group of proponents. On the other hand, US labour opposition to free trade with Mexico mobilized the strongest resistance to the agreement, as the following chapter describes.

Prior to the NAFTA debate, several trade disputes had demonstrated that there can be a conflict between the policy goals of free trade and environmental protection. When the NAFTA plan became known, studies of such experiences with GATT and the CUFTA formed the first warnings for NAFTA's possible detrimental impact. Environmental policy measures that somehow involved controls on import or export had been challenged as obstructions to free trade, implying a limitation of options for national policy-making. However, harmonization of environmental standards might also be problematic.

Although critical environmental assessments of NAFTA were scattered, they show that there was considerable ground for concern about Mexico. Various analyses estimated that the impact of trade liberalization on Mexico's environment would be negative, due to the economic and political asymmetry of the three countries and their different levels of environmental protection. Industrial expansion, structural agricultural reforms and increasing demand for scarce natural resources were the main elements of these forecasts. Studies indicated that without additional arrangements the combination of these trends with the generally weak enforcement of Mexico's environmental legislation would produce environmental damage and social tensions.

For the US, Mexico's weak enforcement of environmental policy might also become a problem. Large differences between actual control on protection efforts of companies were likely to contribute to resistance of the private sector to stringent US environmental standards. The fact that NAFTA would ease location in Mexico might add to the impact of private sector resistance. Similarly, reforms for higher standards in the US would encounter stronger opposition. Besides internal pressures, via NAFTA Mexico might also challenge US environmental regulations and standards relating to trade. These and other concerns about the environmental effects of NAFTA stimulated environmental organizations in Mexico, the US and Canada to become active on NAFTA. The following chapter analyses the first phase of the NAFTA environment debate, which was dominated by ENGOs. In chapter 5, we will turn to the reactions of NAFTA proponents to environmentalist criticism and demands.

CHAPTER 4

Transnational Environmental Opposition to NAFTA

As North American free trade was to involve a range of considerable changes, criticism of the NAFTA plans could be expected. As described in the previous chapter, apart from NAFTA plans there were a few trade-environment conflicts in North America, whereas internationally some environmental organizations had worked on GATT's environmental effects. While some ENGO activities on NAFTA could thus be expected, strong environmental opposition was not foreseen. In particular, the emergence of various transnational relations of ENGOS in Mexico, the US and Canada was a novelty.

Environmental organizations that wanted to ensure that regional trade and investment liberalization would not cause additional environmental damage differed widely. The different structure, constituency, and strategies of organizations was to some extent determined by nationality. On the one hand, these differences formed an obstacle to transnational relations. On the other hand, they were also partly overcome in the NAFTA debate. The emerging transnational arena created new opportunities for opposition (as well as for NAFTA proponents, see chapter 5). ENGOS and their relations in the NAFTA debate will be studied in the first section of this chapter, focusing on the transnational dimension of environmental activism on NAFTA.

The first phase of the NAFTA environment debate lasted from June 1990 until May 1991. This phase was characterized by environmental organizations' exploring the issues as well as the options for cooperation. In May 1991, however, a fundamental difference in the positions of ENGOS came to the fore and split the environmental movement. A number of organizations questioned and criticized not only the immediate environmental effects of the agreement but also the kind of development that trade and investment liberalization would enhance. Hence they demanded broad and fundamental changes in the official proposals. Conversely, other groups accepted the NAFTA initiative (either as desirable or inevitable) and restricted their proposals so that they could be integrated into the agreement as such. Here, these two positions of environmental organizations on NAFTA are named 'critical' and 'moderate'. This scission was transnational in the sense that it occurred in each of the three countries. This difference in position can be traced back to a combination of ideological and political (strategic) preferences. We will return to this point in the second section.

— 4.1 Environmental organizations and transnational relations[1] —

The evidently different nature of environmental organizations as political actors compared to the governments and private sector organizations that supported NAFTA was also reflected in their transnational relations. On the basis of their motivations, transnational relations may be divided into three categories (Keck and Sikkink 1995: 4). First, they can be based on instrumental goals, implying that economic interests are the predominant motivation for cooperation. As chapter 5 will show, the cross-border relations of NAFTA proponents would fit into this category. Second, transnational relations can be based on shared causal ideas, which is the case for scientific groups. Third, transnational relations can be primarily motivated by shared principled ideas or values, creating a transnational issue network. The latter was the case for ENGO cooperation on NAFTA. An important political activity of organizations motivated by values is the interpretation and strategic use of information. Indeed, in the NAFTA debate, the links of environmental groups with academic researchers were strong.[2]

MEXICAN ORGANIZATIONS

In Mexico a number of environmental organizations were active on NAFTA, some of which have been described in chapter 2. In general, they criticized the free trade initiative and government proposals for largely ignoring sustainable development and environmental protection. The compatibility of free trade and sustainability, as presented by NAFTA proponents, was questioned by Mexi-

---

1   The analysis in this section is partly based on information gathered in a number of interviews with persons working in or with environmental organizations in Mexico, the US and Canada.

2   Many meetings and conferences on NAFTA and the environment were attended by both academics and representatives of NGOs. There was a continuous exchange of information and ideas on paper. In addition, several organizations that played an important role in the NAFTA debate combined research and political activities.

can environmentalists, referring to earlier experiences with trade liberalization such as the *maquiladora* sector. There was concern that NAFTA would intensify exploitation and degradation of Mexico's ecosystems and natural resources, and that the agreement would lead to a further subordination of ecological principles to economic expansion (Peña 1993).[3]

Many Mexican ENGOs that actively opposed the official proposals for NAFTA were organized in the Pact of Ecologist Groups (PGE). Initially, the PGE had a diverse membership, but in the tumultuous year of 1988 it was confronted with internal tensions and a divide-and-rule attack by the government after which some moderate groups left and the Pact obtained a more homogenous critical character (Demmers and Hogenboom 1992: 56-8). In the NAFTA process, the Pact acted mainly through Mexico's large NGO network on trade, the Mexican Action Network on Free Trade (RMALC), created in 1991 by nearly 100 NGOs. Besides environmental groups, a wide variety of organizations cooperated in the RMALC: workers and peasants unions, organizations for development and social justice, human rights organizations and women's groups. As such, RMALC had a diverse grassroots base. Although RMALC aimed to integrate environmental concerns with the interests of its various other member organizations, it succeeded more on a theoretical than on a practical level.

RMALC considered NAFTA a project that would be profitable for only a small elite at the cost of the majority of Mexicans and Mexico's environment and natural resources. The network did not oppose commercial exchange as such, but claimed that economic growth alone would not solve Mexico's problems, particularly in the context of North America's economic inequalities and the lack of democracy in Mexico. According to RMALC, trade liberalization could only be beneficial for Mexico if it were part of a development strategy based on popular needs (RMALC 1993c: 157). The network's criticism of NAFTA and its proposals for a social charter were similar to those voiced by the left-wing opposition party PRD.[4] Even though RMALC shared many of its members with the

---

3 Some of these concerns were also expressed by indigenous groups, such as fear of a more rapid exploitation of natural resources. Indigenous groups were also concerned over a further opening to biotechnology companies, which was perceived as a threat to ethnoscience (Peña 1993: 124).

4 For instance, PRD's president Cuauthémoc Cárdenas (1991: 35) stated: "We believe an alternative agreement should include a social charter and be based on common standards for labour, social and environmental rights ... This arrangement should guarantee the sovereign rights of each nation to develop its own natural resources, particularly oil, to meet the needs of its own people".

PRD (Poitras and Robinson 1994: 25), they did not engage in institutionalized cooperation.

The Network's relationship with the Mexican government was ambiguous, partly because of a double strategy of RMALC, combining opposition to NAFTA with thinking along with the government. In the beginning, the network largely worked on informing the public about NAFTA and creating political pressure. Later on, when the trade agreement was signed and the side-deals were negotiated, there were occasions of formal exchange with government agencies. This exchange, however, depended to a large extent on the goodwill of certain officials, and on most occasions was not genuine on the part of the government. As the umbrella organization of Mexican groups that were very critical of NAFTA, RMALC also had to confront several political obstacles, such as very limited access to information and resources, and an attempt at infiltration by a government official in 1993.

The Mexican environmental organizations in the border area with the United States that were most active in the NAFTA debate also opposed the negotiated agreement.[5] They worked with US border organizations and the Mexican universities *Colegio de Sonora* and *Colegio de la Frontera Norte.* These border ENGOs and universities were all members of the binational Border Health and Environmental Network. In general, communication between Mexican border groups and Mexico City-based ENGOs on NAFTA was feeble because of differences in interests and position.

Over 30 moderate ENGOs were organized in the Union of Environmental Groups (UGAM) in 1992.[6] Most organizations in the UGAM perceived NAFTA as a problematic but inevitable stage in the development of Mexico. After initial opposition they started proposing measures to prevent NAFTA from inducing environmental damage. UGAM aimed at a constructive attitude and positive relations with the Mexican government in order to have a say in Mexico's official position on environmental safeguards in NAFTA. In the beginning, their petitions and questions on the environmental aspects of NAFTA were not answered. According to Regina Barba Pírez (1993: 121-3), UGAM's president and a long-time environmental activist, this was because the government was not used to, or equipped for, a political input from society, while strong environmental arrangements were perceived as barriers to free trade. The organization nevertheless persevered in its strategy and continued to propose that environ-

---

5 Predominantly, these were the organizations *Bioconservación, Comité Cívico de Divulgación Ecológica, Enlace Ecológico,* and *Proyecto Fronterizo de Educación Ambiental.*
6 Formally, UGAM was only created in 1993, but from 1992 onwards they acted as a coordinated network.

mental safeguards and an environmental commission be integrated in NAFTA. As one of UGAM's advisors was a prominent environmental lawyer, these proposals were in the form of draft agreements, which gave the Union a certain standing in Mexico and beyond.

Despite their somewhat better relations with the Mexican state, UGAM and its member organizations also struggled with certain political obstacles. Like RMALC, they generally had poor access to official information from the Mexican government on the negotiations. Most of what they received were documents in English obtained by their US and Canadian counterparts. In addition, similar to most Mexican ENGOS, many of UGAM's organizations had to deal with a minimal economic and physical infrastructure (Barba Pírez 1993: 131-2).

Two other well-known moderate ENGOS that were active on NAFTA, independently of UGAM, were the Autonomous Institute for Ecological Research (INAINE) and the Group of Hundred (*Grupo de los Cien*). The INAINE carries out predominantly technical and scientific research for industry and governmental agencies. Although the Institute is not very active in public political debates, it is known to be invited by government agencies. On some occasions, INAINE cooperated with other moderate groups in Mexico and the US on the incorporation of environmental arrangements in NAFTA, and it organized a few transnational meetings with officials and researchers on the issue.

The Group of Hundred's membership is made up of famous artists, writers, intellectuals, and others, who never physically meet but who allow their names to be used to facilitate access to the media. Its formal leader, the poet and writer Homero Arídjis, often operates on his own initiative. The group was divided on the issue of NAFTA. According to Arídjis, around one-third of the members were opposed to NAFTA, whereas two-thirds supported the agreement. This has been denied, however, by a member of the Group of Hundred who claims that opposition to trade liberalization within the group was larger and that only a few members had been consulted by Arídjis. After a period of intensive cooperation with groups of UGAM, Arídjis judged the Union to be too compromising towards the Mexican government and decided to work independently.

There were also various types of environmental groups in Mexico that sidestepped the NAFTA issue. The large Mexican Ecologist Movement (MEM) hardly used its rather easy access to the media to draw attention to NAFTA, which fits in with the general criticism by Mexican ENGOS that MEM does not take a political stand when really needed (see 2.3).[7] Most ENGOS outside Mexico

---

7 At a press conference (Mexico City, 19/VIII/93) its president, Alfonso Ciprés Villareal, declared that MEM opposed NAFTA and perceived it as "ecological neo-colonial-

City focused on local projects and sometimes national issues, and NAFTA was a low priority. Interestingly, some of Mexico's groups in the border region with the US chose to focus their attention on domestic and local policies too. Uncertain about their possible influence in the NAFTA preparation, they worked on other aspects of the government's neoliberal policy, such as the liberalization of agriculture. Their distance from the political centre of Mexico City, a lack of finance and experience, and poor access to information about NAFTA discouraged their participation in the NAFTA debate (Land 1993: 105). As on most national policy issues, Mexico's ENGO activities on NAFTA predominantly originated in Mexico City.

In Mexico, then, the environmental impact of NAFTA did not become the subject of nationwide ENGO activism, let alone of a nationwide public debate. Mexican organizations working on NAFTA were concentrated in Mexico City and to a lesser extent in the Mexico-US border region, and their relations with groups in other areas were relatively weak. This does not mean, however, that ENGOs involved in the NAFTA debate neglected regional issues. RMALC, for instance, put rural issues high on its agenda and included rural development in its analyses and proposals. Another reason why a national debate on NAFTA and the environment never took place was the dissension as well as the traditional distrust among Mexican ENGOs. During the NAFTA process, the relations between critical and moderate groups remained mainly on an informal and personal basis. At times there were joint meetings and initiatives for statements and proposals, but Mexican environmental groups never organised as a whole.

Alongside the weak relations between Mexico's environmental organizations, the general weakness of Mexican opposition to the trade agreement was another reason for the lack of public debate on NAFTA in Mexico. NAFTA criticism was expressed by a range of Mexican organizations. The PRD warned about the probable negative effects of the agreement on labour, agriculture, small businesses and the environment, and criticized the undemocratic manner in which the Mexican government pushed the NAFTA issue (Cárdenas 1992: 35).[8] The PAN challenged the authoritarian practices of the Mexican govern-

---

ism". Yet, these remarks on NAFTA took only a few minutes, and none of the environmental activists I spoke to in August1993 knew MEM's position on NAFTA.

8 Trade liberalization with the US was not repudiated on the whole by the PRD. As early as 1990, Cárdenas denied that he had said he would reverse Salinas' economic programme, including Mexico-US free trade, if he were elected president, and said that he would review the programme "on a pragmatic, not an ideological, basis" (Pastor 1990: 6). During the 1994 Presidential campaign, Cárdenas hardly mentioned the agree-

ment with respect to NAFTA's introduction and promotion in Mexico, but agreed with the policy of economic liberalization. Independent farmers and labour unions, some organized in RMALC, feared the consequences of NAFTA for their members, and opposed the negotiated agreement.

Despite some grassroots support, opposition never really gained momentum. The Mexican government had a strong rhetoric of NAFTA's being favourable to all Mexicans. Also the lack of information on the NAFTA process limited the public debate. At the same time critical groups were weakened by the state through various traditional strategies of silencing dissent (Poitras and Robinson 1994: 21-6). As non-governmental organizations in Mexico were generally not able to force the state to open up to their concerns with respect to the agreement, both moderate and critical groups estimated that their opportunities to change the official position were small. This dilemma at the level of national politics was an important reason for Mexican ENGOs' alignment with foreign groups which had more political clout. However, Mexico's political elite also attempted to repress transnational activities of Mexicans that might add to criticism of NAFTA.[9]

US ENVIRONMENTAL ORGANIZATIONS

The main moderate US ENGOs in the NAFTA debate were the National Audubon Society, Natural Resources Defense Council (NRDC), National Wildlife Federation (NWF), World Wildlife Fund (WWF), the Nature Conservancy, Defenders of Wildlife, and Environmental Defense Fund (EDF).[10] They worked

---

ment. The PRD did not call for a radical revision of NAFTA, but promised to revise it if it came to power (Yanner 1995: 7).

9 This may be illustrated by the following case. With a few other well-known Mexican intellectuals, Adolfo Aguilar Zinser (researcher) and Jorge G. Castañeda (professor) wrote a letter to the Mexican Congress suggesting that social and environmental links to free trade should be discussed. Castañeda and Aguilar Zinser also expressed their concern at a NAFTA conference organized by NGOs in Washington DC (15/1/91). The Mexican press distorted or simply failed to report their views, and for their comments made in the US they were later on accused by a top PRI official on the front page of the prominent newspaper *Excelsior* of betraying the Mexican nation and having become enemies of the country (Aguilar Zinser 1993: 208-9).

10 Critical organizations sometimes referred to them as the 'corporate seven'. Defenders of Wildlife left the group in the summer of 1992. NRDC and Audubon were somewhat more critical than NWF and WWF. While NRDC's president Justin Ward was a proponent of NAFTA, many other members of staff questioned the agreement.

on NAFTA by way of lobbying from within the state, and coming up with legally-based environmental proposals that fitted into the NAFTA plan. They took a pragmatic view and were willing to compromise. This attitude was to help them maintain their reputation for having political weight in Congress. As experienced players in US lobby politics, the power of these ENGOS lay in their public and political relations, and in their ability to influence public opinion (Barkin and Mumme 1992: 21-2). Some of these organizations (predominantly the NWF) were not only involved in the debate on NAFTA but even became active advocates of the agreement. Moderate US ENGOS cooperated loosely with each other on NAFTA.

The major critical ENGOS on NAFTA in the US were Friends of the Earth, Sierra Club and Greenpeace. They found an important ally in the consumer organization Public Citizen, which is also active in environmental issues. As in Mexico, critical organizations cooperated intensively with other types of NGOS, predominantly in formal networks. Through the Citizens Trade Campaign (CTC) and the Alliance for Responsible Trade (ART)[11], Friends of the Earth, Greenpeace and Public Citizen cooperated with smaller ENGOS and groups with environmental concerns, small and medium-sized unions, and NGOS for development, human rights, women, immigrants, Christians and minorities. The large national unions of the American Federation of Labour and the Congress of Industrial Organizations (AFL-CIO) were also represented in the CTC. The groups cooperating in the CTC and ART shared a fear that NAFTA would further enlarge the power of the corporate sector. ART stimulated the debate and focused on the formulation of alternative policy, whereas CTC engaged in lobby activities and mobilized groups around the country. Both worked with RMALC and the Action Canada Network (ACN).

Border groups were a small but important faction in the group of critical US ENGOS involved in the NAFTA debate. They were among the first to warn of environmentally detrimental effects of free trade between the US and Mexico (cf. TCPS 1990; Kelly and Kamp 1991). The Arizona Toxins Information, the Border Ecology Project (BEP), the Environmental Health Coalition and the Texas Center for Policy Studies (TCPS) publicly criticized official proposals and came up with alternatives. Prior to the NAFTA process, border groups had been working for years on environmental damage by industry and health problems stemming from pollution, urbanization and a lack of infrastructure and social services, trying to change corporate behaviour, local policy and communities.

---

11 ART was first known as Mobilization for Trade, Labour and the Environment (MODTLE).

They had established numerous relations in Mexico, not only with NGOs (partly through the Border Health and Environmental Network) but also with local government agencies. The border groups' experience with the environmental effects of economic integration and their relations with Mexican border organizations "lent them a credibility not enjoyed by many national environmental groups" (Land 1993: 104). In contrast with the rather poor relations between Mexican border groups and Mexico City-based organizations, in the context of the NAFTA environment debate US ENGOs in Washington DC discovered the border organizations. Border ENGOs in the US serviced Washington-based organizations with information on the border problems, and they kept in close contact. Moreover, border organizations helped shape the NGO agenda in the NAFTA debate and were an intermediary between US and Mexican NGOs (Land 1993: 103-4).[12]

The key group of NAFTA opponents in the US was organized labour, with the AFL-CIO (with over 14 million members) as their main representing organization. Their basic concern with respect to NAFTA was that investments in Mexico would come at the cost of investments in the US, resulting in job losses, negative wage effects and less job security (more temporary hiring of workers). First, there was a fear that US companies would relocate production to Mexico because of lower wage levels, relatively low union organization, and weak enforcement of labour and environmental standards. Second, labour expected that for the same reasons new investments would be increasingly directed towards Mexico. Moreover, to keep production in the US would require a significant lowering of wages in US industry, US labour unions argued.

The support of labour for environmental demands would significantly add to the leverage and political clout of ENGOs in the US since the unions are powerful actors in Washington DC. The AFL-CIO adopted the environment issue in order to strengthen its position in the NAFTA debate, and established relations with some ENGOs. This move of AFL-CIO to environmentalists was rather uncommon since previously trade unions had often opposed ENGOs and their demands for stringent environmental standards in the US. However, while labour support contributed to the attention on environmentalist proposals, it also strengthened the US focus on industry-related environmental problems at the cost of other ecological issues.

---

12 Some border activists were somewhat sceptical about participating in the NAFTA debate and lobbies. In the experience of the BEP, for instance, environmental protection does not follow so much from national legislation or international agreements as from local activism, implying that environmental arrangements in NAFTA might have little effect on the actual situation in the border region.

CANADIAN ENVIRONMENTAL ORGANIZATIONS

NAFTA and its possible environmental impact was less a political issue in Canada than in Mexico and the US. Very much against the will of critical Canadian NGOs, free trade with the US had already been established, and extending free trade to Mexico was not expected to considerably affect Canada any further. Many Canadians viewed the issue of NAFTA's environmental impact as a Mexico-US affair.

However, the Action Canada Network (ACN), previously called the Pro-Canada Network, was involved in the debate. Similar to RMALC, ART and CTC, this network consists of a heterogeneous group of critical organizations, among which the Canadian Environmental Law Association (CELA) has a leadership position. NAFTA was often the subject of ACN meetings and publications (such as the *Pro-Canada Dossier*, later renamed *Action Dossier*). As well as looking at the national impacts, ACN cooperated with RMALC, CTC and ART on a transnational agenda. The network opposed the negotiators' plans for NAFTA and attempted to abolish the CUFTA. For critical Canadian groups, in contrast with US organizations, NAFTA was not predominantly about Mexico. The agreement was perceived as "one step more down the road of free trade", and involved many broad issues for Canadian organizations.

Canada's moderate ENGO Pollution Probe, in particular its president Janine Ferretti,[13] also worked on NAFTA. Like its counterparts in Mexico and the US, this organization had good relations with government agencies. Pollution Probe at times cooperated with moderate US organizations, especially the NWF. Its links with Mexican groups, however, were rather weak.

TRANSNATIONAL RELATIONS

Before the NAFTA debate, transnational relations between environmental groups in North America were limited, and ENGOs were rather inexperienced with respect to the link between trade and environment. The free trade negotiations between the US and Canada had worried Canadian environmental groups, but as US organizations had been less concerned, it had not given rise to any cross-border cooperation of importance. US-Canada NGO activities were largely restricted to dealing with a few joint problems (e.g. the pollution of the

---

13 Ferretti became the Canadian director of NAFTA's Commission for Environmental Cooperation.

Great Lakes and Acid Rain). Equally, the relations between Mexican organizations and US and Canadian groups were limited. A few Canadian groups had started working with Mexican NGOs only shortly before the NAFTA plans became public. Mexico-US cooperation between ENGOs was more extensive, but was largely restricted to the border region, a case of joint monitoring of World Bank projects, and some conservation programmes. Overall, US ENGOs had hardly dealt with Mexico, had little knowledge of Mexico, and had few contacts with Mexican ENGOs (Barkin and Mumme 1992: 16-23). Despite geographical proximity, Mexican environmental groups only partly focused on their counterparts in the region; European organizations were probably as important for their funding and information as were US sources, whereas Canadian partners were scarce (Kürzinger et al. 1990: 120).

NAFTA preparations were to give a strong impulse to transnational cooperation between ENGOs in the three countries. The announcement in June 1990 that President Salinas and President Bush were planning to negotiate a free trade agreement gave rise to new dynamic discussions and joint activities between Mexican and US environmental groups, and to a lesser extent Canadian organizations. Within three years (summer 1990 to summer 1993) many contacts were to be established, information shared and experience gained in working with each other.

For Mexican organizations there were several reasons to intensify relations with US and Canadian groups when the plan for NAFTA became known. Their main concern was that free trade with the US would speed up industrial expansion, agricultural modernization and the exploitation of natural resources at considerable environmental cost. As Canada had entered free trade with the US in 1989, Mexican groups wanted to learn more about the experiences of Canadian organizations. For access to information on the negotiations, Mexican organizations also needed their counterparts, since little trickled down from the Mexican negotiators, and rhetoric tended to dominate in official declarations.[14]

Politically, transnational cooperation was to help Mexican organizations in two ways. First, it enabled them either directly, or via their US counterparts, to participate in the political debate in Washington DC, where the major decisions on NAFTA were taken. Through this avenue, Mexican ENGOs hoped to influence the future of Mexico's environmental policy as well as more broadly the

---

14 The lack of information on the NAFTA negotiations was the subject of a transnational press release by NWF, PGE, Sierra Club, Community Nutrition Institute, BEP and ACN (26/x/91). They expressed their concern at the general scarcity of information and limited opportunities for public participation with respect to NAFTA negotiations, but stressed that Mexico's case stood out.

nature of economic integration with the US. The fact that, besides numerous representatives of US organizations, a few Mexicans also testified in hearings in the US Congress shows that the US debate was far more open to NGOs than in Mexico.[15] Second, the attention ENGOs attracted in the US might have helped them gain some access to Mexican officials, even though their situation remained far from satisfactory.

For US ENGOs one of the purposes of cooperation with Mexicans and Canadians was to make sure that NAFTA would not run counter to their earlier successes. They feared that free trade with Mexico (with its notorious lack of environmental enforcement) would strengthen US corporate demands for less environmental regulation and create more opportunities to evade such regulations. With NAFTA the roles of the CUFTA seemed reversed, as US concern about its environmental effects was greater than Canadian concern. US groups aimed to form a strong opposition and in this respect transnational relations were useful. In particular, the link with Mexican groups, which implied access to first-hand information on Mexico's problems, gave them a role as intermediaries between Mexican social actors and US politicians, and secured their credibility. As a result US groups were taken more seriously and this supported their position in US forums (Barkin and Mumme 1992: 20-1). The fact that in the context of the NAFTA debate few US ENGOs established structural programmes for cooperation with Mexican groups supports the idea that US cooperation with groups in Mexico stemmed mainly from NAFTA threats and was largely politically motivated (Kelly 1993b: 5).

However, solidarity and a concern about environmental degradation in Mexico (as in other countries) were also reasons for US NGO cooperation with Mexican groups. In this respect, the NAFTA plans seemed to function as an eye-opener and produced interest in Mexico. Numerous transnational meetings, studies and declarations dealt with Mexico's environmental problems. In particular, critical groups in the three countries worked on structural forms of cooperation through the RMALC, CTC, ART, and ACN. In the final stages of the NAFTA negotiations, these organizations developed a joint proposal for an alternative agreement (see 6.2).

Canadian groups were somewhat less involved in NAFTA politics and the trade-environment debate. It was expected that the agreement would affect

---

15 At least two Mexicans testified in US Congress: Homero Arídjis of the Group of Hundred at the joint hearing of the Subcommittee of Labour of the Committee on Labour and Human Resources, and the Committee on Environment and Public Works (23/IV/91); and Carlos Heredia, director of international programs of *Equipo Pueblo* before the Committee on Small Business (20/V/93).

Canada's environment less than that of Mexico and the US. On the other hand, solidarity with Mexicans was an important Canadian motive for action, but financial restrictions limited cooperation between Canadian and Mexican groups. In addition, unlike US ENGOs, critical groups in Canada did not have the feeling that they would really be able to change or obstruct the NAFTA proposal, as a result of their own limited influence in national politics and the weakness of their government towards the US.

Canadian NGOs partly shared this pessimistic perception of their own role in the NAFTA process with many Mexican groups. This was to be a motive for solidarity as well as for developing a different political strategy. Particularly critical organizations in Canada focused more on analyzing the NAFTA process and looking for alternatives coming from the major players, whereas US groups were busy developing their own proposals and helping government officials to formulate their ideas. Mexican organizations tended to combine these approaches. This difference stems partly from the fact that US ENGOs tend to be more single-issue organizations, whereas in Mexico and Canada organizations look at political issues from a broader perspective. For critical Mexican and Canadian organizations, the debate on NAFTA and its environmental implications was always closely linked to the discussion of the neoliberal economic development model behind NAFTA, and to the environmental implications of this model. Critical as well as moderate Mexican and Canadian groups were also very concerned about the US economic and political dominance in the region. Obviously, their distinct views and strategies produced some confusion and dissatisfaction. In the eyes of some Mexican and Canadian organizations, US groups were too preoccupied with their own proposals to be aware of developments in the negotiations. Yet the attitude of Mexicans and Canadians could easily be misunderstood by US NGOs for passivity.

Fundamental differences in the membership and resources of Mexican ENGOs versus US and Canadian organizations also produced distrust. Several groups in the US and Canada have a large number of members (2.3 or even 5.5 million in the case of Greenpeace USA and the NWF, respectively). On the contrary, most ENGOs in Mexico have few official members. Instead of the type of membership whereby people pay contribution and receive the organization's magazine, members of Mexican environmental organizations generally are, or have been, personally active in the organization. This difference in type and number of members sometimes led to reservations among US ENGOs about their Mexican colleagues, because the latter did not seem to (officially) represent a wide group of citizens in the way the former were seen to do. According to Barkin (1994: 351), US ENGOs view Mexico's environmental movement as very incipient or immature, with its activities reflecting its middle-class bias.

Financially, the revenues of US and Canadian organizations also exceed by far those of organizations in Mexico.[16] On the other hand, the fact that various moderate US organizations receive considerable funding from the corporate sector gave occasion for some distrust among Mexican organizations, which were not always sure how much the former cared about the inclusion of environmental provisions in NAFTA, and to what extent those providers of funds influenced the position of the US ENGOs.

To describe the totality of groups and individuals in the three countries who raised environmental issues with respect to NAFTA, we can use the concept of a transnational issue network as developed by Keck and Sikkink (1995). A transnational issue network contrasts with other transnational relations for being primarily motivated by shared principled ideas or values, rather than instrumental goals or shared causal ideas. An important political activity of transnational issue networks is the interpretation and strategic use of information. As Keck and Sikkink (1995: 5) explain, "[i]nfluence is possible because the actors in these networks are simultaneously helping to define the issue area itself, convince target audiences that the problems thus defined are soluble, prescribe solutions and monitor their implementation". There are three stages in which a transnational issue network can be effective: "1) by framing debates and getting issues on the agenda; 2) by encouraging discursive commitments from states and other policy actors; and 3) by effecting actual policy changes in target actors" (Keck and Sikkink 1995: 27).

Indeed, as the above overview of the main environmental organizations and other NGOs involved in the NAFTA debate has shown, principled ideas and values formed the predominant motivation for taking part in the debate. In this respect, cooperation with Canadian groups was of great importance to Mexican organizations. The following section will show that the information on the possible environmental effects of NAFTA (see 3.2) was the main tool for raising issues and framing the debate, resulting in the first environmental commitments of the Bush Administration. Later on, proposals for solutions were also developed. Chapter 6 will discuss the influence and effectiveness of these different activities of environmental organizations and other actors demanding environmental protection within NAFTA. In particular, support for environmental-

---

16 Besides the contributions from members, private funding forms a source of income for US ENGOs. Some moderate organizations in the US are also supported by the private sector. In Canada, government subsidies are common for both moderate and critical groups. ENGOs in Mexico cannot count on structural resources and mainly depend on incidental support and the goodwill of active members who do not claim expenses.

ist concerns from US labour unions and members of the US Congress would significantly add to the efforts of ENGOS.

However, the utility of the concept of transnational issue networks is limited for analyzing the NAFTA environment debate since it does not incorporate the possibility and effects of discord within a network. Obviously, within a group of actors raising an issue, there are to a greater or lesser extent disagreements and conflicts over values, aims, and strategies. As the following section and chapter 6 will demonstrate, after some time political actors raising environmental issues in the transnational NAFTA debate split into a moderate and a critical faction, and this split fundamentally affected the debate and its outcome.

— 4.2 The first phase: ENGO's exploring the issues —

It took a while before environmental groups started to react to the Mexico-US free trade plans announced in June 1990. During the first few months there were only a few incidental ENGO reactions to these plans. In October 1990, Mexican and Canadian groups discussed the trade and environment issue at a joint meeting in Mexico City. From around that time onwards, the NAFTA-environment linkages were explored by environmental organizations in Mexico, the US and Canada. Through assessments, discussions and statements, ENGOS raised numerous concerns and questions, and gradually came to develop demands and proposals. These activities were the start of the NAFTA debate on the environment.

FIRST PHASE OF THE NAFTA ENVIRONMENT DEBATE

The year between the announcement that Mexico and the US planned to negotiate a free trade agreement (June 1990) and Bush's environmental commitments with respect to NAFTA negotiations (May 1991) was a period of exploration of the trade and environment issue by North American ENGOS. Environmentalist criticism and activism emerged slowly as the announcement came rather unexpectedly, and the majority of the organizations had to read up on the issue. Information on the trade and environment link was limited and free trade between countries with such unequal levels of development was a novelty. In addition, as mentioned in chapter 3, it took some time before the probable structure and contents of NAFTA became known, and most studies of environmental effects had an exploratory character. Consequently, developing an underpinned position was not an easy task. The picture was further

complicated by a lack of examples of how to incorporate environmental protection in free trade agreements and the uncertainty of what exactly would be
negotiated.

During this first year, the NAFTA environment debate was open and unstructured. An agenda had not been set yet and on many occasions critical and
moderate groups operated jointly. Through this rather unstructured interaction, ENGOs started to explore what the environmental impact of regional free
trade might be, and what kind of provisions would be able to limit the damage.
Equally, they started to observe each other, nationally and transnationally, and
to examine not only each other's ideas on NAFTA but also the possibilities for
political support and alliances with non-environmental political actors.

The Canada-Mexico *Encuentro* (5-7 October 1990 in Mexico City) was a
meeting of representatives of nearly 30 Canadian NGOs and over 70 Mexican
organizations such as unions, ENGOs and human rights groups. This meeting
of critical organizations was arranged by a working group on continental free
trade, Common Frontiers, with offices in both countries. At the time of the
meeting it was not known that Canada would participate in NAFTA. The purpose was to exchange experiences and ideas, and the trade-environment link
was also raised. A representative of the Canadian Environmental Law Association (CELA), for instance, made a presentation on Canada's experience with
CUFTA, and maintained that a free trade agreement discourages tougher environmental regulation and takes away a country's ability to control the use of its
natural resources (*The Pro-Canada Dossier* 1991, #29).

In January 1991, a trinational public forum on agricultural, environmental
and labour issues with respect to US-Mexico free trade took place on Capitol
Hill. The purpose of the workshop was to stimulate a debate in the US Congress
on social and environmental concerns linked to NAFTA, and to start a public
debate on its possible effects. The programme included representatives of NGOs
and several university professors from the three countries, and the forum was
attended by some 400 persons. The forum was not only an important moment
in the first phase of the transnational NAFTA debate, but also marked the start
of increasing public attention as well as opposition in the US. The majority of
speakers at the Capitol Hill workshop agreed that the goal of negotiating a
North American agreement should be development instead of free trade. In the
words of researcher Adolfo Aguilar Zinser, "the discussion about free trade (..)
puts the cart before the horse" (*U.S.-Mexico Free Trade; Opening Up the Debate*
15/1/91).

Although most of the contributors disapproved the initiative for a free trade
agreement, the general opinion at the Capitol Hill workshop was that it would
be better to work positively and constructively on an alternative agreement

rather than simply opposing the official proposal.[17] Professor Jorge Castañeda suggested that the free trade agreement should include a social charter that would also deal with environmental protection. Stewart Hudson, representative of NWF, supported the idea of a social charter including environmental standards and enforcement mechanisms, and came up with a number of other ways in which environmental concerns should be addressed by US trade negotiators: an environmental assessment of the agreement should be prepared; countries should have the right to use trade restrictions for conservation purposes; and there should be a mechanism to provide Mexico with financial and technical assistance to help it maintain standards equivalent to those in the US (*U.S.-Mexico Free Trade; Opening Up the Debate* 15/1/91).

The declarations and papers produced in the first year of the NAFTA debate raised a host of environmental concerns regarding the agreement. It is not possible to attribute these early issues to groups in particular because they were brought up by various organizations of the three countries. As long as there were no clear ideas on implementation, ENGOs agreed that their concerns should be "included" in trade negotiations. The main points will be summarized here.[18] They can be divided into procedural issues, that is which steps should be taken before and while drafting an agreement, and environmental issues that ENGOs wanted to be incorporated in the agreement.

The procedural issues raised by ENGOs boiled down to three points. First, environmental groups disapproved of the closed and secretive manner in which NAFTA, like any trade agreement, would be negotiated and suggested a transparent process with public participation and access to information. Second, they proposed that each country perform an environmental assessment of the agreement. Third, some ENGOs also stated that participating governments should come up with an environmental action plan to deal with existing and future regional problems.

---

17 It should be noted that during the NAFTA debate, environmental groups had a general habit of raising issues in the form of suggestions and proposals rather than demands.

18 ENGO publications used for this analysis are: Arídjis 1993; Kelly and Kamp 1991; Michael McClosky, chairman of Sierra Club, testimony to the Senate Committee on Foreign Relations, March 22, 1991, on the Mexican Free Trade Negotiations; *Environmental concerns related to a United-State-Mexico-Canada Free Trade Agreement*, 6/11/91, endorsed by ten US NGOs and one Canadian environmental organization. In addition, the overview is based on the following studies: Barkin and Mumme 1992: 16-23; Gallardo C. 1993; Gallardo C. 1994; Gilbreath and Tonra 1994: 80-6; Gregory 1992; Heredia Zubieta 1991.

With respect to legal arrangements, ENGOs agreed that a number of environmental issues should become an integral part of the trade agreement (e.g. in a charter) in order to prevent negative environmental effects of economic liberalization. Many of their suggestions addressed differences between the environmental policy of Mexico, Canada and the US. Free trade and investment in a situation of distinctive standards for environmental protection and unequal levels and forms of implementation of these standards was of special concern to US and Mexican ENGOs. Although some Canadian organizations dealt with the issue, it was clear that for them NAFTA would not have as large an impact as CUFTA.[19]

Harmonization of environmental policy of the NAFTA countries would be a way of tackling the existing differences. It was assumed that the governments (pressed by the US) might choose harmonization in order to take away comparative advantages of producing in a country with lax enforcement (Mexico). ENGOs, however, feared the terms on which this harmonization would take place. Especially US groups opposed harmonization based on a common denominator, as this would reverse stringent US regulations. Together with Mexican and Canadian groups they wanted to prevent harmonized standards from limiting more stringent regulation (common standards as a ceiling) and tougher environmental standards being considered as trade obstructions. Instead, ENGOs proposed common minimal protection standards (common standards as a floor) which would leave federal / national as well as state / provincial and local authorities the right to apply stricter rules.

In particular, Mexican and US ENGOs worried about the effect of NAFTA on industrial production and location given their environmental policy differences. Further liberalization of foreign investment in Mexico was meant to encourage companies to start production there. The lack of infrastructure and control in Mexico would neither help nor push companies to establish clean production processes. ENGOs came up with several proposals on how to internalize the environmental costs of industrial production. There were ideas of drawing up a NAFTA code of conduct for industry or designing criteria for foreign investment. It was also suggested that NAFTA should require transnational industry to obey the legislation of either the country of origin or the country of production, depending on which one is more strict.

---

19 Tony Clark, chairperson of the ACN (then still called Pro-Canada Network) stated that "there is no way Canadians can participate in an alternative strategy unless we abrogate the current US-Canada FTA. The tools have been taken away from us" (*U.S.-Mexico Free Trade; Opening Up the Debate* 15/1/91).

Environmental groups recognized that the problems of Mexico's environmental policy were partly the result of its level of development and inferior infrastructure. Therefore, they proposed that NAFTA should include arrangements to provide Mexico with financial resources for its environmental agencies. There were proposals for environmental loans, or having companies benefitting from NAFTA contribute in some way. In addition, technical assistance for Mexico and environmental cooperation between the NAFTA countries should be included in the agreement, ENGOs argued.

The US-Mexico border was an area of special concern related to the lax implementation of environmental legislation in Mexico. The disastrous state of the border environment after nearly 30 years of this free trade zone served as a clear warning of what weak enforcement can lead to. ENGOs wanted to prevent something like that from happening again. At the same time, environmental organizations in Mexico and the US feared that free trade between their countries would further increase economic activities along the border. In their view, NAFTA arrangements should ensure that North American free trade would not add any stress to the border region. Again, rules for foreign industrial investment and assistance to Mexican environmental agencies were seen as essential elements for solution and prevention.

Natural resource control was also a major issue raised by ENGOs. Mexican and Canadian organizations opposed free trade and investment with respect to natural resources. They expected that US companies and US consumption levels would rapidly lead to a deterioration in their resource base. In their view, natural resources should first serve the national population, in the present and in the future. Control over a nation's resources is a sovereign right and should not be traded away, they argued. In general, US organizations supported this idea and maintained that the opening up of Mexico's resource base would be counterproductive for sustainable development in North America as a whole. Instead of stimulating a more efficient use of resources, NAFTA would sustain the resource-intensive "American way of life". Finally, ENGOs only accepted the inclusion of international property deals if they were adjusted to promote biodiversity.

In April 1991 a Common Declaration on NAFTA was issued by a group of over twenty Mexican, US and Canadian ENGOs, including the Group of Hundred, NWF and Pollution Probe. They demanded the inclusion of environmental issues in NAFTA, a review of the environmental effects of NAFTA, the participation of environmental experts in the negotiations, and the inclusion of an environmental action plan as well as of a trilateral monitoring and regulating mechanism on trade-related environmental problems.

POLARIZATION OF ENVIRONMENTAL ORGANIZATIONS

On 1 May 1991, President Bush presented a set of environmental commitments regarding NAFTA to the US Congress, entitled *Response of the Administration to Issues Raised in Connection with the Negotiation of a North American Free Trade Agreement*, also known as the May 1 declaration or May 1 commitments. This declaration was made prior to the congressional vote on extending the so-called fast track authority, which provides the US government with greater freedom vis-à-vis Congress in trade negotiations. By virtue of fast track authority, US Congress can only accept or refuse, but not amend the outcome of negotiations. As the authority earlier provided for GATT negotiations was to expire, President Bush needed an extension for both GATT and NAFTA negotiations. His May 1 commitments were to convince the growing number of members of Congress who were concerned about NAFTA's environmental impacts that these issues would not be neglected, and to make them vote for renewed fast track authority.

Bush's May 1 commitments showed that the issues raised by ENGOs were to a certain extent recognized by the US government. The document announced that the US Trade Representative (USTR) was to coordinate an interagency review of US-Mexico environmental issues, and that the US would negotiate NAFTA on the principle of maintaining its environmental laws, regulations and standards. Moreover, during the negotiations the US would stand up for the inclusion of trade limits set under certain international environmental treaties, the right to prohibit the entry of goods which do not meet US environmental regulations, and cooperation with Mexico to enhance and enforce environmental standards. Apart from these environmental aspects to be included in NAFTA negotiations, US-Mexico environmental relations were for the greater part to take place via arrangements independent of NAFTA. Bilateral efforts and future plans for the protection of the border environment and the conservation of wildlife were stressed. The most important promise was the preparation of a long-term integrated Border Environmental Plan (U.S. President 1991). The Bush administration thus opted for this so-called parallel track instead of making environmental protection an integral part of the free trade agreement.

The commitments of Bush caused a split among environmental organizations on NAFTA. ENGOs were "presented with the opportunity to embrace the President's concessions and preserve their reputation as team players, or risk those reputations by holding fast in opposition" (Barkin and Mumme: 21). Critical US organizations opposed President Bush's parallel track approach and argued that the commitments were insufficient to enhance sustainable development in the context of NAFTA. Conversely, moderate US organizations proved willing to compromise with the Bush administration in exchange for a constructive role in the NAFTA negotiations. They not only announced their satisfaction with the commitments, but even actively supported fast track authorization.

New avenues were created for this constructive role of moderate ENGOS, which already had good informal relations with government agencies like USTR and EPA. In his Response, President Bush announced that he would increase public participation in NAFTA preparations. For this purpose, Bush did not create a committee on trade and environment, but representatives of a few environmental organizations were invited to join policy advisory committees of USTR. This invitation list of ENGOS turned out to consist of the National Audubon Society, NRDC, NWF, WWF and the Nature Conservancy, in fact the same organizations who, together with the EDF, had shifted their position to support the trade initiative within days of the Response's presentation.[20] In short, through his concessions Bush not only split an important faction of NAFTA opposition, but also secured a new ally for NAFTA proponents.[21]

The discord among US ENGOS confirmed and consolidated similar differences within the Mexican and Canadian environmental movements. The reason for this was the following. Mexican organizations few little illusions about their government's position in negotiations since even moderate organizations were hardly approached to contribute to the process. Moreover, the primacy of the US political process for the contents of NAFTA was evident. Consequently, transnational relations were of considerable importance to Mexican groups. At the same time, the split reconfirmed the differences between Canadian organizations.

The split of environmental organizations, which lasted until the end of the NAFTA debate, created two factions of ENGOS, one moderate and one critical.[22]

---

20 The WWF (whose former President Reilly was by then administrator of the EPA) had not formally opposed NAFTA prior to the May 1 declaration.

21 Another indication that Bush's commitments were partly designed to break environmentalist opposition to NAFTA is that ENGOS who wanted to attend a White House briefing on NAFTA, one week after the commitments, were to sign an agreement not to publicly oppose free trade, which many organizations refused to do (Dowie 1991: 87-8).

22 Other scholars have described them as 'moderate' and 'opposing' groups (Gallardo 1993) or as 'accommodating' (or 'cooperating') and 'radical' groups (Audley 1995). However, these designations are somewhat problematic. Critical groups did not completely oppose a free trade agreement—they did not agree with the governmental proposals. Their ideas were more radical, but their political behaviour could not be deemed as such. As for calling moderate groups accommodating, this seems to give them too little credit as independent political actors. Naming them cooperating is also somewhat mystifying—cooperating with whom, for instance?

Ideologically, the basic difference between moderate and critical ENGOs in the trade debate can be traced back to their positions on dominant economic and political structures, which were in general opposed by critical groups and accepted or ignored by moderate groups. Politically, moderate organizations tended to be more willing to make political compromises, and they had better relations with government agencies and the private sector than critical groups. Here, the different NAFTA positions of ENGOs are deliberately described along ideological and political lines instead of national lines. Taking the ideological and political background of ENGOs as a starting point provides us with a better insight into transnational similarities and relations.

Obviously dissension was based on existing differences between ENGOs, but we will here focus on its significance for NAFTA politics. During the first year of the NAFTA debate, the differences in political position were already expressed but remained in the background of the debate. Some organizations had been explicitly negative about free trade for more than environmental reasons (especially RMALC and ACN). Others were more neutral about economic liberalization, and mainly criticized possible detrimental effects on the environment.[23] As a result of Bush's May 1 declaration this ideological contrast between moderate and critical groups came to the fore.

As the rest of the NAFTA debate would demonstrate, the difference between moderate and critical organizations was not about whether regional integration should take place, but about the nature of integration and development. Moderate groups accepted the NAFTA proponents' claims of the necessity for economic liberalization and growth, or at least perceived this as inevitable, and declared that economic expansion should be accompanied by environmental safeguards. Critical organizations maintained that sustainable development requires not only environmental arrangements, but also democracy, justice, and social and economic redistribution. In the view of moderate ENGOs, the economic growth stemming from free trade, when carefully regulated, could bring new resources to counter ecological destruction. According to critical organizations, on the other hand, economic liberalization predominantly implies more corporate power and fewer possibilities for the correction of adverse effects of economic growth on both humans and the environment. They demanded stringent arrangements to prevent such damage. Thus the differences in views between critical and moderate ENGOs on NAFTA were closely linked to their different attitudes towards the existing political and economic order.

---

23 See, for instance, *Environmental concerns related to a United-State-Mexico-Canada Free Trade Agreement* of NWF (27/XI/90).

While the ideological position of critical organizations was expressed in several documents, moderate organizations were often less explicit on this. An exception is a paper by Stewart Hudson of NWF's international division (presented at a World Bank Symposium), in which Hudson maintains that the concept of sustainable development requires the uniting of trade and environment concerns. In his view, protectionism rewards inefficiency while free trade, through increased competitiveness, can contribute to less polluting production. Sustainable development should be the goal, not free trade, Hudson argues (1992: 57), but "... environmental protection <u>cannot</u> occur in the absence of some level of economic growth ..." (original emphasis). In addition, he recognizes that there are conflicts between liberalizing trade and environmental protection, but believes that they should be dealt with and could be resolved (Hudson 1992: 55-64).

Hudson's expression of the views of moderate groups on environment and development is in contrast to the position of critical organizations. Economic liberalization is a major source of environmental damage, critical organizations argued. In their view NAFTA formed a serious threat of economic and social polarization and even faster environmental destruction. In Mexico, this idea was strongly linked to the North-South asymmetry and the fear that NAFTA would entail domination by the Northern culture of materialism and over-consumption in Mexico (Peón Escalante 1991; RMALC 1992: 25-8). In both Mexico and Canada, critical environmental organizations and the networks they were part of maintained that NAFTA's neoliberal scheme would serve international financial organizations and TNCs at the cost of sovereignty and the common man and woman. They believed that the international economic order should be changed in order to have development for all (cf. RMALC 1991: 93-4; RMALC 1992: 61-81).

A split between groups accepting prevailing power structures and those attempting to overcome them is a general feature in both national and transnational civil society. Following Macdonald (1994) in her useful analysis of theories of transnational politics, the nature of ENGO relations and strategies in the NAFTA debate supports current ideas in critical theory on civil society and transnational alliances. These hold that power is an important ingredient in NGO relations and that NGOs can have strong links to the state and the corporate sector. Moderate groups are more easily invited into policy-making processes, as their demands are not so far removed from state goals as those of critical groups. Moreover, the links of moderate groups to the state or the corporate sector may make them more willing to compromise in return for political and economic gain. Conversely, critical organizations need to really force the state to listen and make changes since their demands exceed its goals. Their ultimate success depends on their ability to build a political counter-power.

This distinction in the political position and strategies of critical and moderate groups was clearly visible in the NAFTA environment debate. Moderate organizations opted for a constructive role (i.e. one close to the decision-makers) in the preparation process and were more willing to accept minimal concessions with regard to their environmental demands, in return for political influence. Critical organizations, with their position differing fundamentally from the thinking of free trade proponents, remained more as an outsiders of the official process. This was perceived by some moderate groups as "staying in the margin". The schism between moderate and critical ENGOs on NAFTA was also linked to their organizational structures and financial situation. Most critical organizations have a grassroots base and limited access to decision-makers and funding. Because of this, and because of their perception of the problems and solutions, in the NAFTA debate critical ENGOs cooperated with other, both new (e.g. human rights and women's groups) and old (e.g. unions) social movements.

Moderate groups held more mainstream views on general issues, were more focused on the environmental issue as separate from other issues, and had better relations with government agencies than critical organizations. Politically, cooperation with other types of NGOs was less necessary than for critical groups, and especially in the US a substantial share of the moderate organizations' attention was drawn to their relations with the government. Through their formal membership of policy advisory committees, and more importantly their informal relations with USTR and EPA as well as the private sector, moderate ENGOs in the US had easy access to the actors preparing NAFTA.[24] In Mexico, moderate groups experienced far less openness for participation, but the leaders of UGAM and the Group of Hundred were involved in some "side-room" discussions during the negotiations of the supplemental environmental agreement (Mexican government source 5/x/95).

Some moderate US ENGOs accepted large sums from companies, including pro-NAFTA companies. In particular the NWF and WWF counted on considerable support of companies which stood to benefit from NAFTA.[25] Even across

---

24 This prominent position is well illustrated by NWF's President Jay Hair, who was close to EPA's administrator, William K. Reilly, and regularly met with corporate leaders of TNCs such as DuPont Co. and Waste Management Inc.. By means of its Corporate Conservation Council NWF has formal ties to large companies like General Motors and Dow Chemical (*Washington Post Magazine* 04/08/91).

25 The WWF, for instance, received a $2.5 million donation in 1993 from Eastman Kodak, a prominent company in the pro-NAFTA lobby (*The Nation* 28/06/93: 894-5). The NRDC formed an exception among major US moderate groups and did not receive any funding from the private sector.

the border, moderate US organizations maintained good relations with the political elite. Most major moderate ENGOs had good relations with President Salinas, environmental minister Colosio, and Mexico's NAFTA office in Washington DC. They also had special interests in Mexico, such as projects, or wanted to open an office or to expand their membership.

The political strategy of moderate and critical ENGOs evidently affected their transnational relations. The need for moderate US organizations to cooperate was relatively limited since the US was evidently the most powerful partner in the negotiations, and moderate groups had both access to government and quite a lot of support in Congress. Apart from discussing ideas with groups across the border and co-signing letters to the governments and negotiators, moderate organizations hardly worked on a transnational position. Critical ENGOs in all three countries had far less access to the governments, and their strategy was "to expand participation through ever wider circles of inclusion" (Thorup 1991: 22). Ideas like small-scale production, strong local communities, equality and equity were matched with ecological care, and many critical environmental organizations became part of the critical networks (RMALC, CTC, ART and ACN) which developed structural forms of transnational cooperation. Various documents were written jointly, and at the later stages of the NAFTA debate critical groups developed a common transnational alternative for NAFTA (see 6.2) and a common lobby against the negotiated agreement.

The differences in transnational relations may be clarified by distinguishing between transnational alliances and transnational coalitions. In the NAFTA environment debate moderate ENGOs participated in a transnational *coalition*, whereas critical ENGOs formed part of a transnational *alliance*. While the transnational relations of moderate groups were limited, pragmatic and predominantly tied to the political moment of NAFTA negotiations, the transnational relations of critical environmental organizations were more profound and directed at more structural cooperation. Rather than being really concerned with Mexico's problems and in solidarity with Mexican counterparts, leaders of moderate US ENGOs primarily thought of transnational ties as useful for attaining their own immediate goals in the NAFTA debate. An interviewed advisor (28/11/95) to moderate organizations even spoke of "an appalling lack of interest in the other countries" among these leaders. However, the term alliance should not lend the transnational relations of critical organizations too much consistency and stability. More profound than the relations of moderate groups, the intensity of exchange between critical organizations in 1992 and 1993 was also bound up to the NAFTA debate, yet of a somewhat more structural nature.

The existence of the environmentalists' split and the interaction of the two factions in the US strongly affected the political struggle over NAFTA and the environment. The input of moderate ENGOS in the NAFTA negotiations was not only the result of their pragmatic attitude but can be equally attributed to the strength of critical organizations. The success of the moderate US organizations' constructive role proved to depend on the continued threat of critical US groups and their ideas, which had produced a lack of a secure majority in US Congress for NAFTA. It was this threat that enabled moderate organizations to gain government concessions. In addition, moderate groups were able to dominate the US ENGO input by not supporting critical initiatives, while convincing critical groups, which needed the legitimacy moderate groups offered, to endorse their proposals (Audley 1995).

— 4.3 Conclusions —

Due to the NAFTA plans, Mexico's environmental policy became an issue of interest and importance outside Mexico. Within a short time, Mexican, US and Canadian environmental and other NGOs became involved in the NAFTA environment debate, and numerous transnational relations were established. An outstanding feature of this transnational political interaction was its diversity. Especially the adoption of environmental issues by non-environmental organizations was an interesting trend in the NAFTA debate.

The nation-wide political debate on NAFTA's environmental impact that took place in the US was not matched by Mexico. Mexican environmental organizations were relatively weak as a result of historical discordance and few relations with groups outside Mexico City and the border region. Moreover, government repression of critical organizations and a general lack of opposition to NAFTA contributed to their feebleness. In this context, Mexican ENGOS chose to extend their transnational relations in order to gain access to information, and to be more successful in changing the official NAFTA proposals. US organizations, on the other hand, succeeded in having the issue discussed both at the grassroots level and within US Congress so that their concerns could not be ignored by the government. To them, transnational cooperation was primarily a means of enlarging their influence on the US government and NAFTA negotiations. In Canada, NAFTA as a whole did not become a major political issue, and a limited number of NGOs were involved in transnational initiatives. For Mexican groups, relations with Canadian counterparts were nevertheless very valuable.

The first phase of the NAFTA environment debate involved the raising and exploring of environmental issues with respect to North American free trade. These activities were a collective affair in which moderate and critical ENGOs seemed to have similar ideas. ENGOs wanted environmental concerns to become an integral part of the trade negotiations. The trade agreement should include arrangements with respect to different levels of environmental legislation and policy enforcement. On the one hand, stringent national or local policy should not run the risk of being disputed as obstructing free trade. On the other hand, NAFTA should provide funding structures to support environmental government agencies in Mexico. ENGOs were particularly concerned about the detrimental effects in the Mexico-US border zone and of industrial expansion and increasing exploitation of natural resources.

The May 1 commitments of President Bush on NAFTA and the environment put an end to this phase of joint moderate and critical activism. With his declaration, Bush split environmental organizations, and two camps came into existence. Interaction between critical and moderate groups continued, but their perceptions of problems and solutions differed considerably, and so did their political strategies. Moderate organizations believed that the integration of a set of environmental safeguards in NAFTA could prevent environmental damage. Critical organizations maintained that negotiations should be slowed down in order to draft a social and environmental charter carefully, and wanted to convert NAFTA into a regional development agreement. This difference was most visible at times of strategic choices. Moderate ENGOs were more willing to compromise with government proposals while critical organizations generally judged them to be insufficient. This difference also affected the transnational relations of environmental organizations. Moderate groups in the US had good relations with their government, and were only to a limited extent interested in cross-border cooperation. Transnational relations among moderate ENGOs thus remained ad hoc and rather limited. Critical organizations, conversely, needed broad networks with grassroots mobilization capacity to obtain political influence. The heterogeneous national opposition networks established strong ties with each other. While moderate environmental organizations cooperated through a transnational coalition on NAFTA, critical organizations were part of a transnational alliance.

The May 1 commitments marked the transition from the first to the second phase of the NAFTA environment debate. The official acknowledgement of the environmental issue regarding NAFTA negotiations shifted the NAFTA environment debate from exploring and raising issues to discussing and designing environmental arrangements. As we shall see in the following chapter, from that time onwards proponents of the agreement and particularly the US and Mexican government became actively involved in the NAFTA debate, and rapidly developed their position on environmental issues. The second phase of the NAFTA environment debate, that centred on the question of how the agreement should encourage and ensure environmental protection, lasted until the end of the trade negotiations in the summer of 1992.

CHAPTER 5

Transnational NAFTA Support and the Environment

The previous chapter has described how Mexico's weak environmental policy enforcement and other environmental issues were raised by ENGOs with respect to NAFTA preparations. While some environmental criticism could have been expected, the Mexican and US governments were not prepared for an important role of environmental issues in NAFTA opposition, nor for the strong resistance to the agreement in the US. As Mexico's entry into NAFTA ran the risk of being hampered by US Congress, and various major interests depended on its passage (see 3.1), strong support and lobbies for the agreement followed.

This chapter analyses the reaction of NAFTA proponents to the criticism of ENGOs. In the first section, we review the main political actors that performed pro-NAFTA activities. Besides several government agencies, after some time numerous private sector organizations in the US and Mexico became involved, and the World Bank did as well. As has been explained in chapter 1, the relations of the Mexican government with the US government and the World Bank had been extended and improved prior to Mexico's decision to join the North American free trade zone. Similarly, the domination of technocrats in the Mexican government had contributed to increasing participation of private sector organizations in economic policy. Cooperation of NAFTA proponents was thus mainly an extension of existing relations.

An important issue that had to be tackled by proponents of NAFTA was the environment. During the first phase of the NAFTA debate, they hardly reacted to questions and critiques from environmental organizations. President Bush's May 1 (1991) commitments marked the end of this phase and the start of the second phase of the debate. Through speeches, documents and press releases the governments presented their position on environmental concerns linked to NAFTA. The second section of this chapter analyses this view as expressed in the main NAFTA-related documents. In addition, plans were presented to improve environmental protection through cooperation, especially in the border region. In chapter 6, we will look into the reactions of environmental organizations to these views and plans, and analyse the struggle over the contents of NAFTA.

— 5.1 NAFTA proponents and transnational relations[1] —

Whereas transnational relations between environmental organizations in Mexico, the US and Canada had been limited before the NAFTA debate, proponents of NAFTA could build on existing cross-border ties. Mexico's involvement in US politics, however, was new. Until then, bilateral activities had predominantly been an affair of government agencies, but NAFTA enhanced a public debate in the US. Here, we will first look at the Mexican political actors that actively supported NAFTA, before reviewing the major Mexican and US lobbies for NAFTA in Washington DC. This sections ends with an analysis of the transnational relations between NAFTA proponents.

ACTIVE NAFTA SUPPORT IN MEXICO

In Mexico, the main force behind the NAFTA plans was the government, or more precisely the technocrats that dominated Salinas' cabinet. This new political elite presented NAFTA as a logical and inevitable undertaking. By stressing the failure of the old model they aimed to dwarf the influence of nationalist *políticos* and their ideas, as these had still leverage in the PRI. At a presentation of the results of the NAFTA negotiations (17/VIII/93), for instance, Trade Minister Jaime Serra Puche claimed that a return to the ISI model was not viable because of its lack of competition, resulting in insufficient efficiency and an insufficient increase of employment and salaries. Serra Puche stated that globalization was the best option for modern economies.

Control by technocrats had increased under Salinas as economic management became a highly presidential field of policy. A pro-free trade policy was also eased by a previous institutional shift, namely the creation of the Ministry of Commerce and Industrial Development (SECOFI) in 1983. As compared to the former trade ministry, more free trade proponents were recruited (Pastor and Wise 1994: 478). Besides SECOFI, the Ministry of Finance, banks, financial institutions and development banks were important supporters of NAFTA within the Mexican government (Poitras and Robinson 1994: 12). Interestingly, despite the technocrats' dominance Mexico insisted to exclude the traditional national activity of oil extraction from NAFTA, and made reservations with re-

---

1   The analysis in this section is partly based on information collected in a number of interviews with persons working in or with government agencies and private sector organizations in Mexico, the US and Canada.

gard to the liberalization of a few other activities (e.g. banking and other energy activities). Although these reservations might be interpreted as a concession towards certain nationalist pressures within Mexico's political system, it is likely that among technocrats too there was concern about losing control of these important sectors, regardless of their general support for free trade.

As mentioned in chapter 1, technocrats had better relations with the private sector than their predecessors, and granted more influence in policy-making to a few organizations that represented Mexico's business elite. This elite also became involved in the NAFTA process after the Mexican government requested business organizations to set up a special coordinating private sector agency. Headed by the business council CCE, the Coordinating Organization of Business Agencies of Foreign Trade (COECE) was created in 1990. It represented eleven major business organizations. Financial capital played a leading role in the coordinating organizations, and like the CCE, COECE over-represented the interests of large companies (Pastor and Wise 1994: 481; Puga 1992: 129).

The central task of COECE during the preparation and negotiation of NAFTA was to handle communication between the private sector and Mexico's negotiators. It did well in this respect and attained an unprecedented degree of communication and cooperation among Mexico's private sector (Bustamante 1991). Mexico's Trade Minister Serra Puche (1992) declared that his team and COECE cooperated in a "constant manner" during the preparation and negotiation of NAFTA.[2] During the negotiations of the trade agreement (not the supplemental agreements on the environment and on labour), COECE also assisted SECOFI in providing information and drafting technical proposals. Officials of SECOFI and COECE cooperated in a working group that commissioned numerous sectoral NAFTA assessments. While the trade ministry was thus served with useful input for the negotiations, key players in COECE obtained valuable foreknowledge of the details of NAFTA (Pastor and Wise 1994: 480-1; Poitras and Robinson 1994: 17).

Officially, private sector participation was also enabled through the government's creation of the Advice Council on the Free Trade Agreement. This council was supposed to channel the participation of labour, agriculture, academic and business sectors, but it did not play a significant role in developing

---

2   Both COECE's president Juan Gallardo Thurlow and executive director Guillermo Güemez were known to have close relations with Mexico's business sector and government. Gallardo, who was close to Trade Minister Jaime Serra Puche and Mexico's chief negotiator Herminio Blanco Mendoza, was continuously kept informed on the advances in the NAFTA negotiations, and even acted as an important spokesman on the negotiations for the press (*La Jornada* 30/VI/93).

Mexico's position in the NAFTA negotiations. It is nonetheless important to note that the business sector's representation in the council consisted of four members of CMHN (the small group of largest capitalists) and five persons who were linked to COECE. Apart from this over-representation of large companies, labour was clearly under-represented with only three representatives.

The Mexican business elite's participation in the preparation and negotiation of NAFTA was unprecedented, but should not automatically be equated with actual political power. Both in the literature and in interviews with Mexican government officials, there were three different accounts of the interaction of Mexico's government and business elite during the NAFTA process. First, there were claims that private sector representatives had a prominent role in the NAFTA negotiations, and that in many areas negotiations were even led by them (cf. Morris 1995: 81). Second, it has been argued that Mexico's NAFTA entry was a state-led process, and that private sector organizations had a merely advisory role (cf. Poitras and Robinson 1994: 17). Third, there were accounts that formal consultation remained poor, but that personal contacts between high government officials and powerful individuals in the private sector became closer (cf. Teichman 1993: 188).

Evidence suggests that Mexico's NAFTA discussions and negotiations were completely government-controlled, but that the government allowed both a formal and informal input from the business elite. The fact that through COECE within less than two years there were over 1,000 meetings between government officials and businessmen, whereas business representatives participated actively in NAFTA negotiations via the so-called side room (staying outside the trilateral negotiations, but discussing the developments immediately afterwards with the negotiators), shows that consultation of the private sector on NAFTA was considerable and that business representatives sometimes had more than an advisory role (Puga 1994: 8). This unprecedented political role of Mexico's business elite, however, was granted, not gained, and could therefore easily be reversed. In addition, this intensified cooperation was restricted to a relatively small group of large companies, leaving many companies with even less access to government than before.

MEXICAN NAFTA LOBBIES IN THE US

In the context of considerable resistance to free trade with Mexico in the US, Mexico's government and business elite actively lobbied for NAFTA in Washington DC. In January 1991, a special NAFTA office was created in the Embassy of Mexico to represent SECOFI in the US. The task of this office was threefold.

First, it aimed at creating a direct liaison between NAFTA efforts in the two countries. This marked a definite shift from the previous Mexican attitude to the US, when Mexico did not want such direct relations. The NAFTA office became the centre of Mexican lobbying in Washington, conveying reasons why NAFTA would be good for the US. Second, during the negotiations the NAFTA office was involved in performing research on possible effects of the agreement. This research was necessary to provide the negotiators with specific, detailed information. The third activity of the office was dealing with US critics of NAFTA. In each of these three tasks the NAFTA office was relatively free, and when necessary it could act relatively independently from SECOFI, which is unusual by Mexican standards. In 1991, SECOFI also created a NAFTA office in the Embassy in Ottawa. This office was important for establishing new relations with private sector organizations in Canada, but was less active in performing studies and lobbying for NAFTA than the office in Washington.

The NAFTA lobbies of the Mexican government in Washington were impressive. The director of the NAFTA office remained in close contact with Trade Minister Serra Puche, Mexico's ambassador to the US, and Mexico's key lobbyists. SECOFI hired numerous well-connected lobby firms as well as former US officials, some of whom had been influential in the early NAFTA preparation process in the 1980s or attained high positions under Clinton.[3] The amount of money spent by Mexico on NAFTA-related activities from 1991 to1993 was approximately $28 million. Compared to other foreign lobbying campaigns, Mexico "mounted the most expensive, elaborate campaign ever conducted in the United States by a foreign government" (Centre for Public Integrity 1993: 1). However, the Mexican lobby for NAFTA was a sensitive political issue in the US. Ross Perot, for instance, accused the Mexican government of "buying Congress". Therefore, the NAFTA office put considerable effort into making its lobbies acceptable and ensuring that they would not jeopardize NAFTA support in Congress. As we will see in the next section, one of the government's lobbying activities involved spreading positive information on Mexico's environmental policy.

Mexican private sector organizations also lobbied for NAFTA in Washington. COECE's US operating budget for promoting free trade amounted to over $0.5 million from April 1991 until October 1992. Among other things, a well-connected trade expert was hired to lobby for NAFTA in Congress, and various

3 The report of the Centre for Public Integrity (1993) gives a detailed overview of the careers of key persons hired by Mexico to lobby for NAFTA. These persons often combined public jobs and private positions, not seldom secretly.

working visits for US congressional staff to Mexico were sponsored. Most of these trips had a broad focus. They included meetings with Mexican government officials working in environmental departments as well as with many others. A few of the trips focused on the environmental issue (Centre for Public Integrity 1993: 26-9).

Another Mexico-based organization that promoted support for NAFTA in the US was the American Chamber of Commerce of Mexico (AMCHAM). It represented US and Mexican companies as well as others producing in Mexico. AMCHAM supported NAFTA through a number of initiatives in which the environment was actively addressed. Letters were written to Congressmen informing them of the policy progress made, and AMCHAM held several conferences on environmental issues in Mexico. Instead of hiring a lobby firm, a few AMCHAM staff members performed some lobby activities in Washington. In addition, the chamber performed studies that addressed some of Mexico's environmental problems and policy, and environmental advances made by its member companies. Reports of these studies were presented in the US and used to support the pro-NAFTA case (cf. AMCHAM 1993).[4]

US NAFTA LOBBIES

Starting in early 1991, when it became clear that there was limited support for NAFTA in US Congress, the US government lobbied hard for the trade agreement and its supplemental agreements. The Bush Administration aimed at an expert consensus that NAFTA was a win-win situation in order to prove opposition wrong, particularly on the labour issue, and numerous studies were performed by think-tanks like the conservative Heritage Foundation and the liberal Brookings Institution (Moody 1995: 103). Simultaneously, USTR and EPA initiated several assessment studies of NAFTA's environmental effects, as will be described in the second section of this chapter. Despite President Clinton's decision on supplemental agreements to NAFTA, he also had to undertake major lobbying efforts to secure sufficient congressional support, eventually involving expensive deals with doubting members of Congress (see 6.2).

---

4   Apart from the evident interests of AmCham's members in NAFTA, the environmental issue was also addressed for another reason. Several of the companies organized in the chamber (and member of its Environment Committee) hoped that NAFTA would stimulate Mexican and US public investment in large environmental and infrastructural projects.

All US economic sectors that stood to gain from NAFTA lobbied in Washington, and a range of private sector organizations were busy promoting NAFTA. The Business Roundtable, the Council for the Americas, the US Chamber of Commerce, the US Council of the Mexico-US Business Committee, Trade Partnership, the National Foreign Trade Council and the National Association of Manufacturers were the most important organizations. In the beginning, the US private NAFTA proponents focused their attention on Congress and US negotiators.[5] They aimed at influencing the contents of the agreement in order to ensure that the agreement would be as liberal as possible. When the agreement was signed in the summer of 1992 they shifted their efforts towards the public as it became clear that the anti-NAFTA alliance received widespread popular support. In addition, these groups wanted to prevent Clinton's supplemental agreements from harming free trade. In their view, environmental provisions could be easily abused for protectionist reasons.[6]

US TNCs producing in Mexico were prominent in USA*NAFTA (US Alliance for NAFTA), an umbrella organization of large companies that promoted NAFTA both at a state and a federal level in the US. Through formal and personal relations these firms kept in contact with NAFTA developments while attempting to convince both the public and members of Congress that NAFTA would be in the interest of their state, the US and North America. For each US state USA*NAFTA appointed a so-called captain, that is a corporation head who tried to convince the public and small companies of the benefits of NAFTA. Practically all these state captains were on the list of the 500 largest US companies, and the vast majority of them already had a base in Mexico. Most of them were also involved in the NAFTA preparation process through their representation in advisory committees of USTR (Anderson, Cavanagh and Gross 1993: 1-3).[7]

---

5 With respect to the congressional vote on fast track authority (see 4.2), for instance, the Business Roundtable, the Association of US-Mexico Businessmen of the Council for the Americas, and the Chamber of Commerce encouraged their members to show Congress their support.

6 Besides promotion activities, some studies were carried out. For instance, the U.S. Council of the Mexico-U.S. Business Committee (1993) financed a study on the environmental requirements in the border region.

7 However, according to Douglas Harbrecht (in *Business Week* 04/x/93: 37), USA*NAFTA was far from successful in its undertaking. "Understaffed, disorganized, and without a clue as to how to conduct a grassroots campaign (...) USA NAFTA is still flailing about (...)".

THE WORLD BANK

Finally, the World Bank had encouraged Mexico's economic restructuring (see 1.2), and was very much in support of NAFTA. According to the World Bank (1993: 7), "NAFTA's long-term impacts on Mexico, as the integration with larger markets to the north and the expedited modernization of the economy take their course, would have major secondary effects as well, on poverty reduction, the environment, human resource development, rural and urban development, (...) and political development. Many of the changes would be positive (...)". The Bank argued that non-ratification of the agreement could lead to falling investor credibility and questionable credibility of Mexico's economic policy.

The World Bank played a small but significant role in promoting NAFTA's passage in the US. Through reports, statements and political contacts the World Bank actively supported NAFTA. Besides the World Bank's general policy of encouraging trade liberalization, its position on NAFTA was also influenced by US interests. Especially shortly before congressional voting on NAFTA ratification in 1993, US interests became dominant in the Bank's NAFTA activities. As we will see in chapter 6, the announcement of an unprecedented environmental loan package of the World Bank for Mexico was largely the result of US pressure.

TRANSNATIONAL PREPARATION OF NAFTA

The relations between the proponents of NAFTA were intensive, in particular in Mexico and the US. Obviously, the governments, predominantly their trade ministries, met constantly while preparing and negotiating the trade agreement and later on the side agreements. But as US and Mexican private sector organizations became actively involved in creating sufficient NAFTA support, the totality of relations of proponents had a transnational character. Pro-NAFTA business had easy access to Salinas' government and the Bush administration, and to a lesser extent to the Clinton administration. The relations between pro-NAFTA US business and the Mexican government were especially strengthened. Mexico's NAFTA office in Washington DC proved to be of great importance for developing relations between the Mexican government and US Congress, US and Mexican business organizations, and on environmental issues also with the seven major moderate ENGOs in the US (see also 4.2). The Mexican government and Mexican private sector organizations encouraged US business organizations and NGOs to support NAFTA. In the beginning, however, US business organizations did not like to work with the NAFTA office openly because they feared being attacked for cooperating with the Mexican government. There were also good relations and regular meetings of Mexican and US private sector organizations.

Free trade proponents had worked on Mexico's entry in the North American market from the early 1980s onwards (see 3.1). During this early preparation process, relations were extended and cooperation intensified, and gradually a common discourse emerged. The latter was reflected in numerous documents, publications, statements and press releases in support of NAFTA, which mainly used the same language and set of arguments, despite their different sources. Apart from regular Capitol Hill activities, NAFTA proponents also aimed to define argument and debate, so-called deep lobbying, as we will see when we review their position on environmental issues. In this context, the leading voices of the US press took a pro-NAFTA stand (*Washington Post* 27/06/93; *Extra!*January/February 1993: 10-2). Particularly during the last few months before US Congress voted on NAFTA ratification in November 1993, hundreds of lobbyists and officials worked actively to make sure that NAFTA would pass through Congress. These pro-NAFTA activities were well coordinated through weekly meetings of government officials, private sector representatives and hired lobbyists (*National Journal* 30/10/93: 2595).

Despite strong transnational relations, major efforts of the US and Mexican governments, and the largest North American panbusiness effort ever, NAFTA did not get through US Congress easily (see 6.2). Some argued this was due to a late start of extensive lobbying by US business organizations. Another explanation is that the pro-NAFTA alliance could not produce proof of one single tangible US issue that would improve with NAFTA (*Mexico & NAFTA Report* 28/10/93: 2; *The Wall Street Journal* 25/04/91: A16). This setback stemmed from the expectation that only large companies and a few economic sectors in the US stood to gain considerably from trade and investment liberalization, while labour and environmental opposition to the agreement was influential.

The transnational relations of NAFTA proponents shifted over time, as will be described extensively in chapter 6. Under Bush, the US private sector attended congressional hearings but was less involved in the public debate since the president held similar views on what NAFTA should look like. Clinton's plan for supplemental agreements, however, clashed with the position of all the other proponents and caused tensions within the alliance. Mexican business had tighter and more constant relations with its government, but hardly an independent approach on NAFTA. In the end, the interests of all proponents merged again in ensuring the ratification of the NAFTA package, which required a strong joint effort. The NAFTA experience thus formed the basis for increased and new political and economic cooperation between Mexican and US actors as well as between Mexican and Canadian government agencies and business organizations.

As a result of the NAFTA environment debate, contacts on environmental matters between trade ministries, environmental ministries, business organizations and moderate ENGOs increased nationally and transnationally. Within the private sector cross-border initiatives for the environment were set up, such as the cooperative programme between the U.S. Council for International Business and the Mexican Confederation of Chambers of Industry (CONCAMIN), which focused on training (USCIB 1993). The relations between Mexico's NAFTA office and moderate US environmental organizations were reported to be friendly, which comes as no surprise in the light of the organizations' position on NAFTA and their interests in Mexico (see 4.2). Chapter 6 further analyses the transnational relations that emerged in the NAFTA environment debate. In the rest of this chapter we will review the position of NAFTA proponents on trade-linked environmental issues.

— 5.2 Proponents' position on environmental concerns —

Shortly after Mexico and the US signed a declaration advocating free trade, the link between trade liberalization and environmental protection became an issue of transnational debate. As described in the previous chapter, ENGOs in the US questioned the environmental implications of free trade with Mexico. In particular, organizations on the border with Mexico spread information on the disastrous environmental damage that had resulted from earlier trade liberalization with the US (the *maquiladora* sector). This criticism received widespread media attention and had political leverage. Next, Mexican concerns over NAFTA and its possible environmental effects attracted attention in the US. Only a few months after the official declaration on free trade between Mexico and the US, Mexico's lax environmental policy developed from a low-priority political issue at the domestic level into a high-priority issue in North America.

After the first phase of the NAFTA debate, when environmental criticism was expressed, proponents rapidly started to present their views and ideas on trade and environment. In the second phase of the debate, proponents attempted to prove critics wrong with two main arguments. First, they claimed that the link between trade and environment is generally positive. Second, they maintained that NAFTA would help to solve specific Mexican environmental problems through an increase in financial resources and an increase in North American cooperation on the issue. In addition, in order to improve Mexico's image in the us, proponents pointed to the recent policy progress that had been made (see 6.3).

In the context of a general strengthening of transnational relations during negotiations, the joint effort of NAFTA proponents on the environmental issue was strong, and a transnational pro-NAFTA position came into being with respect to environmental effects. Initially, the reaction to environmentalist criticism was predominantly a governmental affair, with which major private proponents agreed, and only at a later stage would private sector organizations become involved. In this section we will look at the position of NAFTA proponents regarding the links between the trade agreement and Mexico's environmental policy. Here, the focus will be on the second phase of the NAFTA debate, lasting from May 1991 until October 1992. First, we will see how the reaction of NAFTA proponents fitted into the more general claim that free trade is positive for environmental protection. Second, we will review the most important pro-NAFTA documents on environmental issues. Finally, ideas of NAFTA proponents on the Mexico-us border region will be discussed. Chapter 6 discusses the reactions of environmental organizations to the position of NAFTA proponents, and analyses how the debate was shifted again by the decision to negotiate a supplemental environmental agreement.

Positive trade-environment links

The position of NAFTA proponents with regard to Mexico's environmental policy was in the first place based on general arguments that free trade is beneficial for the environment. Trade liberalization produces more economic growth, and economic growth allows better environmental protection, the basic reasoning goes. In the NAFTA debate, depending on the speaker, the occasion and the audience, the positive relation between trade and the environment was presented either as a simple and automatic cause and effect or as a more complex interaction. Mexico's Trade Minister Serra Puche stated simply in the Mexican Senate (17/viii/93) that the more developed a country, the cleaner its environment. Social Development Minister Donaldo Colosio (who was also responsible for Mexico's environmental policy) stated that "free trade and a better environment go hand in hand ... [and] a North American free trade zone would increase sensitivities to the environment ..." (Border Assembly 25/vi/92). President Salinas argued more cautiously that trade liberalization is an opportunity for better environmental protection that needs to be supported by a good policy (*International Wildlife* Sept-Oct 1992). Similarly, the Bush administration maintained that "[w]hen coupled with environmental sensitivity [...] policies which stimulate economic growth are an indispensable element in improving environmental protection" (USTR 1992a: 223).

A first argument used for underpinning the idea that free trade is good for environmental protection is that free trade enhances access to and resources for advanced technologies and manufacturing processes that pollute less and use natural resources more efficiently. The abolition of trade barriers renders the import of foreign technologies, like other products, cheaper and easier, while investment liberalization stimulates new investments in economic modernization. Above all, the argument goes that increased economic growth stemming from liberalization would provide the public and private sector with more resources for environmental protection.

A second argument behind the idea that free trade benefits environmental protection is that trade liberalization helps the environment by enabling economies of scale, encouraging specialization and competition, and increasing the choice of locations for industry. Because of these tendencies productivity will rise and efficiency will grow (cf. World Bank 1992b: 66, 68). Combined with the help of new technologies, products may be produced with less natural resources and energy. Finally, there is an argument that increased economic growth as a result of free trade may give rise to more political pressure for environmental protection. With increasing incomes people are more likely to shift their attention from subsistence to other issues. "As incomes rise, the demand for improvements in environmental quality will increase" (World Bank 1992b: 39). With respect to fast track authority, the Bush administration argued accordingly that rejecting NAFTA would not be in the interest of a new environmental approach in Mexico. "The Government of Mexico will be less likely to get support from most Mexicans for environmental protection if they are struggling to find work or are eking out their existence" (U.S. President 1991: 1).

The first argument—increased resources and technology through growth—was the most prominent in the position of NAFTA proponents regarding Mexico's environmental policy. According to the US government, Mexico had shown a strong commitment to protecting its environment, and "the major remaining obstacle to improved environmental quality in Mexico is not standards or enforcement but the availability of economic resources" (U.S. President 1992: 5). NAFTA would deal with the problem of resources as "NAFTA-led growth will generate substantial resources, providing funding for environmental projects and enforcement of environmental laws and regulations" (SEDESOL, undated a: 1.5). In the words of Salinas, "[o]nly through widespread prosperity can we have the resources to channel toward the protection of land, air and water" (Government of Mexico, undated b). In short, proponents presented NAFTA as a solution to Mexico's environmental policy weaknesses.

NAFTA proponents opposed ENGO proposals to include an arrangement for environmental funding in the trade agreement. Linking environmental protection to trade (e.g. cross-border trade taxes) would create new trade barriers, thereby countering liberalization. The Mexican government maintained instead that "[a] strong Mexican economy is the best way of creating resources for environmental improvement" (SEDESOL, undated a: 1.6). Another reason behind this resistance was that the inclusion of environmental funding in NAFTA implied that such an arrangement would also apply to any new country entering the trade bloc.

Taken together, the perception of positive trade-environment linkages is characterized by a great faith in the good of economic growth and technology. Economic growth would bring technologies and prosperity, rendering growth sustainable. Environmental protection was thus predominantly presented as a money problem for which economic expansion would provide the solution. The notion that economic growth, due to more production, consumption and transport, is likely to produce additional ecological damage was largely rejected. Instead, "President Bush and President Salinas believe that the two [i.e. sustained economic growth and environmental protection in both countries] are complementary and must be pursued together" (U.S. President 1991: tab 4-1). We will return to this point when reviewing ideas on the Mexico-US border region.

MEXICO'S ENVIRONMENTAL POLICY AND NAFTA

The first major political defence against environmental criticism on NAFTA was President Bush's May 1 commitments to US Congress (see 4.2). Bush promised that a few environmental concerns would be included in the trade negotiations, and that a review would be made of US-Mexico environmental issues. However, environmental relations would predominantly be dealt with bilaterally, outside NAFTA. As we saw in the previous chapter, the May 1 commitments shifted the NAFTA environment debate from raising and exploring issues by environmental organizations and other groups to a discussion between ENGOs and the US and Mexican governments on how to integrate environmental arrangements in the trade agreement. The contents of Bush's commitments caused a split between moderate and critical environmental organizations, which would have a decisive effect on the course of the debate. The commitments were also an important demonstration of the reluctance to turn the environment into an integral issue for negotiation. The commitments signalled that the North American economic integration plan was not open to fundamentally considering environmental concerns.

With the support of moderate US environmental organizations, US Congress granted the government fast track authorization. However, critical as well as moderate groups continued to put pressure on the negotiators, and Congressional hesitation on NAFTA remained. Worries about job losses and weak economic sectors prevailed in the US, but environmental issues contributed to the opposition. Convincing the public, NGOs and Congress that trade and investment liberalization would not affect the environment in a negative way became a lasting task of NAFTA proponents.

US government reports that followed after May 1991 dealt with Mexico's environmental problems, its environmental legislation and the advancements made in policy performance. These reports tended to focus on the border region, and will therefore be reviewed later. Even the review of US-Mexico environmental issues (USTR 1992a) turned out to deal largely with border concerns. An exception to this border bias was EPA's *Evaluation of Mexico's Environmental Laws and Regulations*. In the report, EPA (1991: 45) concluded that "Mexico's environmental laws, regulations and standards are in many respects similar to those in the United States" and that Mexico had a strong commitment to environmental protection. This legislative similarity between the US and Mexico's environmental policy was often repeated by proponents of NAFTA. A lack of adequate resources was the critical factor behind Mexico's weak monitoring and enforcement of compliance, according to EPA.

In Mexico, the SEDUE initially performed an environmental impact study of NAFTA, possibly inspired by the US plans for an environmental review. Compared to other publications by the Mexican government on NAFTA and environmental protection, the draft environmental impact report was remarkably informative rather than propagandistic. Whereas other documents mainly reported on the great progress made, this study summed up how economic development had damaged the environment in the past, and how the growth of production and trade due to NAFTA could harm Mexico's environment in the future. The following sentence would be unthinkable in any of the other publications distributed by the Mexican Government: "The chemical and engineering industry are especially aggressive for the environment, but this is even more so when its processes are technologically backward and when equipment for the control of emissions is lacking, as is the case in the majority of these industries in Mexico" (SEDUE undated: 3.5, my translation).

However, the draft study was never revised or released. According to an insider in Mexico's environmental politics, the study was covered up because it contained too much evidence (in particular through its data) that NAFTA would cause major environmental damage in Mexico (Mexican ENGO source 18/VIII/93). The US environmental review referred to the forthcoming Mexican environmental review for an extensive treatment of the environmental impact of growth in Mexico away from the border, since the US review was mainly restricted to the border region (USTR 1992a: 5). With mounting transnational criticism and opposition, however, the Mexican government feared that the draft's information could be used by opponents to stop NAFTA, and was therefore set aside.

The Mexican government's political defence of NAFTA against environmental criticism aimed to counter its poor image in the US. Speeches, press releases and publications all stressed recent progress in environmental policy performance, if necessary by providing unreliable figures.[8] Sergio Reyes Lujan, Sub-Minister of Ecology and later on president of the National Ecology Institute, attended many meetings in the US to inform participants on the progress of his policy, such as the new environmental standards, the number of plants inspected, and the increasing environmental budget (see 6.3). Also the new structure of environmental government agencies in 1992 (replacement of SEDUE by the Ministry of Social Development, SEDESOL) was presented as an important means to improve Mexico's policy implementation. Through Mexico's embassy and NAFTA office in Washington DC, brochures in English were distributed in the US (cf. Embassy of Mexico 1992; Government of Mexico, undated a and b). The ambassador wrote letters to Congress members, for instance to the influential Democratic NAFTA opponent Richard Gephardt (*Inside U.S. Trade* 10/VII/92), to convince them of Mexico's commitment to sustainable development. In addition, lobby firms and former officials were hired to make brochures, press releases, public statements, and to make presentations at Congressional Hearings.[9] In these image-building activities, much reference was made to the environmental awards won by Salinas: the Earth Prize in 1991, and the World Conservation Leadership Award in 1992.

While Mexico could rightfully point to policy progress, symbolism was another ingredient of its image-building activities. An illustration of this was the permanent closure of Mexico City's largest (PEMEX) oil refinery at Azcapotzalco in March 1991, at the time that fast track authority for NAFTA negotiations was heavily debated in the US. Both inside and outside Mexico, the closure was presented as a proof of the government's determination to combat air pollution in the capital, and it was repeatedly mentioned in NAFTA-related documents.[10]

---

8 As we shall see in greater detail in section 6.3, the so-called Fact Sheets of the Embassy of Mexico (1992) contained unreliable data on Mexico's environmental budget.
9 For instance, the lobby firm Burson-Marsteller, which received $5.4 million from SECOFI, produced thousands of copies of the brochure entitled "Protecting the Environment" to improve Mexico's image (Center for Public Integrity 1993: 20).

According to official sources, the closure of the refinery cost about $500 million and 5,000 jobs, and was expected to reduce industrial air pollution by 15 per cent (SECOFI 1993: 75). However, the fact that the plant was reassembled in the industrial city Salamanca without additional environmental equipment was not made public (*Los Angeles Times* 17/11/91: A18).

In Mexico itself, where pro-NAFTA propaganda was strong and environmental criticism received little public attention, much less of an effort was made to weaken arguments of ENGOs on NAFTA. The environmental issue was largely dealt with through some remarks of government officials which were reproduced in the media. SEDUE's successor SEDESOL did produce an "informative file" on NAFTA and the environment, but it consisted of a hotchpotch of agreements, statements, and texts from unclear sources (SEDESOL undated a). Compared to the brochures made for the US, the quality of the informative file was poor.

The US private sector hardly reacted to the environment debate until late 1992. The reason for this was that Bush's approach of largely excluding environmental issues from the trade negotiations satisfied the private sector, which felt no need for an independent environmental lobby. On the other hand, through the NAFTA-enhanced relations with the EPA and moderate ENGOs, US business organizations were not excluded from early in-door discussions. After Clinton's plan for supplemental agreements, US business organizations extended their activities with regard to the environmental debate to more public initiatives. They believed that NAFTA-linked environmental arrangements should be based on cooperation, not supranational policy. They supported claims that NAFTA by itself would be beneficial for environmental protection, and argued that stringent safeguards would be abused by protectionist actors (6.3).

A politically important academic report in the NAFTA environment debate was that by Grossman and Krueger (1991) of Princeton University. The paper was prepared for a conference on free trade between Mexico and the US that was sponsored by SECOFI. As it pointed to possible positive effects of NAFTA on Mexico's environment, the paper attracted considerable attention. In fact, it was adopted as the scientific evidence of the position of NAFTA proponents. For a discussion paper, it was remarkably often quoted.[11]

---

10 I came across this example in: Embassy of Mexico (1992: 32); SECOFI (1993: 75); U.S. President (1993: 36).

11 The occasions in which I found Grossman and Krueger's paper quoted are: Embassy of Mexico (1992: 38, 41); Government of Mexico (undated a: 9); U.S. President (1992: 5); U.S. President (1993: 76); by EPA's Alan Hecht at the Washington Environmental Industry Association's annual conference, 09/IX/93: 6; by EPA's administrator William

The most quoted part of the Grossman and Krueger paper is its first section, that deals with the relation between GDP and three air pollutants: sulphur dioxide (SO2), smoke and suspended particulates. This analysis is based on data from 19 to 42 cities (depending on the pollutant) in the world, none of which are Mexican. The authors found that sulphur dioxide and smoke stop rising with increasing economic growth when a country reaches a per capita income level of about $5,000. They subsequently conclude that "economic growth tends to alleviate pollution problems once a country's per capita income reaches about $4000 to $5000 US dollars" (Grossman and Krueger 1991: 35-6), which was the case in Mexico.

This conclusion was not unchallenged. There was criticism that the findings of the report's first section had very limited application as one cannot generalize on overall pollution on the basis of a few air pollutants. That the links between economic growth and environmental pollution are more complex than presented by Grossman and Krueger is supported by the *World Development Report 1992* (World Bank 1992b: 10-1), which shows that there are three emerging patterns regarding these links. Some problems, such as unsafe water and inadequate sanitation, decline with an increase in incomes. Some problems initially worsen but then improve as income increases, like urban concentrations of particulate matter and SO2, although this improvement is not automatic but the result of policy choices. Finally, environmental problems like municipal waste and CO2 emissions worsen continuously with rises in income.

Also the link between trade and increase of income as presented in the Grossman and Krueger report was questioned. Predictions regarding the effects of free trade are in general hard to make, but even if GDP rises there is still the point of income distribution, which has been notoriously unequal in Mexico. It seems improbable that a society with a few ever richer families and a continuously large number of poor will live, produce and consume in a more environmentally sustainable manner than before (Lee 1992).

In the second section of their paper, Grossman and Krueger (1991) analysed whether under NAFTA US companies were likely to move to Mexico because of lower pollution abatement costs; an issue that was of great concern not only to ENGOs but also to US labour. Their findings pointed out that evading stricter environmental standards had not been a significant motive for US firms to move production to Mexico, since environmental abatement costs were mostly

K. Reilly in his statement before the Subcommittee on International Trade of the Committee of Finance of US Senate, 16/09/92: 4; and by Mexico's Trade Minister Serra Puche in the Mexican Senate (17/VIII/93).

too small when compared to other production costs.[12] While later studies have reached opposite conclusions (cf. Molina 1993), there was also criticism that Grossman and Krueger had posed the wrong question. It was suggested that it is more important to find out whether firms that do move to Mexico, for instance because of lower labour costs and cheaper natural resources, pollute more than they did in the US (Lee 1992). At the time of the NAFTA environment debate, US-owned *maquiladoras*, although having access to and resources for modern equipment, did not comply with Mexico's environmental legislation (see 6.3).

The third and last section of the Grossman and Krueger report dealt with the relation between economic liberalization and resource reallocation. Because of a limited data-base (Mexico did not collect data on pollution generated by different industries), confusion over the final contents of NAFTA when the paper was written, and limitations in the model applied, the analysis remained quite speculative, as the authors admitted. Their conclusions nonetheless provide an interesting indication of the possible environmental impact of NAFTA. On the one hand, "[s]ince Mexico enjoys comparative advantage in a set of activities (agriculture and labour-intensive manufactures) that on the whole are 'cleaner' than the average, the composition effect of *trade liberalization* may well reduce pollution there" (Grossman and Krueger 1991: 35, my italics). *Investment liberalization*, on the other hand, might have an opposite effect. With a presumed 10 per cent increase of Mexico's capital stock, manufacturing industry was expected to expand. Grossman and Krueger predicted that this industrial expansion would entail increased emission of air pollutants and toxic waste. In short, the report expected investment liberalization to be negative for Mexico's environment.[13] In their final conclusion, however, Grossman and Krueger did not repeat the results of their investment liberalization scenario, only of the trade liberalization scenario. NAFTA proponents quoting this report never mentioned its negative environmental predictions regarding investment liberalization, even when it was clear that NAFTA would include national treatment of investors from member countries.[14]

---

12 USTR's review (1992: 163, 171, Executive Summary: 7) comes to a similar conclusion based on three arguments: environmental compliance costs for US industries on average are only 1.1 per cent; trade barriers for industries with high pollution abatement costs were already generally low prior to NAFTA; and new foreign investors have to submit an environmental plan to the Mexican authorities.

13 Based on research by Peat Marwick, a similar conclusion with respect to all productive sectors was reached by SEDUE (undated: 1.3.1).

14 For instance, in its folder *A better Mexico * a better environment*, the government of Mexico (1992, undated) quoted the Princeton study like this: "Trade liberalization may

THE MEXICO-US BORDER REGION

NAFTA proponents argued that environmental cooperation, predominantly be-tween Mexico and the US, would flow from NAFTA. Mexico and the US had expressed their willingness to protect the North American environment, and NAFTA would contribute to this by fostering closer relations and cooperative efforts with regard to common environmental problems as well as other issues. The *Review of U.S.-Mexico Environmental Issues* carried out by a US inter-agency task force coordinated by USTR, as committed by Bush in May 1991, pictured future environmental cooperation as depending considerably on NAFTA. "The negotiation of the NAFTA is likely to be an important stimulus to maintain high levels of cooperation and commitment to address [environmental] problems", USTR (1992a: 70) maintained. Conversely, "in the absence of a NAFTA, Mexico may have less incentive to fully develop and enforce its environmental legal and regulatory regime in respect, for example, to U.S. concerns to transboundary impacts" (USTR 1992a: 73).

The border region was the most important area of Mexico-US environmen-tal cooperation, as chapter 2 has shown, but *maquiladora* pollution was also a central issue of NAFTA criticism. However, according to NAFTA proponents the agreement would "facilitate solution of the existing environmental problems in the border area" (SEDESOL, undated a: 1.6). Besides enhanced cooperation and increased economic growth, the border environment would improve because NAFTA might stimulate new industrial investment to take place in areas other than the border strip, reducing congestion at the border (USTR 1992a: 4). The latter, however, was an over-simplified conclusion of the review's findings. Besides a no-NAFTA scenario, the review described two NAFTA-scenarios: 1. NAFTA with extra growth in the border area; 2. NAFTA with less growth along the border, as new investments might disproportionately be directed to the rest of Mexico.[15] Absence of NAFTA might result in a 5 to 15 per cent annual growth in the border region until 2002, whereas scenario 1 was assumed to produce a

---

increase Mexican specialization in sectors that cause less than average amounts of envi-ronmental damage, improving environmental quality". No mention was made of the findings on investment liberalization.

15 After its early years, the maquiladora programme was no longer restricted to the border area but extended to Mexico as a whole. Yet as the programme only promoted production for export, the overall majority of *maquiladoras* remained located close to the US. With NAFTA, conversely, production for the internal market by foreign investors would be liberalized, which might be an incentive for these investors to produce in other regions of Mexico, among others to be closer to the consumer market.

6 to 17 per cent border growth and scenario 2 a 4 to 13 per cent growth (USTR 1992a: 64-8). Which scenario would be closest to reality was uncertain, but it is clear that no matter which development would take place, border growth would remain rather high and border congestion would consequently increase. In fact, USTR (1992a: 225) acknowledged that "economic growth and industrialization in the border region will continue, and possibly accelerate, whether or not a NAFTA comes to pass".

A major share of USTR's review dealt with various possible environmental effects of NAFTA in the border region. The results depended to a large extent on the scenario applied. Mexican border air emissions, for example, might change 0 to 165 per cent with scenario 1, or -20 to +85 per cent with scenario 2 (USTR 1992a: 88). The change of air emissions in a no-NAFTA scenario would depend on the impact of the absence of free trade on future environmental cooperation. Less cooperation might give way to a 40 to 225 per cent increase of Mexican air emissions, whereas no free trade with a continuing high level of environmental cooperation could result in a -10 to +125 per cent range (USTR 1992a: 88). In short, a considerable increase of air emissions was likely in each scenario.

With respect to border water quality, USTR (1992a: 113) also estimated that scenario 1 would mean a worse situation but scenario 2 a better situation when compared to no NAFTA. Domestic and industrial waste were expected to increase with growth, but growth might simultaneously provide resources for environmentally-sound disposal. Wildlife was expected to be harmed by free trade (spurring export agriculture), free investment (increasing pressure for industrial and recreational development of sensitive areas) and subsequent extra economic growth in Mexico (more production, infrastructure, prosperity). In the short term, health problems on the Mexican border side were expected to worsen under all scenarios as health infrastructure would not be able to keep up with the growing population, while NAFTA-scenario 2 might in the long term have a positive effect (USTR 1992: 132-9, 155-9). Taken together, the tentative analyses of USTR's review showed that most of the border problems were likely to exacerbate with or without NAFTA, and that a positive effect of NAFTA depended on additional growth taking place outside the border region. As the US review did not deal with problems in the interior of Mexico, and the Mexican review was covered up, the optimistic claims of NAFTA proponents on Mexico's environment remained rather ill-founded (see also 6.1).

With the development of the Integrated Environmental Plan for the Mexico-U.S. Border Area, the two governments made a rapid start with expanding environmental cooperation in the border region. With his May 1 declaration, President Bush had made a commitment to accelerate the creation of a border environment plan, which was agreed upon by Bush and Salinas in November

1990. As early as August 1991, SEDUE and EPA presented a draft of the Border Plan's first stage, covering the 1992-1994 period. The goal of the plan was to provide for the long-term protection of health and natural ecosystems along the border by means of strengthening laws, reducing pollution, and improving planning, training and education, as well as knowledge of the border area (SEDUE and EPA 1991).

The draft Border Plan presented an overview of major environmental problems in the border region, especially water and air quality, and waste and hazardous materials. Next, it described the existing institutional framework for the border environment, and the policy priorities. The final section on the implementation of the draft contained a list of plans with respect to monitoring and pollution control, environmental regulatory activities, resources for pollution control, and programmes for pollution prevention and voluntary action. Apart from several infrastructural works, many of the implementation plans involved opening talks, developing plans, recommending solutions, evaluations, analyses, consultations, and the completion of existing projects (SEDUE and EPA 1991). The Border Plan's draft was heavily criticized by environmental organizations for being too weak, among other things because it did not address the relation between NAFTA and possible environmental damage in the border region (see 6.1).

NAFTA proponents thus repeatedly presented economic integration as a prerequisite for intensified environmental cooperation, but this argument was questionable. "The alternative in which a NAFTA is not established would likely portend less cooperative environmental relations between our two countries, and a less adequate solution to those border environmental issues that do arise" according to USTR's review (1992: 63-4). However, before the decision on Mexico-US free trade, cooperation between the two countries on environmental issues had already expanded in areas such as wildlife protection, tropical forests and marine resources. In addition, Bush had stated that the proposed parallel track activities were "scheduled to occur whether or not a NAFTA is adopted" (U.S. President 1992: 73).

There did seem to be a relation between publicly known plans for Mexico-US economic integration and increased bilateral efforts in the border region. Border activities, most importantly the Border Plan, were speeded up when President Bush and President Salinas met in November 1990, a few months after the announcement of trade negotiations, "to discuss important issues of interest to both countries" (SEDUE and EPA 1991: 1-1). From that time on, SEDUE and EPA met to develop the Border Plan. The elaboration of NAFTA produced an intensification of environmental cooperation between Mexico and the US, as NAFTA proponents argued, but beside the preparation of the agreement it was the widespread criticism which the NAFTA plan evoked that formed an important motive for increasing bilateral cooperation on environmental problems.

NAFTA proponents nonetheless strongly maintained that economic integration is better for environmental cooperation. There are at least three political reasons for this position. First, this logic rendered integrating strong arrangements on environmental protection and cooperation in the trade agreement unnecessary. Second, it supported the image-building attempts of the pro-NAFTA alliance to improve the public perception of the agreement and its proponents. It was, for instance, argued that "[a]s momentum has built behind a North American Free Trade Agreement, the nature and extent of such [environmental] cooperative activities has expanded" (USTR 1992a: Executive Summary-1). Third, the Bush administration also reasoned that "[i]t would be a great mistake to replace this increasingly successful cooperative approach with a series of dictates" which Mexicans might perceive as "impugning their own commitment and as a form of eco-protectionism" (U.S. President 1991: 10). This terminology clearly confers a negative image on ENGO plans to include stronger environmental arrangements in NAFTA than those envisioned by the neoliberal alliance.

A more fundamental, puzzling aspect of the environmental position of NAFTA proponents was its stand on growth and economic integration, in particular with regard to the border. On the one hand, it was acknowledged that the disastrous environmental state of the border stemmed from rapid expansion of the *maquiladora* sector. On the other hand, the argument ran that the solution to these growth problems was further growth. Why did the earlier growth not give way to increased environmental protection, and why would increased economic expansion not lead to more environmental damage? NAFTA proponents attempted to deny the growth dilemma by arguing that Mexico's recent commitment to improving the environment and the expected resource-providing growth made a difference with the past, but this argument remained somewhat ambiguous.

— 5.3 Conclusions —

In the context of the preparations and negotiations of NAFTA a transnational alliance of proponents emerged. This alliance first of all consisted of government agencies and the presidents of Mexico and the US, while during the later stages of the NAFTA debate also private sector organizations and the World Bank reacted to criticism and developed major lobbies in close relation with government efforts. The relations between these NAFTA proponents at the time of the debate were rather profound when compared to their previous relations. With the prospect of North American free trade, these new and strengthened relations obtained extra weight as the basis for future integration.

The pro-NAFTA alliance reacted actively on criticism with respect to possible environmental damage stemming from trade and investment liberalization. In documents and speeches, proponents presented their position on the NAFTA-environment links. As it was predominantly US Congress, and indirectly the US public, that had to be convinced of the good of NAFTA, the Bush administration produced the majority of documents. After denouncing its environmental review, which was unsuitable for the pro-NAFTA effort, the Mexican government mainly published image-building brochures in English. An early academic report claiming NAFTA would be beneficial for Mexico's environment (Grossman and Krueger 1991) was adopted by both governments for the NAFTA cause. Business organizations largely refrained from public activity on the environmental issue as long as the Bush administration, assisted by the Mexican government, seemed able to deal with the critics. The World Bank maintained an equally distant position from the public debate.

The most important pro-NAFTA documents on environmental issues were interrelated. Regularly, these documents used the results of the others' studies and brochures. Another regularity is the simplification of results, either of their own data or when quoting other documents. Whereas most reviews contained a large amount of complex data predicting a range of possible environmental effects of NAFTA, conclusions and summaries lacked caution and depth.

NAFTA proponents attempted to change the negative image of Mexico's environmental policy by highlighting recent improvements. Large amounts of money were spent on lobbying for the same purpose. In addition, proponents maintained that free trade is environmentally beneficial as it leads to economic growth. Their argument went that this growth produces the resources necessary for environmental protection. Moreover, free trade would enhance environmental cooperation between the US and Mexico. Mexico's environment would thus be better off with than without NAFTA, and the inclusion of environmental arrangements and funding in NAFTA would be a redundant measure according to the pro-NAFTA alliance.

The environmental position of NAFTA proponents was notable for its narrow approach. Regarding Mexico, most attention was paid to the border region with the US and to industrial pollution, with the exception of Mexico City and conservation of wildlife, forests and marine resources. This distortion of the link between NAFTA and Mexico's environment can be partly attributed to the US dominance in the NAFTA environment debate. Weak enforcement of

Mexico's environmental legislation as a source of US job losses, and pollution at the border was what worried the US public most, as the previous chapter showed. With the US Congress divided on NAFTA, the border environment and Mexican industrial pollution, was the main issues to be addressed by NAFTA proponents. However, the pollution focus was also strong within the Mexican government, as has been shown in chapter 2. In short, the reaction of NAFTA proponents to ENGO criticism strengthened a limited approach to Mexico's environmental problems and policy.

CHAPTER 6

Mexico's Environmental Policy
and NAFTA Negotiations

Between 1991 and 1993, Mexico's environmental policy became an issue of transnational political interest in the context of the NAFTA environment debate. After the early criticism of environmental organizations on free trade plans in the first phase of the debate, as described in chapter 4, the environment became an element of the trade negotiations. However, the proposals and activities of the Mexican and US governments and other NAFTA proponents in this respect, which have been analysed in the previous chapter, gave rise to new criticism and heated discussions. Mexico's weak enforcement of environmental legislation was central to the second and third phase of the NAFTA environment debate. These developments were an important motivation for the Mexican government to speed up improvements of its environmental policy and implementation.

This chapter analyses the simultaneous processes of environmental politics and policy-making in Mexico, and the transnational NAFTA environment debate in the period 1991-1993 (see Table 6.1). The main questions that will be addressed are how the NAFTA debate changed environmental politics in Mexico, and how the debate affected Mexico's environmental policy. In order to answer these questions, we will review the transnational struggle over NAFTA and the changes that took place in Mexico at that time. The effects of the NAFTA debate will be analysed both from the immediate changes in Mexico and from an assessment of the implications of the NAFTA package. An overview of the first NAFTA experiences is beyond the scope of this study. Describing two different but linked processes that evolve simultaneously poses a problem for structuring a text. In the first two sections of this chapter the NAFTA environment debate is analysed. Section 3 then assesses the changes that took place in Mexico during the same time span.

This chapter starts with the second phase of the NAFTA environment debate, which lasted from May 1991 until September 1992. This phase involved the interaction between transnational proponents (chapter 5) and critics (chapter 4) of NAFTA with respect to the environmental provisions of the trade agreement, as well as the Mexico-US arrangements for environmental cooperation. Formally, these bilateral arrangements were not linked to NAFTA, but they were very important for the NAFTA environment debate. After reviewing the main proposals and reactions, the first section provides an overview of the environmental provisions included in the trade agreement that was completed in the summer of 1992, and the political reactions to these provisions.

The third phase of the NAFTA environment debate that started in October 1992 and lasted until November 1993 will be described in the second section. After the completion of the trade negotiations the NAFTA process was not finished. Insufficient support in the US Congress, and the US presidential elections in November 1992, slowed down the implementation of NAFTA. With the electoral victory of Bill Clinton, the NAFTA environment debate centred around a supplemental environmental agreement. While US political dynamics had been crucial to the way in which the NAFTA debate had evolved so far, during this last phase the US impact was the strongest. Consequently, the second section pays more attention to internal US politics. The section reviews the discussions and negotiations on the supplemental agreement, their outcome, and a comparison of the contents of the supplemental agreement with the positions of the main actors involved.

TABLE 6.1 *The Three Phases of the NAFTA Environment Debate*

Phase	Major issues	Main actors and positions
I (June 1990 – April 1991)	Environmental effects of free trade	ENGOs: environmental concerns and public participation in negotiations
II (May 1991 – September 1992)	NAFTA's environmental provisions and Mexico-US cooperation	Critical ENGOs: environmental charter Moderate ENGOs: environmental safeguards NAFTA proponents: no environmental safeguards
III (October 1992 – November 1993)	Supplemental Environmental Agreement	Critical ENGOs: sustainable trade and development Moderate ENGOs: a strong CEC Clinton administration: strong CEC and trade sanctions Other NAFTA proponents: no supranational CEC, no sanctions

Next, we will focus on the changes that took place in Mexico's environmental politics and policy at the time of the NAFTA debate, and assess to what extent these changes were likely to be caused by the debate. Some of the NAFTA-related developments resulted from the criticism expressed during the debate's first phase (chapter 4), while other trends may be understood from the transnational processes that took place during the second and third phase. Finally, in the concluding section we will combine this information on the immediate effects of the NAFTA environment debate on Mexico with the findings of the first and second sections in order to understand the broader and long-term implications.

— 6.1 The second phase: bilateral plans and trade negotiations —

During the second phase of the NAFTA environment debate, for most of the time the so-called parallel track efforts and border problems were the main issues. President Bush' parallel track strategy accentuated the domination of US concern about pollution at the border, and the fear of relocation of US industries to 'the other side'. The Mexican government did not resist this focus, which at least limited the scope of criticism. As noted in the previous chapter, not only the Border Plan, also the Environmental Review of the USTR mainly considered Mexico-US border issues. Environmental organizations criticized this limited geographical scope of official initiatives, but only a year after the start of the debate's second phase they began to come up with proposals for environmental safeguards. Whereas the negotiating teams presented NAFTA in August 1992 as the greenest trade agreement, both critical and moderate ENGOs condemned its environmental provisions.

THE BORDER PLAN AND OTHER BILATERAL PROGRAMMES

In August 1991, SEDUE and EPA released the draft for the first phase of the Integrated Environmental Plan for the Mexico-US Border Area (1992-1994). The objectives of the Border Plan were multiple (see also 5.2): enforcement of existing laws; reduction of pollution; increasing cooperative planning; training and education; and improving understanding of the border environment (SEDUE and EPA 1991). The presentation of the draft Border Plan was followed by ten public hearings in the US and seven in Mexico (organized by EPA and SEDUE respectively) to consult local communities on the plan. These attracted hundreds of people. Border environmental organizations testified at various of these hearings and submitted written comments.[1]

Border groups were very critical of the draft as they missed commitments, detailed programmes and financial arrangements for policy enforcement and infrastructure, and they were dissatisfied with the arrangements for public participation and access to environmental information.[2] Because of its vagueness on implementation, the draft was called a "plan to plan" and a scoping document. The draft did not mention the NAFTA, and EPA officials denied that the Plan was linked to the trade negotiations, whereas ENGOs wanted the plan to be incorporated in the NAFTA. Finally and fundamentally, the draft plan was criticized for its growth focus, instead of aiming at sustainable development (Gilbreath 1992a; Kamp 1991; Kelly 1991).

The release of the draft Border Plan and the subsequent public hearings attracted additional attention in the US for environmental problems in Mexico's border region. The US media presented a range of horror stories and pictures, and described the weaknesses of Mexican government agencies. While the governments presented the Border Plan as separate from NAFTA, it was an important issue in the transnational debate on the agreement. Apart from ENGO criticism, US labour unions illustrated their opposition to the agreement with examples of non-enforcement of environmental regulations in the *maquiladoras*. As a result, border environmental concerns became more and more articulated in US Congress.

The rapid response of the Mexican government to the border environment issue shows that it was greatly concerned about the effects of this negative publicity and criticism. In October 1991, SEDUE Minister Patricio Chirinos stressed that Mexico would not wait until the release of the final Border Plan but would start immediately to make improvements with a budget of $460 million. Nearly half of the funds would be spent on water supply and waste water treatment plans. Transportation infrastructure would consume another quarter, while municipal solid waste and territorial reserves for housing were two other areas for government support. Chirinos stressed that SEDUE was making major efforts to strictly enforce environmental legislation in the border region. The number of inspection personnel would be doubled to 200, and SEDUE's border budget was to increase by approximately 450 per cent to $6.3 million in 1992

---

1 Border organizations also organized two public forums (one in Mexico and one in the US) where they informally discussed the Border Plan's draft and the NAFTA plans with concerned citizens.

2 Border ENGOs extended the issue of participation to the role of the International Boundary and Water Commission (see chapter 2), demanding that either its mandate should be limited, or it should open up for broader public participation. Another proposal was the creation of a binational environmental and natural resources agency.

(Speech by Patricio Chirinos in Ciudad Juárez, 23/x/91). The fact that the English translation of Chirinos' speech was distributed in the US shows that these commitments were to boost Mexico's image on the "other side".

A few days after the speech of Chirinos, the trade ministers of Mexico, the US and Canada agreed to include labour and environmental issues in the NAFTA talks at a trilateral meeting in Zacatecas (25-27/x/91). The Zacatecas meeting marked the start of the second round of NAFTA negotiations, namely the beginning of drafting the trade agreement. While the trade ministers discussed the official agenda, a wide range of labour unions and NGOs from the three countries held a parallel international forum on alternatives in Zacatecas.[3] Environmental organizations presented their common transnational agenda, demanding as before (see 4.2): access to information and genuine public participation; legal mechanisms that allow for strong environmental protection in the three countries; a resource depletion tax and pollution prevention programmes; a regional environmental commission with NGO representation; and mechanisms to ensure sustainable use of resources.

In a joint press release produced in Zacatecas by the NWF and critical groups like the PGE, BEP and ACN, the official messages and the role of the environment in the agreement were questioned. While the US public was told that environmental issues would be integrated in the agreement, in Mexico they were portrayed as separate. These different messages clearly fitted the national political agendas. The US public and Congress had to be reassured that their environmental concerns were taken into account, whereas Mexicans feared that free trade with the US would entail increasing US political interference in Mexican affairs. In the context of Mexican concerns for NAFTA coming at the cost of state sovereignty, in Mexico the agreement was characterized as a purely commercial agreement.

The Border Plan was revised considerably after the hearings, including more issues and data, and the final version was released in February 1992.[4] During the three-year period of the plan, the two governments were to invest over $1 billion in cleaning up the border area. Mexico had already committed $460 million, but the US (with about 25 times Mexico's GDP) was only prepared to provide $380 for the first two years. Proponents praised the plan for being the most comprehensive border environment cooperation programme in the world, and the first extensive collaboration between a developing and a developed country. They claimed that there was a clear recognition that NGOs as well as business

---

3   A report of this meeting was produced by RMALC (1992).
4   According to Arídjis (1993: 3), the revision had minimal Mexican input.

organizations and local government agencies had to play key roles in the co-operation process (Atkeson 1992).

Conversely, despite the improvements, border ENGOs found the plan to fall short of the region's needs and criticized the commitments made by EPA and SEDUE.[5] The final plan was not, as environmental organizations had pleaded, directly linked to the NAFTA negotiations, nor did it strengthen the La Paz agreement between Mexico and the US on the border (see 2.3). Due to its focus on urban and industrial problems, many serious issues were still neglected. The final plan did not mention a new binational agency for environmental protec-tion, or at least a restructuring of the existing International Boundary and Water Commission, which was even given greater responsibilities as the major agency to deal with new funding. With respect to public participation and ac-cess to information, the final version of the plan did include some progress as compared to the draft, but proposals of Mexican groups for public access to policy documents and information on environmental hazards were not ad-dressed (Gilbreath 1992a: 27).[6]

The resources for the Border Plan seemed impressive, at least from the per-spective of Mexico's total government budget for environmental protection, but they were insufficient to deal with the existing border problems and the problems that were to be expected with continuous economic growth. A study performed by a border organization of business people and officials, for in-stance, estimated that the region's need for infrastructure projects required nearly $5.7 billion (Gilbreath 1992b: 165). Similarly, the U.S. Council of the Mexico-U.S. Business Committee (1993) concluded that approximately $6.5 billion was needed within a ten-year period in order to reach internationally acceptable standards for water supply, waste water, and waste disposal in the border region. With approximately $4.5 billion available through existing mechanisms, a gap of $2 billion remained. The US contribution of $380 mil-lion, then, was considered small, and nearly half of this sum had already been covered by planning. The plan did not include a funding mechanism for a pri-

---

5 Over half of the commitments involved information exchange, meetings, training and plant "visits", another 17 per cent concerned developing a plan or conducting a study, and 10 per cent of the commitments were basically promises to enforce existing laws (TCPS 1992: 1).

6 The Mexican and US governments each set up a border public advisory committee to advise their environmental Ministry, and to funnel information to local communities. Although lacking actual authority, in the US the committee did permit some public input into governmental border initiatives. In Mexico, however, the government never appointed the committee's members (Barry and Sims 1994: 86-7).

vate sector contribution to environmental protection, as environmental groups had proposed (Gilbreath 1992b: 166). The limited us resources for environmental protection in the border region showed that there was no genuine commitment to this matter, notwithstanding NGO pressure and government intentions for further economic integration.

The bilateral initiatives were useful in the sense of focusing political attention on the area and promoting cross-border cooperation between institutions. Rather than enforcement, the joint border activities had an education and info-sharing emphasis.[7] Implementation of plans to improve infrastructure and monitoring moved slowly. Other programmes were initiated for conservation, and plans were made for sister reserves on both sides of the border. As a side effect of government attention and efforts, it became somewhat easier to attract private finance for projects such as the construction of water infrastructure (Barry and Sims 1994: 77; Meacham 1993: 278, 280).

Besides this border focus, us and Canadian involvement in other Mexican environmental affairs also expanded during the NAFTA debate. One way in which us-Mexico environmental relations changed was through programmes of the us Agency for International Development (USAID). USAID increasingly supported the protection of rain forests and energy efficiency, as well as NGOs working on environmental education. Mexico and Canada signed an agreement for environmental cooperation for 1992 and 1993. Within this context, the Canadian government supported Mexico's institutional reinforcement with Canadian $1 million annually (Mexican government source 17/x/95). These bilateral initiatives for environmental protection were beneficial to Mexico, but were ad hoc efforts to deal with structural problems.

ENVIRONMENTAL REVIEW

In February 1992, besides the Border Plan, the Environmental Review prepared by the office of the USTR was released (see 5.2). The general conclusion of the Review was that the NAFTA would not lead to more degradation of Mexico's border environment as compared to a no-NAFTA scenario. This prognosis was based on the idea that NAFTA would only moderately affect border growth while stimulating us-Mexican environmental cooperation, modernization of certain

---

7 Among other things, bilateral efforts involved data collection, training, technology transfers and pollution monitoring. For instance, the us funded inspector training and the Environmental Technology Clearinghouse, a computerized data system indexing more than 500 databases on pollution control and energy conservation techniques.

Mexican economic sectors, and the end of the notorious *maquiladoras* as such. The Review discounted the view that NAFTA would stimulate the location of polluting production in Mexico (USTR 1992a, Executive Summary: 4-7).[8]

Like the Border Plan, the Environmental Review was an important subject for transnational activism. A draft of the Review released in October 1991 received considerable criticism from environmental organizations. For instance, NRDC, INAINE and Grupo de los Cien (1991) jointly wrote a report on this draft, arguing that the Review ignored potential environmental impacts of NAFTA outside the US-Mexico border area, that the recommended measures of funding and institutional arrangements were inadequate, and that alternatives proposed by ENGOs were not examined. In their opinion, the Review produced far too little evidence to support its conclusion that NAFTA would be positive for Mexico's environment. The NWF commented on the draft Review's suggestion that environmental degradation in Mexico would be reduced because NAFTA would cause an investment flow away from the border. While this tendency was most probable, NWF argued that it would not result in a reduction in net pollution, but that the burden on the environment and environmental agencies in Mexico would increase. Due to its border focus, however, the draft Review did not touch upon the environmental effects of a spreading of *maquiladoras* throughout Mexico (NWF 1991). In January 1992, INAINE, NRDC and NWF organized a regional forum in Mexico City, where a large number of NGOs gathered to discuss NAFTA-related environmental issues.

The final version of the Review was labelled inaccurate by most environmental organizations. One point of criticism concerned the failure to outline mechanisms or provisions to protect environmental standards from being attacked as barriers to free trade (Barry and Sims 1994: 76). Environmental organizations were also disappointed that despite their comments the Review gave little attention to environmental issues outside the Mexico-US border region. The USTR (1992a: 4) defended this void by claiming that an analysis of NAFTA's environmental consequences in the interior of Mexico was not feasible. Like the Border Plan, the Review focused on industrial environmental effects. While it did consider wildlife conservation, natural resource depletion was largely absent.

---

8 As analyzed in chapter 5, these rather optimistic conclusions were a simplification of the report's calculations.

MINIMAL ENVIRONMENTAL SAFEGUARDS

After the Border Plan and the Environmental Review had been released and debated, environmental organizations worked on proposals for minimal environmental safeguards in the NAFTA. Hardly any information on the negotiations was available, with the exception of a copy of the NAFTA draft that leaked out to environmental organizations on 23 March 1992, the so-called Dallas Composite. As a result, ENGOs worked on "green" provisions that could be included in the Dallas Composite. While there were various transnational contacts on these safeguards, they were largely developed by ENGOs cooperating at the national level.

In May 1992, Mexico's UGAM sent a text for Environmental Safeguard Clauses in NAFTA to Mexico's Trade Minister Serra Puche. As one of UGAM's advisors was a prominent environmental lawyer, these proposals were in the form of agreement articles, something which gave the proposals as well as the UGAM a certain standing in Mexico and beyond. UGAM proposed to maintain the most stringent environmental standards, that environmental impact assessments of any policy or activity that might have environmental effects should be obligatory, and the creation of an independent panel to control NAFTA's environmental impact based on as much public participation as possible.[9]

In the US, a group of national and border organizations started drawing up minimal safeguards, but their opinions differed over the contents. As a result, in June NWF presented a proposal together with Canada's Pollution Probe, which was endorsed by the EDF. The proposal dealt with issues like the harmonization of environmental standards, public participation, having the most stringent environmental standards prevail, and the creation of a North American Committee on Trade and the Environment with monitoring, investigating, recommending and enforcing tasks. Simultaneously, the NRDC released its safeguards position, which was endorsed by three border organizations and eleven national ENGOs, including moderate and critical groups. Organizations in the US-Mexican border region also wrote a separate letter to the negotiators in July with a list of solutions to environmental problems that were urgent with or without NAFTA.

The environmentalists' demands for environmental safeguards were adopted by several Members of the US Congress.[10] Although the Bush administration

---

9 While UGAM later opposed trade sanctions (the suspension of some of the abandoned trade tariffs under the agreement) in the event of non-enforcement of environmental policy, the May 1992 proposal allowed the panel to suspend a country's membership of the agreement completely.

was not willing to make many environmental commitments, the fact that in-fluential members of Congress responded positively to proposals of environ-mental organizations was crucial for the latter's influence. As before, the adop-tion of environmentalist ideas by Congress legitimized these ideas within the US political arena, and brought them into the heart of the decision-making on NAFTA. Again, due to these circumstances and the asymmetries of the three countries, US ideas and interests dominated the NAFTA environment debate, both at the governmental and non-governmental level.

A month before the trade negotiations were finished, 51 organizations from the three countries signed a joint letter to the NAFTA negotiators. In this July 1992 letter they urged the inclusion of environmental safeguard clauses in NAFTA as proposed by ENGOS. They stressed that despite differences in details, their proposals for elements to be integrated in the agreement's text were largely similar: public participation; improved enforcement of environmental legisla-tion; more funding for ecological programmes; and protection of environmen-tal standards and laws at the national, state and local level. The 51 signatories stated that their support for NAFTA depended on this inclusion.

NAFTA'S ENVIRONMENTAL PROVISIONS

The NAFTA does not contain an environmental chapter. Instead, it deals with environmental protection in several chapters. The preamble (introductory chapter) of the agreement describes some general goals, also regarding the envi-ronment. It states that the elimination of trade barriers will be pursued consist-ently with environmental protection and conservation. The importance of en-vironmental concerns is recognized, sustainable development will be pro-moted, the development of environmental laws and legislation will be encour-aged and the enforcement of environmental standards strengthened. Although these general aims express the recognition of a link between trade and environ-ment, they are unenforceable because they are only included in the preamble and not in the agreement itself.[11]

---

10 Especially the position of Senator Max Baucus (a free trade proponent and chairman of two congressional committees) was important. He argued that under NAFTA environ-mental legislation should not be treated as trade barriers; that a commitment should be included to ensure that future growth, trade and investment would be environmentally sound; and that there would be an ongoing review of the environmental commitments and impact of the agreement (Shrybman 1993: 285-7).

11 On the other hand, it has been argued that the environmental language in this sec-

Two relatively strong environmental sections of the agreement concern sanitary and phytosanitary measures[12] (chapter 7B) and standards-related measures (chapter 9), which may be partly due to the stress on the importance of high standards by US ENGOs and Congress. With respect to human, animal and plant life or health, the agreement establishes the right of a party (any government that has signed the agreement) to set its own "appropriate level of protection" in order to protect its citizens (art. 712.1), while each country has the right to maintain and enforce its environmental, health and safety standards, if necessary by prohibiting import of products that do not meet domestic standards (art. 904.1). However, no distinction is made between standards regulating the finished product and standards regulating the production process. This omission restricts a country's ability to ban imports of goods that are produced in an environmentally unfriendly way (Houseman and Orbuch 1993: 735-9).

Other provisions are similarly ambiguous with respect to the tension between national environmental standards and free trade. Parties have the right to determine the acceptable level of risk with respect to the protection of environment, health and safety, and in case of absence of adequate scientific information to do so, the parties are free to use available information (art. 904.2 and 907). On the other hand, the agreement prohibits environmental standards that create an "unnecessary obstacle" to trade (art. 904.4). If the GATT's interpretation of "necessary" is followed, only the "least trade restrictive" regulation available to attain the end sought would be acceptable (Housman and Orbuch 1993: 741).[13] According to the agreement, sanitary and phytosanitary measures may not create a disguised restriction on trade (art. 712.6). However, what may be a legitimate measure for one party could be viewed as a disguised trade restriction by another (Housman and Orbuch 1993: 742).

NAFTA's harmonization provisions contain stronger environmental components than the GATT. The use of international standards is required (art. 501.1), and domestic regulatory standards can be higher than international measures (art. 905.3). In other words, international measures determine minimal and not maximal levels of protection. The parties are encouraged to harmonize their regulations (art. 906.2), and—contrary to GATT's toleration of downward harmonization of standards— "upward harmonization" principles are introduced

---

tion of the agreement is important since the preamble forms the basis for interpretation, implementation and dispute settlement (Hustis 1993: 621).

12 These measures are to protect human, animal or plant life from risks associated with pests, diseases, toxics, contaminants, and additives in food.

13 Based on this GATT interpretation, asbestos-producing Canada opposed a US ban on imports of products containing asbestos.

(art. 714 and 906). However, principles and encouragement are rather weak as compared to obligations.

Dispute settlement (chapter 20B) within NAFTA takes place through a three-step resolution process, consisting of consultation, settlement by the Free Trade Commission, and an arbitration panel. An arbitration panel may seek the opinion of NGOs or request a group of independent scientists to write a report. However, citizens and other interested actors are not allowed to submit documents on their own initiative, only parties (governments) are allowed to participate in the resolution process (art. 2004 and 2013), and panel activities and reports are confidential (art. 2012.1B). NAFTA's provisions place the burden of proof on the complaining nation (art. 914.4 and 723.6), in contrast with GATT arrangements where the offended country has to prove that its policy is consistent with the free trade provisions. As a result of this difference, a country that raises its environmental standards has in general a stronger position under NAFTA than under GATT provisions.

With regard to certain international environmental agreements, an exception is made to the rule that the NAFTA takes priority over other international agreements between the parties. In the event of a contradiction of NAFTA with the Convention on the International Trade in Endangered Species (CITES), the Montreal Protocol (on ozone depleting substances) or the Basel Convention (on hazardous substances), these three environmental agreements prevail (art. 104). This is also the case for the La Paz agreement between Mexico and the US on the environmental improvement of the border region. International environmental agreements or conventions that are approved by all the parties in the future will also predominate over NAFTA obligations. Existing agreements, however, need to be explicitly added to the NAFTA in order to prevail, therefore greatly depending on the political willingness of all parties.[14] Moreover, a party has to choose the means of complying with the environmental obligation that is most consistent with NAFTA, as long as these means are equally effective and reasonable available. Vagueness on this part of article 104 might form a loophole for challenges to environmental measures (Hustis 1993: 622).

Environmental considerations with respect to investments are also dealt with in the NAFTA (chapter 11A). The parties are allowed to take measures "to ensure that investment activity in its territory is undertaken in a manner sensitive to environmental concerns" (art. 1114.1). Relaxing domestic environmental, health or safety measures to encourage investment is labelled "inappropriate"

---

14 The NAFTA thus breaks with international trade law tradition, and renders environmental agreements less vulnerable.

(art. 1114.2). The article states that a party *should* (instead of *shall*) not waive from such measures as an encouragement for investments, and that if a party considers that another party has offered such an encouragement, it may request consultations with the other party (and no dispute settlement). In other words, instead of an obligation, only an unenforceable recommendation is made with respect to lowering environmental standards for the encouragement of investments.

CRITICISM OF THE ENVIRONMENTAL PROVISIONS

Whereas high-level US officials claimed that the NAFTA was the greenest trade agreement ever negotiated, environmental organizations in the three countries were widely dissatisfied. Their main points of criticism were:

1 The lack of enforcement mechanisms to deal with a country that does not implement its environmental legislation;
2 the lack of "strong" language on upward harmonization, and the failure to adopt minimal environmental standards;
3 the omission of arrangements to finance environmental infrastructure and cleaning up operations;
4 the lack of transparency and opportunities for public participation;
5 the failure to establish an environmental commission.

With respect to the first point, the trade agreement did not contain mechanisms, such as the withdrawal of trade benefits (a form of trade sanction), for the enforcement of a country's environmental laws. On point 2, upward mobilization principles with respect to environmental standards were included but not mandatory. Harmonization of environmental standards was encouraged, but process standards and a time-table for harmonization were not included. As to the third point, while financial restrictions had been an important limitation on the enforcement of Mexico's environmental legislation, and the Mexico-US border region was in great need of environmental infrastructure, the NAFTA did not arrange for funding, such as a tax or levy on direct foreign investment to use some of the NAFTA revenues for environmental purposes, and the creation of a trilateral fund. In this respect, environmental organizations in Mexico and the US continued to oppose the decision of the governments to deal with the border problems on a "parallel track". Compared to the demands of environmental organizations for public participation, the fourth point of criticism, NAFTA's provisions were poor. Citizens' "right to know" was not guaranteed, and ENGOs could hardly participate in dispute settlement, let alone challenge a country. Finally, NAFTA provisions did not provide for a trinational environmental commission which could serve as a forum for public participation, monitor the environmental situation in North America, and enforce NAFTA's environmental provisions.

An issue widely criticized in Mexico and Canada was that NAFTA only dealt with pollution control and nature conservation, while excluding the use of natural resources. Even though NAFTA's preamble mentions the promotion of sustainable development, which is internationally recognized (in the Declaration of Río) to include access to natural resources and a rational distribution of their costs and benefits, natural resource issues were not incorporated in the agreement. The absence of measures in NAFTA dealing with future changes in the use of natural resources could lead to environmental degradation, but also to social problems since growing demands for and a polarizing access to natural resources could have serious consequences at the social level too (Sánchez 1993: 8-9). The Mexican government was accused of partly evading NAFTA's provision on the inappropriateness of relaxing environmental measures to encourage investment (art. 1114) through the 1992 reforms of natural resources legislation. According to Mexican ENGOs, these reforms effectively dismantled legislation on forestry, water, mining, fishery, tourism and land use (Székely, undated).

The strong environmentalist criticism of NAFTA contributed to additional arrangements. Shortly after the completion of the trade agreement and transnational ENGO disapproval, in September 1992, the three governments agreed in principle to the creation of a North American Commission on the Environment (NACE). This agreement was initiated by the US in order to address some of the environmentalist concerns. At the time the governments approved the creation of NACE, its functions and jurisdiction were not defined. The general goal of NACE would be to raise environmental standards and enforcement practices. Despite this concession, no environmental organization except the NWF endorsed NAFTA. ENGOs demanded that NACE perform independent research, publish annual environmental reports and function as a policy forum. During the following year, the NAFTA environment debate focused on a supplemental environmental agreement. This third phase of the NAFTA environment debate will be analyzed in the following section.

— 6.2 The third phase:
the supplemental environmental agreement —

As the position of the US Congress on NAFTA remained largely negative, despite the agreement on an environmental commission, Bush decided to delay the vote on NAFTA ratification until after the US presidential elections that were to be held in November.[15] As a result, the NAFTA became an electoral issue. While Bush vigorously supported NAFTA, Clinton was uncertain and requested input from organizations that supported his candidacy. The Sierra Club and Friends of the Earth encouraged Clinton to reject the NAFTA text, but NWF and WWF urged him to endorse it and helped him to develop his position. Other factors of influence were Clinton's reliance on US business support, and the general tendency among US presidents to reject protectionism (Audley 1995: 17; Audley and Uslaner 1994: 32, 34). In October, Clinton announced that he would support NAFTA on condition of supplemental agreements for the protection of the environment and workers. The main aim of these agreements would be to ensure that NAFTA countries would enforce their own environmental and labour legislation, and to prevent lax enforcement from attracting companies. In October 1992, a start was made with trilateral discussions on the Environmental Commission NACE, but the meetings were called off by Mexico and Canada until after the US presidential elections.

Bill Clinton was elected as the new US President in November, and his position on NAFTA produced tensions in the trilateral relations. The Mexican and Canadian governments were reluctant to negotiate supplemental agreements, and even more to renegotiate the NAFTA text. Both Mexico and Canada feared US interference, in particular since about one-third of the House of Representatives opposed NAFTA. Especially the Mexican government was in a problematic position, as it very much wanted NAFTA but had to accept demands that were largely directed at removing US public concern about integration with the Mexican economy. At first, there was still unclarity on whether Clinton wanted the original NAFTA text to be reopened, but at a meeting with President Salinas in January 1993 he promised not to do so.

During the third phase of the NAFTA environment debate, the lax enforcement issue gave rise to a heated fight over sanctions. Some US members of Congress wanted sanctions as an ultimate penalty for dispute settlement for countries or industries that did not enforce environmental policy. They argued that a dispute panel should have the right to impose a fine (economic sanction) or to suspend some of the trade advantages of NAFTA (returning to pre-NAFTA trade tariffs). The latter kind of sanctions are trade sanctions, which may cause considerable damage to the producers of goods involved. The Mexican and

---

15 Delay seemed better as NAFTA was not popular with the electorate, and a pro-NAFTA vote could seriously harm a member of Congress' chances during the forthcoming elections.

Canadian governments resisted trade sanctions because of the North American asymmetric relations.

Despite Clinton's decision not to renegotiate the NAFTA, critical US organizations decided to work with the new president in order to make the supplemental agreement satisfy their demands. On March 4, a large number of critical US ENGOs sent a letter to the US negotiator on the supplemental agreement. Their concerns and proposals corresponded to the five points of criticism mentioned above, calling for sufficient funding (for environmental cleaning up operations, the trilateral commission's administration and the creation of a regional development bank), an enforcement mechanism, clarification on environmental standards, more public participation in dispute settlement, and a strong regional environmental commission. The enforcement mechanism should at least consist of access to domestic courts by private parties (for compensation from individuals and companies), and the possibility of trade remedies in cases of continuous lax enforcement or transboundary / global pollution.

The negotiating team under Clinton predominantly intensified cooperation with moderate environmental organizations.[16] The limited overture to critical groups was the result of the domestic and regional political situation with respect to NAFTA. Although there was a need to satisfy some environmentalist demands to obtain sufficient US congressional support for ratificaion, there was also (Republican) pressure in Congress opposing stronger environmental safeguards. Moreover, the Mexican and Canadian negotiators resisted these safeguards. Consequently, the environmental opposition had to be weakened by the Clinton administration for NAFTA to pass, and the attitude towards ENGOs became increasingly stratified.

Moderate US environmental organizations reacted strategically to this impasse by lowering their demands. The reinforced split of moderate and critical ENGOs, then, was not only the result of Clinton's strategy, but also a deliberate step by the main moderate groups (advisor to ENGOs 28/IX/95). On May 4 1993, the so-called "Group of Seven" (Defenders of Wildlife, EDF, the National

---

16 There were no new environmentalists added to USTR trade committees, and Friends of the Earth, Greenpeace and Public Citizen received limited attention. On the other hand, NRDC was for instance contacted for a proposal on citizens rights related to the environment, which was adopted by the US government and presented to Mexico and Canada in May1993 (Spalding 1995: 146).

Audubon Society, NRDC, NWF, Nature Conservancy and the WWF) wrote a letter to US Trade Representative Mickey Kantor, in which they declared they would support NAFTA if a number of provisions were included in the supplemental agreement. INAINE (Mexico) and Pollution Probe (Canada) took similar positions. The May 4 provisions went less far than the ones proposed by critical organizations. Funding for the creation of a regional development bank was no longer a demand. The Environmental Commission would not need to have the authority to impose or recommend trade sanctions. Access to domestic courts by private parties in Mexico and Canada was not mentioned either. On the other hand, within six months of NAFTA's implementation, a start would have to be made to negotiate production process standards. Although critical organizations and some influential Congress members in the US did not agree with the moderate position, the May 4 letter became the standard by which the NAFTA was judged in the US (Audley and Uslaner 1994: 32-4).

In Mexico, trade sanctions were the most sensitive issue of the supplemental agreement, also among environmental organizations. Although the May 4 letter of moderate US ENGOs no longer mentioned trade remedies as a NAFTA tool to enforce environmental policy, the US negotiating team left the demand on the table. Mexican environmental organizations generally opposed the inclusion of trade sanctions as they feared US abuse of trade sanctions for economic reasons under the guise of environmental protection (according to Mexicans this had happened with the dolphin/tuna case, see 3.2). With the asymmetric relation between Mexico and the US, Mexican ENGOs expected that the US would have more success in imposing trade sanctions on Mexico than vice versa. In addition, Mexican environmentalists were not convinced that trade sanctions would automatically serve the environment. They wanted to make sure the sanctions would really affect the contaminators and serve to undo the damage, instead of serving as pretexts to contaminate in exchange for money (cf. Restrepo 1993).

According to UGAM the US sanction proposals were clearly directed at Mexico and were totally unacceptable, as they would infringe on state sovereignty. Instead, UGAM proposed that the Environmental Commission include an independent group of experts from governmental and non-governmental sectors. In the event of a country's allowing industry to exceed an environmental standard, the group's most powerful instrument would be exposure of such information to public scrutiny. For the sake of transparency, all meetings and documentation should be open to the public. As a possible way of funding it proposed a 1 per cent tax on cross-border trade for environmental protection (UGAM 1993).

RMALC proposed to complement the trilateral Environmental Commission with a Mexican commission in order to protect sovereignty and allow for a strong and effective institution at the same time. The Mexican Commission would have the authority to produce studies, recommendations, and action plans. Instead of the trilateral commission, this independent national commission would recommend sanctions in cases of non-compliance with environmental laws and standards that harm the environment or health. In the view of RMALC, the creation of a North American Fund or Bank for Environment and Development was necessary to solve existing environmental problems and to finance the regional and Mexican Environmental Commission (RMALC 1993a).

To a limited extent, involvement of Mexican environmental organizations in the negotiations on the supplemental agreement increased via the Mexican government. In contrast to the period of the trade negotiations, during the supplemental agreement negotiations there was for instance formal contact between RMALC and SECOFI. However, this contact was disappointing for RMALC as it did not involve genuine exchange (Mexican ENGO source 23/V/94). Moderate Mexican ENGOs had somewhat better access to government officials and were allowed a more constructive role in the negotiation process. There are indications of involvement by UGAM and the Group of Hundred in discussions of the Mexican team and working groups during the negotiations.[17]

In Canada, ENGOs were largely critical of the official plans for the supplemental agreement and cynical of the supplemental negotiations. Canadian organizations were concerned that the natural resources issue would again be neglected, and that the supplemental agreement would not protect stringent local and provincial environmental legislation sufficiently. While Pollution Probe joined several transnational proposals, critical groups felt that Canada had little influence in the negotiations, therefore not expecting to have leverage. This explains why most Canadian organizations did not come up with proposals, but focused on analyzing the official processes (see 4.2). Limited input was nonetheless realized via the membership of seven representatives of ENGOs in the ad hoc consultancy group that was created by the government for the supplemental environmental agreement.

The transnational environmentalist relations during the third phase of the NAFTA debate were marked by a deepened distinction between the moderate and critical groups. The increased access of US moderate ENGOs to their negotiating team complicated the links with Mexican counterparts. As it was clear that support of some major US organizations was needed for ratification of the

---

17 While two interviewees (Mexican academic source 15/IV/94; Mexican government source 5/X/95) mentioned this, information on the role of these organizations is absent. The interviewed members of the ENGOs in question never mentioned involvement, but this may be due to the fear of being labelled 'co-opted'.

agreement, Mexican groups tried to influence US organizations. However, this was an unbalanced situation (US ENGO source 12/IV/94). Moreover, the trade sanction issue entailed an estrangement between Mexican and US moderates. Mexican ENGOs opposed trade sanctions, and although moderate US organizations like the NWF and the WWF did not demand sanctions, they did not support the Mexican position either.

On the other hand, critical organizations from the three countries made efforts to overcome their differences and prepare a transnational critical position. After a transnational meeting in Washington in March 1993, critical organizations and networks started to develop a joint document entitled *A Just and Sustainable Trade and Development Initiative for North America*. As before, they protested against secrecy of the official NAFTA process, the agreement's focus on the movement of goods and capital, and the prevalence of the interests of large companies, while presenting a set of alternatives for starting anew with regional integration.[18]

Although critical groups had been working together for some time since the beginning of the NAFTA debate and were agreed on many issues, sanctions continued to divide them. US and Canadian ENGOs proposed to use trade sanctions against countries for compliance with minimal regional environmental standards (which would have to be developed). Mexican groups organized in RMALC strongly objected to such sanctions. They proposed that polluting firms clean up the environmental damage inflicted, rather than having them pay for the damage, as direct corporate responsibility for environmental damage would avoid bureaucracy and corruption. US organizations preferred wider measures, because in their view non-compliance of companies generally implies a lack of responsibility of governmental institutions as well, and wide sanctions would be an incentive for more effort and control from that side as well.[19] In the final document released in September 1993, proposals for fines and trade sanctions were excluded, while the Polluter Repairs principle was adopted.

---

18 The document focused on: new principles for North American economic integration (including respect for basic human rights, promotion of democracy, environmental sustainability, and the reduction of economic inequalities); measures for addressing inequalities (funding mechanisms, reform of multilateral institutions, debt reduction and trade adjustment); international rules on corporate activities, concerning labour and environmental rights and standards, as well as codes of conduct for companies; policies for sustainable development; and the Mexico-US border. Several drafts of this document circulated in the summer of 1993, and the final version was released on September 28.

19 The differences in views of the organizations emerge from the draft version of 30/VIII/93.

PRIVATE SECTOR POSITION

The US presidential shift changed the role of the US private sector in the NAFTA environment debate. While Bush's parallel track approach had coincided with the position of the private sector (see 5.2), the latter opposed Clinton's idea of supplemental agreements. When it turned out that these agreements were likely to be added to NAFTA, US private sector organizations started to take the initiative on environmental issues. In March 1993, the US business community came up with a proposal on the supplemental environmental agreement, supporting the creation of a regional environmental commission that would encourage cooperation, discussion and information-sharing. They opposed a commission that would hear citizen or NGO complaints, investigate these complaints, and impose penalties or trade sanctions on non-enforcing countries or companies. However, the US business community found that Clinton's team was not very accessible to them (in contrast with the Bush administration). On the other hand, the US business community was in constant contact with the SECOFI representative in Washington DC, while there were also meetings with Mexican business organizations (US private sector source 19/IV/94).

These contacts with SECOFI followed from the similarities of the position of the US private sector and the Mexican (as well as the Canadian) government on the supplemental agreements. No supranational powers for the environmental commission, no trade sanctions, no environmental taxes, and no obligatory harmonization of environmental standards were their main demands. US business opposed the May 4 letter of moderate US ENGOs on two points. First, a high degree of independence of the Environmental Commission's secretariat was in their view unacceptable, and especially the authority to investigate private interests was condemned. Second, they would not agree to a clarification of NAFTA standards if this changed the nature of the trade provisions (*Inside U.S. Trade* 7/V/1993: S-2).

Mexico's private sector continued to be hardly active on environmental issues. Few individuals in Mexico's private sector were interested in the negotiation of the supplemental agreement on the environment, and they were seldom involved (Mexican government source 5/X/95). According to a US private sector source (19/IV/94), the Mexican government mainly told the Mexican private sector what to do on environmental issues. Interestingly, in a poll among 260 Mexican business executives 74 per cent supported the idea of a trilateral environmental commission, because in their view it would help to eliminate corruption, ensure compliance with environmental laws and improve vigilance through shared responsibility (*Expansion* 7/VII/1993).

THE NEGOTIATIONS

The negotiations on the supplemental environmental agreement were long and troublesome as a result of four factors. First, the reason to negotiate the agreement was largely internal US politics, and in none of the negotiating teams (not even the US) was there real conviction and motivation to establish the supplemental agreement. Second, as NAFTA support in the US Congress was tight, the pressure on the negotiators was larger than usual. Third, the US demands very much contrasted with Mexico's and Canada's position. Due to the asymmetries between the US on the one hand and the two other countries on the other hand, US proposals that seemed to infringe on state sovereignty were very sensitive for Mexico and Canada. Fourth, there was no international experience with environmental supplements to trade agreements. In short, unmotivated negotiating teams that violently disagreed with one another had to come to grips with a rather innovative issue.

The most problematic issues of the negotiations were dispute settlement and the authority of the environmental commission. Although the May 4 letter of the main moderate ENGOs in the US no longer demanded trade sanctions as a means of enforcing NAFTA provisions on the environment, the US negotiating team considered that sanctions were necessary for congressional ratification of the NAFTA. It was a major issue for the Mexican as well as the Canadian government because it touched upon state sovereignty.

Linked to the dispute settlement issue, the US focus on Mexico's non-enforcement of environmental legislation was perceived by the Mexican government as prejudiced and exaggerated, motivated by protectionist US tendencies. Rather than non-enforcement, government officials pointed to non-compliance by companies as the main weakness. While a government can be held as much accountable for non-enforcement as for non-compliance, there is an important difference between the two. Non-compliance by companies implies a lack of consciousness and government control (and punishment), which can be mended by more information and inspections. This is largely a matter of resources, training and time. Non-enforcement of legislation, on the other hand, is associated with a lack of priority or willingness, and Mexican government officials resisted this perception.

The US enforcement focus also contrasted with the Mexican preference for a supplemental agreement stimulating cooperation instead of arranging punishment and creating a supranational commission. There was great concern for US paternalism and domination, a fear that sanctions might be abused for US protectionist purposes, and doubts as to whether the US environmental aims were sincere. There were similar sentiments in Canada. A Canadian government source (21/IX/95) claimed that the side agreements were mainly for Clinton to show the Congress that he had succeeded vis-à-vis the other countries, since proposals by the Canadian and Mexican negotiators for progressive environmental safeguards were refused by the US. Despite these similarities, the Mexican and Canadian teams did not form an alliance in the supplemental negotiations. Canada was less concerned than Mexico, as US proposals were primarily designed to deal with Mexico's weak policy enforcement.

Perception of the negotiating process differed within Mexico's team. Among SEDESOL officials, there was irritation and frustration because of the enormous US criticism and the lack of credibility in the advances made in Mexico (Mexican government source 7/IV/94). SECOFI officials wanted NAFTA to be implemented and were less critical of the supplemental agreement than SEDESOL officials were. The Mexican team as a whole objected to US proposals for changing Mexico's laws in order to enable citizens to start a lawsuit against government institutions (*Inside U.S. Trade* 21/V/1993; 24/V/1993). Mexico also resisted transparency of the regional Environmental Commission, as it had experienced that negative information could be used for US mobilization against Mexico.

On some issues the US government clearly mirrored the proposals of moderate US ENGOS. This was the case with their proposals for a relatively independent Environmental Commission's secretariat with investigating authority on citizens' complaints; a regional (not national) public advisory board; public access to the Environmental Commission's Council; the opportunity for citizens to submit complaints; and citizens' right to know. These positions were all in opposition to the Mexican negotiators' position. With respect to sanctions and the reporting functions of the Environmental Commission, the US government's proposals were somewhat less far-reaching than those of the moderate environmentalists. On harmonization of environmental legislation and prevalence of higher domestic laws, ENGO proposals were not adopted by the US government.[20]

At the last stage, during the summer of 1993, the negotiations went through a phase of secrecy and seemingly endless struggle, and final dates were postponed several times. Press releases gave little information, and statements of considerable progress and an imminent conclusion of negotiations alternated with statements of serious obstacles. Regarding the negotiation process in general, the time-span of these final negotiations, and the ambivalent press releases, the conflicts were probably very large. This impression is supported by interviews with government officials who were involved in the supplemental

---

20 This comparison is based on an overview by Kelly (1993a).

negotiation process.[21] The negotiations on the supplemental agreements on the environment and labour were concluded in August 1993.[22]

While the supplemental environmental agreement was being negotiated, Sierra Club, Friends of the Earth and Public Citizen were involved in a lawsuit versus the Clinton administration. On June 30, a federal judge decided that the administration first had to make an Environmental Impact Statement (EIS) on NAFTA before it could have Congress vote on ratification. This decision was based on the National Environmental Policy Act (NEPA) that requires impact statements on significant governmental actions affecting the environment. For both sides the verdict came as a surprise. Critical organizations hoped that this decision would buy time for a more thorough analysis and debate concerning NAFTA's environmental implications. NAFTA proponents worried that the decision would derail NAFTA because an environmental impact assessment could take many months and would prevent NAFTA from coming into force on the first day of 1994 as planned.[23] The Clinton administration, however, besides lodging an appeal against the judge's decision, continued the negotiations on the supplemental agreements as before. In August, the administration won the appeal.

THE NORTH AMERICAN AGREEMENT ON ENVIRONMENTAL COOPERATION

The obligations of the supplemental environmental agreement reinforce some of the environmental provisions of NAFTA. The agreement requires each NAFTA

---

21 There is, however, another explanation, according to a Mexican government source (9/XIII/93), namely that the whole thing was a "puppet-show", arranged to give the impression of a troublesome process. The aim of giving such an impression would be to convince US critics of the Clinton administration's perseverance. Critics would have to believe that the outcome was the ultimate that could be reached and that renegotiation would not produce any other results.

22 Mumme and Stevis (1995) provide a useful comparison of the Labour and Environmental Cooperation Agreements from the perspective of social regulation of capital mobility. According to information gathered in my interviews, the negotiations on the labour agreement were more complicated because it was a more sensitive and controversial issue, not only between the countries but also between unions and the corporate sector.

23 According to Gilbreath and Tonra (1994: 54), most moderate US ENGOs, "particularly those that had set up offices in Mexico and undertaken cooperative programs with the Mexican government, were disturbed by the federal district court rule for a NAFTA-related EIS".

country to report periodically on the state of the environment and the NAFTA environmental impact. Environmental education, research, technological development and the use of economic instruments are to be promoted (art. 2). A party may establish its own levels of environmental protection (art. 3). This last point can be positive for a country that wants high standards, which might otherwise be considered as obstructing free trade, but it also allows a country to establish low legal standards.

The supplemental agreement on the environment provides for the creation of an environmental commission. The Commission for Environmental Co-operation (CEC, instead of NACE) comprises of a council, a secretariat and a public advisory committee. The Council consists of the three cabinet-level environmental representatives: the Mexican Minister of Social Development, the EPA Administrator, and Canada's Minister of the Environment. As the governing body, the Council oversees all CEC activities. The trilateral Secretariat has about 32 members of staff to support the Council and the committees created by the Council. The Joint Public Advisory Committee (JPAC) with 15 members (5 from each country) may advise the Council and provide technical information to the Secretariat. The supplemental agreement allows each party to convene a national advisory committee.

Central to the supplemental agreement is article 5, that requires each party to enforce its environmental laws effectively. If not, dispute settlement may be set in motion, the process of which is very complex.[24] The CEC is the institution responsible for responding to allegations of non-enforcement of environmental laws. This happens through one of two procedures. First, if the complainant is a person or an NGO, the CEC's Secretariat decides whether a response by the accused party is called for. If this is the case, the party must respond, unless it states that the matter is the subject of a pending judicial or administrative proceeding, which means the end of the investigation. After this response the Secretariat may require a factual record to be prepared, at least if the Council approves this with a two-thirds vote, which is the ultimate "penalty" under this procedure. The Council also has to approve with a two-thirds vote for this report to become public (even to the complainant).

The second procedure is triggered if the complainant is a party, who must allege a "persistent pattern" to "effectively enforce" an environmental law.[25]

---

24 What follows is a very condensed description of the agreement's dispute settlement provisions as described by Van Pelt (1994: 129-32).

25 The rather broad definitions of the two terms are advantageous to the accused party. The effective enforcement definition, for instance, seems to allow a party to escape responsibility for non-enforcement in the event of insufficient resources.

This procedure starts with a request for consultations. If the matter is not resolved, this is followed by a special session of the Council, an evaluation by experts, and actual dispute settlement by an arbitration panel. In the event of non-enforcement, this panel can first recommend the implementation of an action plan by the accused party. In case of disagreement on the action plan or non-implementation of the plan, the panel may order a country to pay a fine.[26] Due to this large and complex process, it is unlikely that a party will actually be faced with a fine.

The response to non-payment of the fine was the most problematic negotiation issue, as both Mexico and Canada resisted the application of trade sanctions. At a very late stage, Canada managed to escape trade sanctions through a special arrangement in the agreement. If Mexico or the US fails to pay a fine, the panel can impose trade sanctions in the form of a withdrawal of NAFTA benefits and a return to pre-NAFTA trade tariffs. In the case of Canada, the national courts can enforce the NAFTA order (no appeal possible). In short, fines and trade sanctions for countries that do not enforce their environmental laws are a novelty in free trade agreements, but the supplemental agreement contains a range of provisions that can prevent such measures from being used, even in the event of a clear violation of the supplemental agreement.

In the text of the supplemental environmental agreement, the Secretariat of the CEC is less powerful with respect to disputes than in US proposals. This was an important concession to Mexican fear of supranational influence and transparency. The governments presented the CEC as an agency that would stimulate and support a range of environmental processes: public debate, domestic enforcement of laws, and regional cooperation. However, the commission is most likely a reactive device for disputes rather than directing and regulating policy processes, as the CEC *may* submit policy proposals and recommendations for a government's consideration, and *may* prepare annual reports on the state of the environment and environmental policy (Mumme 1993: 92). During consultation and evaluation by experts, the Secretariat plays an important role, but the decision to start the actual dispute settlement process falls under the authority of the environmental Ministers. Indirectly this provision limits the role of public participation, as persons or NGOs can direct their complaints of violation to the CEC, but even if the Secretariat's investigation supports a complaint, the Ministers are not legally bound to set up a panel to investigate it. The Sec-

---

26 The maximum of the fine is proportionally linked to the flow of North American Trade. For the first year of NAFTA the maximum fine per offense was established at $20 million.

retariat's power is also limited as the supplemental agreement allows govern-ments to refuse to provide the commission with information on their enforce-ment level.

The enforcement provisions of the supplemental agreement concern envi-ronmental laws and are explicitly non-applicable to domestic regulations that primarily regulate exploitation and harvesting of natural resources, and to envi-ronmental matters that are not connected with trade. The exclusion of natural resources laws stemmed from Canada's insistence on this point,[27] which was supported by the Mexican team. It implies that a wide range of economic activ-ities that do have environmental consequences (forestry, fishery, mining, etc.) are not covered by these provisions (*Inside U.S. Trade* 20/VIII/1993), although specific environmental protection provisions of domestic natural resource legislation are not exempted. According to US Trade Representative Mickey Kantor, "trade-connected means an issue has to be 'somehow' involved with trade, such as having a trade or investment impact" (*Inside U.S. Trade* 16/VIII/1993: S-8). Consequently, sectors or areas which are of little interest to North American trade and economic sectors that are excluded from NAFTA (e.g. Mexi-can oil) will not be affected by the enforcement provisions.

The supplemental agreement contains several provisions with respect to public participation and transparency. First, citizens seeking environmental en-forcement or compensation for environmental damage have the right to go to court. Second, the agreement contributes to transparency and citizens' right to know through requirements such as the publication of policy enforcement pro-cedures and non-compliance, and public comment prior to the adoption of legislation. Finally, there are several opportunities for citizen input in the CEC (see above), and the commission is obliged to make some of its reports public (Spalding 1995: 146-9).

The funding and management of infrastructure and environmental cleaning up operations in the Mexico-US border area were not provided for in the sup-plemental agreement. Instead, in October1993 Mexico and the US agreed on the creation of the bilateral North American Development Bank (NADBANK)[28] and the Border Environmental Cooperation Commission (BECC). The BECC's tasks involve assisting border states and communities in the coordination and design of environmental infrastructure projects. Officially, the composition of its board of directors and advisory council is to allow for maximal local and

27 The logging industry of British Columbia and Alberta might have been the major interest group pressurizing the Canadian position.
28 The NADBANK was a proposal by Hispanic groups and members of Congress in the US, and its creation served to win support for NAFTA.

public participation. The NADBANK is to provide part of the funding (loans at the lowest commercial rates, and guarantees) for border environmental projects in Mexico and the US that are certified by the BECC. In addition, 10 per cent of the NADBANK's capital is to be used for the support of NAFTA-related community adjustment and investment (which may be outside the border region in both countries). The bank will provide $2 to $3 billion for credits, for which Mexico and the US have a 50/50 responsibility. The bank will furthermore assist borrowers in finding additional private and public funds for projects (*Fact Sheet on the U.S./Mexican Agreement on the BECC and the NADBANK*). Due to this parallel arrangement of the BECC and the NADBANK and to regulatory omissions, there are no explicit links between these bilateral institutions and the CEC.

REACTIONS TO THE SUPPLEMENTAL AGREEMENT

The reactions of the major actors in the NAFTA environment debate to the supplemental environmental agreement provide insight into the political value not only of this agreement, but of the NAFTA package as a whole. In Mexico it was widely felt that its negotiators had made unacceptable concessions. In particular, the fact that trade sanctions could be imposed on Mexico (while Canada had arranged an "escape") was widely perceived as harming state sovereignty. Both in government and non-government circles, the sanctions were a source of worry. What would happen if small Mexican companies without resources did not comply with environmental measures? To what extent might the US be able to use sanctions against Mexico for economic reasons? Was there anything positive to expect from this possible avenue of US interference in Mexican politics?

In public announcements, President Salinas and negotiator Serra Puche attempted to play down these concerns by stating over and over again that Mexico's sovereignty was guaranteed by the supplemental agreement. They stressed the unlikelihood of the application of sanctions and the advantages of environmental cooperation. For instance, in a meeting with Mexican senators (17/VIII/93) Serra Puche declared that they should not worry about the possibility of trade sanctions because the complexity of the procedure of dispute settlement would render it very unlikely that a trade sanction would ever be used.

Indeed, the complex procedures for dispute settlement render the chance of actual application of trade sanctions minimal, and also on other issues US demands were mitigated in the agreement. The Mexicans gave in with respect to the regional character of the Public Advisory Committee, although an additional national committee remained optional.[29] On the other hand, Mexico successfully limited transparency and public access (citizen submissions, public access to the CEC Council, and citizens' right to know) as proposed by the US government. While the initial US negotiating position reflected many ideas from US moderate ENGOS, the supplemental agreement's provisions demonstrated that US negotiators had mainly succeeded on a relatively powerful CEC while giving in on public access issues.

While in each of the three NAFTA countries official announcements on the supplemental agreement applauded the "green" achievements, government officials and private sector organizations had their doubts. Several interviewed officials expressed their cynicism about the negotiation of the supplemental agreement and the agreement itself. The domination of US politics and the lack of conviction within the negotiating teams were mirrored in the outcome, they argued. Not only in Mexico was there a sense that the CEC and the two border institutions had too much of a political incentive. Government officials would have preferred more 'technical' institutions, while the efficiency of two new border agencies was very much questioned. As part of the lobbies for ratification, private sector organizations also announced support for the NAFTA package and praised it for being green, although they found CEC's authority too extended and were disappointed with the supplemental agreement.

Both critical and moderate ENGOS in Mexico opposed the trade sanction option in the supplemental agreement. While on other points the agreement was acceptable to organizations like UGAM and the Group of Hundred, with respect to the dispute settlement it was not. In the eyes of RMALC the final text did not meet the demands made by NGOS at all. RMALC's main points of criticism were that the participation of NGOS in the CEC remained vague, and that the funds for environment were restricted to the border region (RMALC 1993b). The supplemental agreement allowed for national environmental committees as counterparts to CEC's public advisory committee, but it was not obligatory as RMALC required.

Critical environmental organizations in the three countries were disappointed and labelled the supplemental agreement insufficient. Many weak spots in the trade agreement were not repaired, they claimed, and the provisions on the CEC did not satisfy the demands of critical groups. The NAFTA package had little in common with their ideas of 'just and sustainable trade and development'. Critical US ENGOS maintained that the supplemental agreement fell short on each of their five points of priority. The CEC was not the strong

---

29 Although the Mexican government preferred national committees, it did not create a national public advisory committee when the US and Canadian governments did.

institution critical ENGOs had pleaded for, and especially the Secretariat's dependence on the Council went against their demands. Both critical NGOs and members of Congress in the US claimed that the supplemental environmental agreement had "no teeth". US environmental organizations thus remained very divided on NAFTA until the end. One day after 300 US grassroots ENGOs and public interest groups expressed their opposition to the NAFTA package (13/IX/93), six of the seven moderate organizations announced their support and attacked the opposing groups.[30]

Even though the Mexico-US border was the major beneficiary of the NAFTA environment debate through the creation of new institutions and funding mechanisms for the region, problems with border environmental management continued. Because of the absence of a basis for a common administrative system and comprehensive planning of the border environment, coordination between the various government agencies on both sides of the border was bound to remain difficult. The NAFTA (parallel) arrangements for the border promised to improve the region's infrastructure considerably, but neglect of ecosystem issues was likely to persist. While solutions to existing problems as well as dispute settlement were taken more and more seriously, preventive measures were hardly considered. Finally, both the older and the new (NAFTA) arrangements were insufficient to secure participation by border constituencies (Mumme 1993: 95-6). This criticism was partly confirmed by EPA's Public Advisory Committee in August 1993, when the committee reported that the Border Plan had failed in many respects. Based on the plan's experience, the committee called for better cross-border coordination, greater responsiveness to border communities, and more rational funding allocations (Land 1993: 107).

PASSING THE NAFTA IN THE US

Although some Canadian provinces opposed certain provisions of the NAFTA package, US Congress was the stumbling block for the creation of the free trade zone. Labour opposition to NAFTA posed a great problem to President Clinton,

---

30 While a comparison of the environmental side agreement with demands of critical ENGOs results in a rather bleak picture, environmentalists were rather successful when compared to labour activism and the labour side agreement. Mumme and Stevis (1995) argue that environmental organizations in the three countries were more flexible in their political relations than labour unions, and more independent vis-à-vis their government, while the novelty of the trade-environment linkage allowed for political innovation.

who had to achieve the agreement's ratification without the support of one of the traditional allies of the Democratic Party. Despite the concessions of the Mexican and Canadian governments in the supplemental negotiations on labour and on the environment, the ratification of the NAFTA package by the US Congress was not secured. A considerable number of members of Congress either opposed the agreements or remained in doubt, so that proponents further intensified their NAFTA lobbies.

At this stage, the World Bank gave its strongest and most public pro-NAFTA support. In September 1993, the Bank announced that it would provide an unprecedented environmental loan of $1.8 billion for Mexico's northern border region. This major sum to deal with problems that were stressed by US public opinion and Congress was clearly aimed at weakening NAFTA opposition. The announcement was a publicity stunt. In reality, it was not a loan but a declaration of intent, and the projects involved (waste disposal, water supply and sanitation, transport) were already prepared as social projects. Moreover, the Bank was not simply supporting the NAFTA passage, it was clearly under the influence of the US government as it stopped pursuing its own priorities by focusing on the border.[31] After the disastrous $120 million environmental loan, it was most questionable whether Mexico could handle $1.8 billion (World Bank source 11/IV/94; World Bank source 16/V/94).[32]

Other NAFTA proponents also intensified their lobby in the US (see 5.1). The Clinton administration, SECOFI's NAFTA office in Washington, and corporate organizations worked together to secure sufficient congressional support. Some of the moderate US environmental organizations that supported the NAFTA package actively attempted to convince members of Congress to vote for the agreement. Although the environmental issue was important in the US debate on NAFTA, in the end economic arguments dominated in the congressional decision-making. The final stage of the lobbying process involved major deals by the Clinton administration with members of Congress who still doubted.[33]

---

31 According to an earlier World Bank report (1992a), Mexico's major environmental problems were: air pollution in major metropolitan areas; water scarcity and water pollution; soil erosion; deforestation and destruction of natural ecosystems.

32 According to the World Bank (1994a: 18-20), the objective of the project was to improve the environmental conditions on the border, for which purpose the Mexican government had requested Bank assistance in April 1993.

33 Clinton could not count on his own Democratic Party for NAFTA support, predominantly because of the vigorous opposition of its labour constituency. He therefore needed the Republicans as well as enormous side-payments to secure enough supporting votes (cf. Public Citizen 1993).

On 17 November 1993, the House of Representatives accepted NAFTA with a 234 to 200 vote, and thereby the last serious obstacle to NAFTA had disappeared. On November 20, the NAFTA passed the Senate by 61 to 38 votes. The NAFTA and the supplemental agreements became operative on the first day of 1994.

— 6.3 Mexico's environmental politics and policy 1991-1993 —

As described in chapter 2, the environmental efforts of the Mexican government at the beginning of the presidency of Salinas were first of all motivated by domestic politics. In the context of rising environmental consciousness, demands of ENGOs for major policy improvement touched a sensitive point. After the presidential elections of 1988, which demonstrated the lack of legitimacy of both the state-party system and the economic restructuring programme, the environment was adopted by the incoming president to obtain more support. However, due to a lack of resources and genuine priority of environmental protection, regulatory and instrumental progress was limited and policy enforcement remained weak in 1989 and 1990. To change this pattern, Salinas actively sought to attract foreign funding, which implied a certain degree of transnationalization. Here we will analyse the changes in Mexico's environmental politics and policy-making during the second and third phase of the NAFTA environment debate, between 1991 and 1993.

TRANSNATIONALIZING ENVIRONMENTAL POLITICS

Besides NAFTA, several issues were important to Mexican environmental organizations between 1991 and 1993, and like the NAFTA issue they involved international processes or interests. Especially the United Nations Conference on Environment and Development (UNCED), known as the Earth Summit, that was to be held in 1992 in Río de Janeiro stimulated NGO activism and led to a temporary joining of environmentalist forces. In June 1991, the Mexican Forum for Rio 92 (FOROMEX) was created, which at first included largely Mexico City groups, but after a few months a range of networks from other regions joined in. The forum emphasized this nation-wide aspiration by also having regional meetings (outside of Mexico City). Beyond the borders, there were some relations with US and Latin American networks. However, FOROMEX was not prepared for a genuine dialogue with popular sectors and did not succeed in opening a national debate (Barkin 1994: 359; Umlas 1996: 100-44).[34]

FOROMEX's heterogeneous constituency had both negative and positive consequences. About 70 NGOs were involved, with more than half of them environmental organizations and the rest development or social organizations. The Forum experienced decision-making problems, discord and a lack of consensus. The Mexican government's tendency to meet not with the Forum as a whole, but only with some of its members added to the internal tensions. This approach became particularly apparent a few days before the Río conference, when government officials invited a number of NGOs, including members of FOROMEX, to sign a document entitled 'joint proposals of the government of Mexico and the social groups', which some organizations did.[35] After Río, Mexican ENGOS became divided again because of old tensions and the refusal of some groups to continue the Forum. Its experience nevertheless resulted in the incorporation of environmental issues in non-environmental organizations, new national and international links, and increased mobilization and coordination of regional groups (Barkin 1994: 359; Umlas 1996: 100-44).

The increased international attention to Mexico's environment and the strengthened transnational relations at times proved useful for Mexican ENGOS. Apart from the NAFTA environment debate and the Earth Summit, this was the case with the opposition to a highway in the Chimalapas rain-forest in Chiapas. The national committee fighting this plan consisted of various local, Mexico City-based and national groups, and had ties with organizations in the US, who rapidly communicated with each other by fax. The fact that a key member Mexican group received funding from the WWF helped to put extra pressure on President Salinas. The UNCED process and the NAFTA debate added to initiatives of the committee and its member organizations. The conference in Río even enabled some of the Chimalapas committee's members to approach President Salinas and environmental Minister Colosio on the matter. Moreover, the

---

34 Besides UNCED matters, FOROMEX also commented on national policy. In addition, some of the regional networks worked on a diagnosis of their state's environmental situation.

35 For a previous research I once attended a meeting of SEDUE officials with NGOs on UNCED (23/1/92). This meeting was earmarked for information and consultation, but it was most striking that every time an NGO member criticized SEDUE, officials replied that the meeting was meant for exchange of information, not for discussion. Equally dubious was the fact that there was no information on the government's position with respect to the summit's issues. According to an environmentalist, the Mexican government had not invited NGOs for consultation as prescribed by the UN until Mexican groups sent a letter to the UNCED organizing committee. According to Barkin (1994: 342), at the last stage the Mexican government tried to incorporate some ENGOS into the official Mexican delegation to the Earth Summit.

importance of Mexico's international image with respect to environmental protection rendered the government more vulnerable to criticism (Umlas 1995).

On major policy issues, however, the domestic political influence of Mexican environmental organizations remained very limited.[36] This was the case in the making of new legislation on natural resources. In 1992, article 27 of the Mexican Constitution was reformed (see 1.3), and linked to this reform new laws on agriculture, forestry and water were created. These reforms involved a major liberalization of natural resources, which since the Mexican Revolution had been characterized by a relatively high level of state control (see chapter 2). They were part of Salinas' programme of a more market-dominated economy, and were speeded up because of the NAFTA plan. Neoliberal reforms thus produced deregulation of natural resource use, instead of the much needed protection measures. Among environmental organizations as well as a range of popular organizations (unions of farmers and fishermen, *ejidos*, local communities) there was great concern about the privatization of natural resources.[37] Environmentalists stressed the importance of a central role of local communities in the use and protection of natural resources, and criticized the failure to include strong measures for conservation of natural resources. However, neither nationwide mobilization nor international attention came about, and the reforms came into force.

What may have gradually improved was environmental consciousness. Several polls show that Mexican citizens are very much aware of environmental problems, while classifying environmental protection as one of the first policy priorities, especially in Mexico City. Also interest in environmental issues in Mexico's business sector increased slowly. Private sector organizations and their publications paid more attention to environmental degradation, policy and company initiatives. Motivated by the NAFTA environment debate, the Study

---

36 In interviews with Mexican government officials and external advisors, different views were expressed. Limited consultation was sometimes attributed to a lack of (technical) expertise and knowledge of environmental organizations. On the other hand, other interviewees were positive about ENGOs and their role in stimulating environmental consciousness and policy.

37 As most of the *ejido* farmers were very poor, they were likely to cash their plot if necessary (e.g. in case of illness) despite their dependence on the land. Large-scale (transnational) landownership and an increasing use of machinery and chemicals were expected to follow. The new forestry law was criticized for being focused on the most commercialized regions, while neglecting the variety of forests, the different levels of degradation, and the fact that more than three-quarters of all forests are owned by *ejidos* and communities (instead of private persons).

Centre of the Private Sector for Sustainable Development (CESPEDES) was created in 1993. Even though the centre is very small for its immense task of convincing the majority of Mexican companies that environmental protection
needs to be taken seriously, its very creation shows that the environment is
becoming more of a priority in the private sector too.

TRANSNATIONAL POLICY SUPPORT

An important factor behind the transnationalization of Mexico's environmental politics was the international efforts of Salinas. First of all, Mexico's image
of a model debtor willing to restructure its economy and heading towards integration in the North American free trade zone provided credibility and confidence. Second, the early environmental initiatives of Salinas had demonstrated his aspiration to improve Mexico's protection record. Finally, Mexico's
commitment to a number of international environmental agreements improved its environmental image, rather than having large policy effects.[38]

As we have seen, bilateral environmental cooperation with the US and
Canada was extended in the context of the NAFTA plans. Most Mexico-US
activities were directed towards the border, implying unprecedented attention
for environmental degradation and threats to that region. Other external funding was directed to air pollution in Mexico City (see 2.4), and to conservation
and a sustainable use of natural resources. The Tropical Forest Action Plan
(PROAFT) for instance, had been internationally developed by organizations
like the Food and Agriculture Organization (FAO) and the World Bank to enhance sustainable management of forestry resources. The Mexican programme
was financially supported by (among others) the Ford Foundation and the governments of the US, Canada and the United Kingdom. Interestingly, the Mexican PROAFT was not incorporated in a government agency but organized as an
NGO, in order to ensure continuity of the long-term programme. Salinas also
managed to attract new debt-for-nature swaps. In 1992, the Interamerican Development Bank (IDB), for instance, agreed to lend Mexico $100 million to buy
back shares of its foreign debt at a discount in order to use the proceeds for a
reforestation project in the mountain area around Mexico City (*The IDB* July

---

38 By the end of 1991, Mexico was the first country to sign the Montreal Protocol (on
Substances that Diminish the Ozone Layer), and had subscribed to the Basel Convention (on Transborder Movement of Hazardous Wastes) and the Convention on International Trade of Wild Plant and Animal Species (CITES). At the Earth Summit in 1992,
Mexico signed the Biodiversity Treaty and the Convention on Climate Change.

1992: 8). However, some of these externally induced conservation programmes were criticized by local communities and Mexican environmental organizations for their lack of local participation.

In 1992, the World Bank approved its Mexico Environmental Project (MEP) for the strengthening and decentralization of Mexico's environmental policy. The project involved a $50 million loan by the Bank, a $30 million grant from the Global Environmental Trust Fund (GET), while the Mexican government was to cover $46.6 million. As the MEP would increase the recurrent costs of the ecological sub-ministry by about 30 per cent, it would affect Mexico's environmental policy beyond the project's term. Of the project budget, 44 per cent was to be spent on conservation of biodiversity, and 29 per cent on the monitoring and control of air and water contamination. With respect to institutional matters, 6 per cent of the MEP budget was reserved for strengthening the administrative sector, especially with respect to environmental standards and Environmental Assessment Projects, and another 5 per cent for a pilot programme of supporting administrative decentralization to five states (World Bank 1992a).

This major World Bank loan became a disaster. The predominant cause was the reform of SEDUE (see below). The MEP was supposed to support the institutional strengthening of SEDUE (the Bank was to contribute $4.5 million to this programme), and the World Bank was to be actively involved in the planning of institutional reforms. On this matter, the Bank and the Mexican government had agreed that in July 1992 the latter would submit the reports of consultants to the World Bank, and that by December 1992 the government would present an action programme for SEDUE's reorganization, taking the World Bank's recommendations and comments into account (World Bank 1992a: 25). In reality, SEDUE was replaced in May 1992, and as SEDUE's reform followed a path different from what was agreed upon with the Bank, it became an obstacle to the execution of the MEP, causing suspension of disbursement (World Bank source 11/IV/94; World Bank source 16/V/94).[39]

In 1993, the World Bank praised the steps taken by the Mexican government to protect the environment, but simultaneously argued that as "the approach has been largely piecemeal and (...) not enough has been done (...)" a "much more comprehensive assault is needed" (World Bank 1993: 10-1). Therefore, the

---

39 It seems that the Mexican government had not expected the SEDUE reform to derange MEP's implementation. Even before the agreement on the MEP, the Mexican government had been contracting and paying potential employees, and buying material for the project, for millions of dollars (*Proceso* 881, 20/IX/93: 30-1). Also a $220 million World Bank programme on air pollution in Mexico City, approved in December 1992, had still not started in 1994 (World Bank source 16/V/94).

Mexican government and the World Bank started cooperating on a more comprehensive approach to Mexico's environmental problems. For this purpose, the Bank was to further expand its analytical work, policy dialogue, and lending to Mexico. One of the Bank's proposals was a greater use of economic instruments, instead of command-and-control measures in Mexico's environmental policy. Next, the Bank aimed at better policy implementation and enforcement, and improving the legal and regulatory framework by the creation of environmental norms and standards to support the existing laws. In order to help Mexico achieve these goals, the World Bank planned to allocate 33 per cent of its total Mexico budget for 1993-1996 to environmental projects, as compared with the 20 per cent reserved for 1992-95. The Bank also encouraged Mexico to privatize and decentralize its environmental policy apparatus. The private sector's role was particularly to be increased in the water, sanitation, and waste management sectors (World Bank 1993: 12-5).[40]

In sum, the success of President Salinas in attracting foreign environmental loans and grants improved Mexico's financial resource base for policy implementation substantially. In a NAFTA publication, the Mexican government even claimed that in 1991 over 70 per cent of SEDUE's environmental budget was financed by external credits, while in 1992 an increase of government resources had brought this share down to less than 40 per cent (Embassy of Mexico 1992: 15). However, the major share of this external support was attributed to the Mexico Environmental Project of the World Bank. As we know that the Project only started in 1992 and problems led to the suspension of disbursement, these figures should be taken with more than a pinch of salt, as indicating trends rather than of reflecting facts.

The additional external resources for Mexico's environmental policy had several effects. First, they allowed the improvement of existing projects and the taking on of new programmes. Second, international ties gave rise to external pressure on the Mexican government because of its image and certain conditions imposed.[41] Third, large foreign contributions affected policy priorities, as

---

40 One interviewed World Bank source (11/IV/94) had mixed feelings about the Bank's impact on Mexico. On the one hand, he expected the Bank to have influenced Mexico since considerable funds were provided. On the other hand, he wondered whether the Mexicans had "played a nice game", because he could not judge to what extent enforcement had really improved.

41 The Organization for Economic Cooperation and Development (OECD), for instance, requires an Environmental Performance Report from its member countries. Since OECD membership is highly valued by Mexico's Ministry of Trade, evaluation of environmental policy has been taken more seriously outside environmental government

will be demonstrated below. The external focus on the border with the US and on industrial pollution and conservation not only directed foreign resources but also Mexican funding because most external contributions involved an additional local share in finance. Credibility and again a good image with respect to efforts on externally valued policy fields had to secure foreign support. Finally, international relations were important for cooperation, training and information. The World Bank even acted as a sounding board through open discussions on policy issues with Mexican government officials.

INSTITUTIONAL REFORM

In May 1992, SEDUE was replaced by the Ministry of Social Development (SEDESOL).[42] The SEDESOL had sub-ministries on regional development, urban development, and public housing. An important activity of SEDESOL involved the administration of the National Solidarity Programme PRONASOL, Salinas' neopopulist social programme (see 1.4). The environmental tasks of SEDESOL were formally exercised by the National Ecology Commission (CONADE), which was created in 1985, but CONADE's environmental responsibilities were executed by two agencies that were technically and administratively autonomous from SEDESOL. The National Institute of Ecology (INE) was responsible for the formulation and implementation of policy. The Office of the Attorney General for Protection of the Environment (PROFEPA) was responsible for the enforcement of this policy and penalization for non-compliance.

In practice, the expected advantages of SEDUE's reform were limited. Some of SEDUE's environmental tasks were directed to ministries other than SEDESOL in order to integrate conservation functions with regulation and management of the natural resources involved, as separation had proved inefficient.[43] However, since the transfer was not followed by a structural reform of these ministries, the problems with conservation remained. Similarly, although there were certain advantages of autonomous environmental agencies (flexibility, less bureaucracy), coordination between these agencies and the sub-ministries was

---

agencies (Mexican government source 17/x/95).

42 In early 1995, SEDESOL was replaced by the Ministry of Environment, Natural Resources and Fisheries (SEMARNAP).

43 The management of national parks and flora and fauna reserves as well as the task of imposing bans on hunting and cutting down trees were moved to SARH. Sea and river flora and fauna, and water reserves were transferred to the Ministry of Fisheries (SEPESCA).

weak and the merging of policy areas did not come about. Consequently, the fact that environmental protection became part of the Ministry of Social (instead of Urban) Development had few practical implications. Finally, the creation of SEDESOL was presented as serving policy decentralization as established by the environmental law of 1988. State and local governments could formally enact more stringent standards than federal legislation. However, a lack of funding structures, capable personnel[44] and the still highly centralized system hampered a successful decentralization process.[45] Summarizing these three tendencies, SEDESOL could be described as a missed opportunity (Carabias and Provencio 1994: 411-4).

   Not surprisingly, Mexican environmental organizations did not favour the institutional reform. They feared that SEDESOL would be a more bureaucratic and less powerful institution than SEDUE, and were especially concerned about the split of environmental responsibilities (Arídjis et al. 1992). In their view, the National Institute of Ecology was a decentralized institution without enforcement capacities, employing the same group of officials that had been criticized for lax and inefficient working. Mexican ENGOs criticized PROFEPA for having mainly conciliatory and recommendatory powers; this was not the autonomous enforcement authority they had pleaded for (Székely, undated: 7). Although SEDESOL's Minister Luis Donaldo Colosio Murrieta immediately promised ample possibilities for popular participation (*La Jornada*, 26/05/92), and he was said to be more sympathetic and open to environmental NGOs than predecessors, Mexican environmentalists did not have particular confidence in or approval of the new ministry.[46] With the establishment of SEDESOL, the National Council for the Protection of the Environment and councils for INE and PROFEPA were also created, in which environmental organizations, groups of industrialists and political parties participated. However, the role of these councils and their members remained dubious. The PROFEPA council, for

---

44 Apart from a lack of well-trained technical experts, there were very few Mexicans with an environmental law degree because this degree could not be obtained at a Mexican university.

45 The mining town Cananea, close to the US border, could not wait for these slow decentralization initiatives. In this rather exceptional case, the mayor—supported by a large sector of the community—created an environmental commission, contacted US experts for assistance, and requested the federal government to hand over information, resources and authority. Several US ENGOs (including BEP) contributed to this initiative (*San Francisco Chronicle* 30/x/93: A12).

46 Positive accounts were expressed in interviews with Mexican government officials, but not supported by ENGO sources.

example, only incorporated moderate ENGOs, and in its first two years of existence met only three times.

The political background of the creation of SEDESOL remains rather mysterious. The construction of INE, PROFEPA and the Council contrasted with plans discussed with the World Bank only shortly before. According to the World Bank (1992a: 25), SEDUE's Sub-ministry of Ecology was to be transformed into a highly qualified second-tier organization, supervising and coordinating environmental work carried out by other levels of government, other federal agencies and private sector firms. Taking into account that high-level World Bank officials doubted the openness of the Mexican government, and considering the backlash of the Bank's Environmental Project caused by SEDUE's replacement, it is probable that the World Bank was not informed about and involved in the plans for creating SEDESOL. In the context of the NAFTA environment debate, the consultancy firm McKinsey was hired by the Mexican government to advise on its environmental institutions, but this study was preempted by the creation of SEDESOL and never finalized (US government source 25/x/95).

The transnational NAFTA environment debate might have speeded up reform plans, but it does not suffice to explain SEDESOL's rapid creation. PROFEPA was presented behind closed doors as the enforcement agency the US wanted (US government source 25/x/95), and indeed a separate agency for control on compliance cannot be separated from the strong US criticism of weak policy enforcement and environmental practices of companies in Mexico. However, the World Bank's Environmental Project and McKinsey events suggest that there was a sudden domestic political need to rush the reform of SEDUE instead of awaiting external advice. The choice of Colosio as Minister of SEDESOL supports the idea that the pace of SEDESOL's creation stemmed not only from external political incentives. Colosio left his position as chairman of the PRI, and he was perceived as one of the contenders for the next PRI presidential candidate. On the one hand, orchestrating prestigious environmental programmes and PRONASOL added to Colosio's image. On the other hand, with PRONASOL and Colosio, SEDESOL became a highly politicized institution (Barry and Sims 1994: 79).[47]

---

47 According to an interviewed high-level Mexican government official (17/x/95), SEDESOL was one of Salinas' most important ministries, with possibly the most important minister.

POLICY PRIORITIES

International influence was evident between 1991 and1993 in all prioritized environmental policy areas. The additional attention for conservation of biodiversity in this period reflected international concerns and processes and could equally count on foreign support, as has already been indicated. Mexico expanded the surface of protected areas that were part of the Programme of Protection of Natural Zones from 3.1 per cent of its national territory in 1992 (SEDESOL 1993: 105-6)[48] to 4.8 per cent in 1994 (SEDESOL 1994a: 98-9). Plans were made with the US to expand protected areas at the border and to coordinate protection efforts on both sides of the border. In addition, in 1992 the coordinating National Commission for the knowledge and use of biodiversity (CONABIO) was created, co-funded by the Mexican government and private contributions.

New environmental standards were to improve the enforcement record of Mexico's environmental policy, but their number remained behind the official goal. As foreseen by the General Environmental Law of 1988, Salinas aimed to establish more than 200 environmental standards for air pollution, hazardous waste and water pollution. Plans for new standards were regularly mentioned at international forums, and SEDESOL (1994b: 7) presented their creation as a reply to new legal measures as well as to commitments taken on in the NAFTA and the OECD. By the end of 1992, seventy to eighty standards had been developed (Embassy of Mexico 1992: 9; Rebolledo 1993: 159) and there were serious intentions to triple this number of new standards.[49] However, due to SEDUE's reorganization, most attention went to rewriting existing norms rather than preparing new standards (World Bank official 16/v/94). In Mexico City, on the other hand, worsening air contamination, increased local pressure, and external attention for Mexico's industrial emissions stimulated SEDESOL to establish more air pollution measures.

A nationally and internationally important policy challenge for the Salinas administration was improving the industrial compliance record. This was predominantly done by expanding inspection personnel. Whereas in 1990 SEDUE had only 9 staff members for industrial inspection in the Federal District (Mexico City), in 1992 this number had increased to 59, while the Mexican government claimed that in that same year 200 inspectors were working in the

---

48 According to Quadri de la Torre (1994: 374), in 1989 Mexico's protected areas also encompassed 3.1 per cent, which is very little from a global and regional perspective.
49 The World Bank's Environmental project was to finance technical studies that were necessary to support the preparation of over 100 technical standards.

border states and 75 in the rest of the country (Embassy of Mexico 1992: 18). Although these figures have to be used with caution, as they were part of Mexico's image-building in the context of the NAFTA environment debate, they do indicate increasing efforts in pollution control and the special focus on the Mexico-US border region. The Mexican government announced that it would start working with industrialists on renovation and modernization of production, while intensifying controls and becoming more strict on compliance.

The fact that SEDESOL's environmental priorities were more urban than rural suggests that existing policy tendencies were further accentuated by external criticism, although the border focus diverted from the earlier priority of Mexico City, Guadalajara and Monterrey. Among high-level officials in INE there was a concern that due to external pressure Mexico was focusing too much of its energies on the external concerns of border issues and air pollution, at the cost of efforts to fight Mexico's great environmental threats of water contamination and conservation, deforestation and depletion of natural resources (Stern 1993: 191).

Policy efficiency was also stressed between 1991 and 1993. Privatization of former state functions was one element of this efficiency policy. A start was made with moving pollution and compliance monitoring, licensing, inspection and the design of standards to private contractors. Efficiency might indeed improve, but the incidence of corruption and conflict of interest (consultants acting both as plant inspector and consultant to a given firm) might also increase (Barry and Sims 1994: 80). Another policy initiative that was linked to improving policy efficiency was the development of economic instruments for environmental policy, such as the polluter pays principle, eco-taxes and eco-subsidies, tradeable pollution permits, ownership rights, the incorporation of environmental costs into consumer prices, and environmental accountancy. Economic instruments were to complement and partly replace so-called command-and-control measures, on which Mexico's policy had relied heavily.[50] Although they remained a relatively small policy initiative, Mexico's efforts in this new area were linked to transnational initiatives and received substantial external support, including $1.2 million from the World Bank (1992a: 26).[51]

---

50 Apart from requiring extensive (and expensive) government controls, disadvantages of command-and-control measures are their inefficiency (one rule for different regions), that they do not encourage future efforts towards sustainable development, and that they do not provide the state with funding for protection (Quadri de la Torre 1994: 380-2).

51 For the development of national environmental accountancy and an "environmental GDP", Mexico cooperated with the World Bank, the United Nations Statistical Bureau,

POLICY ENFORCEMENT AND IMPACT

During the second half of Salinas' presidency the budget for environmental protection strongly increased. With large amounts of external support and a major expansion of government resources, the environmental expenditure of SEDUE (and later on of SEDESOL) multiplied. The above analysis of external and internal political pressures for environmental protection in Mexico suggests that the NAFTA environment debate was an important incentive for this budgetary rise. Apart from US criticism and bilateral cooperation, the US government had encouraged Mexico to raise the INE budget from $30 million to $70 million (US government source 25/x/95).

While Mexico's environmental budget rise was undoubtedly substantial between 1991 and 1993, actual expenditure remains obscure. The exceptional release of figures in a NAFTA publication of the Embassy of Mexico (1992: 15) showed a tenfold increase of SEDUE's environmental expenditures between 1989 and 1992 (1989: $6.6 million; 1990: $11,8; 1991: $38,5; 1992: $78.2). However, as mentioned above, the fact that these Fact Sheets (sic) considerably exaggerated World Bank funding means that its figures are unreliable.[52] In addition, there is no information on how resources were spent. According to the same NAFTA publication, only a very small proportion of the official federal expenditure on environmental protection was channelled through SEDUE and SEDESOL,[53] but further information on environmental programmes of government agencies other than SEDUE and SEDESOL is lacking. Given the propagandist nature of the NAFTA publication, it is likely that a wide range of projects were earmarked 'environmental' simply to raise the figures.[54]

---

and the United Nations Development Programme (Jarque 1994: 216). With support of the European Economic Community (EEC), INE organized a workshop with representatives of the World Bank, OECD, and EEC (SEDESOL 1992b).

52 It is also curious that these figures show an increase in SEDUE's environmental expenditure between 1988 and 1989, whereas other sources referred to 1989 as the leanest year for the ecological sub-ministry (see 2.4).

53 The publication claims that in 1991 federal expenditure on environmental protection by SEDUE was $38.4 million, whereas the Department of the Federal District spent $650 million for that purpose, and the Ministry of Energy, Mines and Parastatal Industry (SEMIP) $748 million (Embassy of Mexico 1992: 14).

54 According to the World Bank (1992a), the budget of the environmental sub-ministry accounted for less than 0.2 per cent of the total federal budget. On several NAFTA-related occasions, however, the Mexican government claimed to spend more than 1 per cent of its GDP on environmental protection, stressing that it was a high percentage for a developing country.

The area in which the most efforts were made for improving the policy record was industrial compliance with environmental legislation, but serious
problems remained. First, despite the remarkable expansion of inspecting staff,
their number was still insufficient. Most inspections took place in large companies and the most polluting industrial sectors, leaving many companies un-
inspected. Second, there were problems with contracts, salaries and payment of
inspectors, which enhanced corruption. In November 1991, for instance, it was
reported that SEDUE had cut 48 per cent of its inspection personnel (Barry and
Sims 1994: 80). Of the border inspectors only about one-fifth worked as full-
time government employees, while the rest worked under contract, and many
of them had to wait months to receive their salaries (*BorderLines* July 1993: 8).
Third, most inspectors were still badly trained, while those that were well-
trained were soon offered a better contract in the private sector.

The increase of technical staff was accompanied by a continuing increase of
company inspections and temporary or partial shutdowns.[55] This focus on
compliance had some positive effects. An environmental survey conducted
in1993 by AMCHAM among its manufacturing members points to considerable
policy and enforcement improvements. Enforcement measures were more
stringently applied by government agencies, inspections were particularly
frequent in areas and sectors with high pollution levels (large cities; chemical
and electronics companies), and the quality of inspectors had improved. As a
consequence, companies surveyed by AMCHAM considerably increased investment in environmental equipment and staff (AMCHAM 1993). In contrast with
these findings, nearly three-quarters of 260 business executives polled that same
year claimed that control and vigilance for pollution prevention were lacking
(*Expansion* 7/VII/1993). These contrasting findings may be explained by the approach of PROFEPA to focus on large companies, as members of AMCHAM are
among larger US and Mexican companies with international interests. As small
companies make up the main share of Mexico's private sector, there was still a
lot to be done.

Apart from the increased number of inspections, another improvement concerned a gradual "hardening" of the governmental attitude towards large industry. Apart from environmental protection purposes, this focus on large industry

---

55 Inspections performed by PROFEPA between August 1992 and June 1994 were reported to include: 25,493 visits to verify industrial emissions (more than 50 per cent in
Mexico City); 344 inspection visits to parastatal companies (mainly PEMEX); and 2,541
verification visits at protected natural resources areas. During the period, 54,111 polluting cars were rejected and in total nearly $10 million of fines were imposed (SEDESOL
1994c).

was clearly motivated by the NAFTA environment debate. The mix of US environmentalist criticism (focusing on the *maquiladoras* at the border), labour and protectionist concerns (for unfair competition with Mexico-based companies or even industrial relocation to Mexico) turned non-compliance of internationally competitive industries into a major transnational issue. According to Stern (1993: 188), Attorney General Santiago Oñate "applied his authority with some intensity", pressing transnational companies as well as PEMEX to improve their environmental records. In fact, it appears that PROFEPA often applied the strategy to extract "voluntary" agreements from companies under threat of serious sanctions.[56] A problem in this respect was that some of Mexico's environmental standards were set too high (too soon), leaving most industries unable to comply (Mexican government source 7/IV/94).

To what degree the improvements noted above resulted in actual progress of industrial compliance is unclear, but the limited information available supports the idea that compliance predominantly increased in large companies. A NAFTA-related (English) brochure of SEDESOL (undated b) claimed that in 1991 55 per cent of the *maquiladoras* complied with operating licenses. However, as in other NAFTA publications, this figure might have been "raised" for political purposes. Later on, SEDESOL (1994c) reported irregularities in more than 70 per cent of the inspected industrial facilities nation-wide. Both figures might be more or less accurate if one considers the government's focus on large industrial companies.

While external pressure directed the Mexican government's attention towards large industry, most of the polluting activities of other companies were neglected. This was shown not only by the limited inspections in these companies, but also by the persistence of obstacles to compliance for smaller companies. Especially a lack of accessible, long-term financing for environmental equipment continued to be a bottle-neck. In general, bank credit is very restricted in Mexico (except for the largest firms), interest rates are high, and terms are short. Mexican and US initiatives to support environmental credits for Mexican companies failed as the commercial banks that operate as intermediaries are unexperienced with environmental loans (Robinson 1994). A second major problem for environmental protection in industry was the lack of consciousness and limited knowledge of legislation.[57] Third, the lack of environ-

---

56 From the companies PROFEPA inspected in its first two years, 1,537 had to partially close down and 271 were closed completely (SEDESOL 1994c). However, it is not mentioned whether these closures were temporary or definite.

57 A poll held in 1993 among 260 business executives demonstrated that only 12 per cent of them were "aware" and 50 per cent were "partly familiar" with the General Environmental Law, which they perceived as a dead letter (*Expansion* 7/VII/1993).

mental infrastructure such as sewerage and waste-disposal also inhibited environmentally-sound production. The AMCHAM survey showed that companies found government investment especially needed in hazardous waste collection and disposal, and water treatment and supply (AMCHAM 1993).

A short overview of some other scattered figures and inside information supports the assessment that enforcement of environmental policy and compliance with environmental standards still left much to be desired. René Altamirano Pérez, an assistant director of INE, estimated in1993 that more than 90 per cent of Mexican industry did not comply with the ecological norms for management of contaminated residuals (*El Financiero* 7/VII/1993). The enforcement of Environmental Impact Assessment regulations also proved to be problematic. Even among (large) US majority-owned maquiladores compliance was poor. Of six companies in a US sample, none had prepared the Environmental Impact Assessment new companies are required to make (United States General Accounting Office 1992). According to university professor Beatriz Silva Torres, due to a lack of resources and personnel INE faced an enormous backlog in approvals for Environmental Impact Statements (*The News* 13/VII/93). A former high-level SEDESOL official revealed that INE's staff lacked knowledge of environmental risks, and that a very large number of the environmental impact assessment reports received by INE presented invented data (Ezcurra 1995: 35-6).

In sum, the NAFTA environment debate strongly affected Mexico's environmental politics and policy between 1991 and 1993, and contributed to several improvements. Although domestic pressure and other external incentives also stimulated the increasing government efforts, the major initiatives for improving the compliance of large industrial companies with environmental legislation point to the importance of the NAFTA debate. On the other hand, the way in which SEDESOL was created indicated that increasing external influence did not stop a certain internal "logic" from continuing. Moreover, while the Mexican government tried hard to improve its image in the NAFTA environment debate, many problems were tackled only partly or cosmetically.

— 6.4 Conclusions —

During the NAFTA environment debate, regional environmental relations and cooperation at the governmental as well as non-governmental level strengthened, but also regional differences came to the fore. As described in chapter 5, economic interests and views on development and economic growth united the governments and major business organizations from Mexico, the US and Canada together with the World Bank in an alliance of NAFTA proponents.

Until the completion of the trade negotiations in the summer of 1992, this transnational alliance in general agreed on the approach to integrating environmental issues in the trade agreement. This consensus ended with the demand of the incoming President Clinton for supplemental agreements on the environment and labour, which created major tensions among the NAFTA proponents. Improved relations and cooperation with the US did not avert a strong sense of distrust among Mexican negotiators. This reinforced Mexico's reserved and cautious attitude towards the NAFTA process, as it was feared that openness might eventually provide US environmentalists or protectionist groups with information that could harm its entry into NAFTA. Mexico had always been uncomfortable with US criticism of its weak policy enforcement, and this worsened as US pressure forced the Mexican government to make major concessions in the supplemental agreement. The negotiations of the supplemental environmental agreement stressed the Mexico-US inequalities. The agreement's final contents were partly directed at protecting US interests against non-enforcement of environmental policy in Mexico. Trade sanctions and the creation of the CEC, which allowed policy monitoring and some NGO input, were hard to swallow for Mexico's government.

For the commitments and resources that were generated as a result of the NAFTA environment debate, Mexico's border region with the US was the most important beneficiary. With the US NAFTA politics dominating the debate, and the border and industrial pollution dominating the US political agenda, the border focus was almost inevitable. Environmental organizations protested against this focus, but it was not resisted by the Mexican government. Supported by the other NAFTA proponents, the border problems were presented as a technical problem that could be solved by planning, resources for infrastructure, and plant controls. The Border Plan, the NADBANK, the BECC, and the World Bank's $1.8 billion loan for the border environment were the main products of this approach, implying major external support for the environmental policy of the Mexican government. However, to what degree these arrangements will contribute to genuine Mexico-US policy coordination is questionable.

From a pre-NAFTA perspective, the package was a step forwards for regional environmental protection. Apart from the cooperative and financial effects, the trade agreement and the supplemental environmental agreement created avenues for policy monitoring. With this monitoring, Mexico is likely to remain sensitive to external criticism. Especially the CEC provides for governmental and non-governmental discussion, cooperation, and progress. From the Mexican perspective, one may expect two important obstacles to the CEC avenues. Policy monitoring requires reliable information. Mexican government agencies are unfamiliar with producing this, what is more, the distrust and fear of abuse of information are likely to continue limiting Mexico's openness. The CEC possibilities for NGO participation will probably be used by the same groups that were involved in the NAFTA environment debate, so that a middle-class, Mexico City bias will continue to dominate Mexico's nongovernmental input.

Environmental organizations played a crucial role in the second and third phase of the NAFTA environment debate. Building on a much broader (labour-oriented, protectionist) resistance to NAFTA in the US, environmentalists analysed and criticized official plans and developed proposals and alternatives. While the first phase of the NAFTA environment debate was marked by ENGO criticism without a response from NAFTA proponents (see chapter 4), during the second and third phases there was constant interaction between proponents and the environmental movement. Although many environmental organizations opposed the final NAFTA package, their ideas and activities made an important contribution to its environmental provisions.

At many points in the NAFTA environment debate, ENGO activities were transnational, involving organizations from at least two of the three countries. On the one hand, efforts were made to understand and accept differences in order to establish equal relations. On the other hand, US dominance was evident. Apart from differences in resources and professional staff, NGO relations reflected the region's asymmetries. As internal US politics were the strongest determining factor in the NAFTA process, US ENGOs dominated the transnational environmentalist relations. For critical organizations this was less the case as US critical groups had limited access to their government, while making genuine efforts to overcome inequalities. Despite the more or less unbalanced situation, critical as well as moderate Mexican environmental organizations built strongly on the newly established transnational relations, both in their NAFTA activities and in domestic struggles.

When estimating the immediate impact of the transnational NAFTA environment debate on Mexico's environmental politics and policy between 1991 and 1993, one should be aware of the other processes that played a role in that period. Mexican environmental organizations continuously attempted to influence policy decisions and to move the government to better enforcement. The fact that after a repressive period in 1988 government agencies allowed some controlled participation of moderate ENGOs is partly due to the activities and qualities of these organizations. At the transnational level, the NAFTA environment debate coincided with the Earth Summit in 1992, which encouraged contacts between the government and NGOs on environment and development matters. In addition, Salinas' successful attracting of external funding for ecology projects also implied increasing transnational influence. Without acknowledging this context, the effects of the NAFTA environment debate may easily be exaggerated. Most US interviewees, for instance, thought the NAFTA process to have been decisive for the changes in Mexico, as their perspective was the NAFTA debate and not Mexico's circumstances as a whole. Mexican interviewees had more diverging ideas, with the NAFTA debate's effect ranging from very influential to not important at all.

On the basis of the above analysis, it may be concluded that between 1991 and1993 the politics of Mexico's environmental policy-making became considerably influenced by external processes and actors, and that the transnational NAFTA environment debate was crucial in this respect. Strong US environmentalist criticism, and the fact that this was taken seriously in the US Congress, linked North American economic integration with environmental care, and created an urgent need to improve Mexico's environmental image. Environmental protection became a prioritized policy issue for the Mexican government as a whole, resulting in a very substantial increase of federal resources, the establishment of a number of environmental standards, institutional reform, and more industrial compliance. Based on limited information, one may conclude that between 1991 and1993 policy enforcement improved, despite a range of persistent problems. Also a review of the policy areas and issues that were stressed showed that the NAFTA debate was important. While earlier policy had also focused on pollution control in Mexico's major cities, the border efforts were rather new. Similarly, the relatively rapid progress made with policy compliance of large industrial companies cannot be separated from the sudden external pressure at this point.

Generally, the NAFTA process reinforced the environmental policy priorities in Mexico: urban over rural problems; industrial pollution and nature conservation over natural resources issues. As a result, the external resources and attention to Mexico's environment produced by the NAFTA environment debate were hardly directed at solving excessive threats to Mexico's natural resources. Only with respect to water did the NAFTA debate improve the policy attention to resources. Nature conservation attention was largely directed at certain species and special ecosystems (i.e. turtles and rain forests), while a more comprehensive approach did not come about. Possible long-term implications of this outcome will be discussed in the concluding chapter.

Within Mexico, the changes in environmental politics were limited. The NAFTA environment debate contributed to the process of consciousness-raising, and was important for the integration of ecological concerns outside environmentalist circles. This was not only the case for non-environmental government agencies, but also for Mexico's private sector. Even though the sector's involvement in the NAFTA environment debate remained marginal, environmental awareness was gradually emerging among companies and private sector organizations. The input of Mexican environmental organizations in the NAFTA environment debate was enhanced by transnational relations established in this context, but at the national level participation of critical groups remained minimal, whereas moderate groups experienced only a slow increase of access to government agencies. The lack of openness and public access to information on policy initiatives and performance persisted, and structural avenues for NGO influence improved only slightly. In that context, the international attention to Mexico's environmental situation and policy, and the new transnational ties of Mexican ENGOs, allowed these organizations to express their concerns outside the Mexican political arena.

CHAPTER 7

Conclusions

For Mexico's political elite, entry into NAFTA was not only an economic project, but also an important political project. Apart from the expected advantages of free flows of goods and capital, the agreement served the consolidation of Mexico's restructuring programme initiated in the 1980s. Securing and expanding the historical economic integration into the US seemed the most realistic and rapid means to anchor the neoliberal development model. The anticipated economic growth should provide some relief for the many Mexicans who were impoverished by the sequence of crises and previous restructuring measures. This was to diminish the criticism of the state-party system, and the opposition with respect to the new model from within. If in spite of this Mexico's political elite was replaced, NAFTA membership would function to embed the new development strategy. A return to more regulation and protection would require the abandonment of the free trade agreement. Apart from direct economic loss and the domestic and foreign pressure this would arouse, such a decision was likely to harm Mexico's global creditworthiness to an unacceptable degree, no matter what the preferences of a future government might be.

While the announcement of the NAFTA plan in June 1990 came as a surprise to the larger public, so did the intensity and the transnational character of environmental protests to the proponents of the agreement. The plan for North American free trade and investment gave rise to a range of concerns about environmental consequences, which fundamentally touched upon the question of how to match development with environmental care, and on the role of the state in protecting the environment. Despite inexperience with trade issues, a history of limited cross-border cooperation, and diverging interests and ideas, environmental organizations from Mexico, the US and Canada succeeded in jointly making the environment an important issue in the trade negotiations.

The principal reason for the intensity of environmental protests against NAFTA was the uncommon situation of economic integration of a developing country bordering on a highly industrialized country. In general, free trade between countries with different environmental policies may have considerable ecological and economic implications, and combined with strongly diverging development and wage levels concerns are likely to be great. In the NAFTA debate, environmental issues and environmentalist demands became linked to other (economic, social) interests and concerns. In Mexico, fear of bankruptcy of many small companies, or of an exodus of subsistence farmers interfered with questions of diverging environmental standards and sustainable development, although government propaganda and weak organized opposition to NAFTA in Mexico prevented a national NAFTA environment debate. In the US, unfair competition and employment concerns were linked to the idea of Mexico's becoming a pollution haven. With the US Congress adopting many of these issues, transnational activities were primarily directed towards Washington DC.

The transnational NAFTA environment debate between governments, NGOs, private sector organizations and other political actors went through three phases. During the first phase of the debate, from June 1990 until April 1991, environmental organizations explored the issues at stake. Through studies, declarations and transnational meetings, ENGOs exchanged ideas and got to know one another. As a majority in the US Congress linked environmental concerns to fast track approval, in May 1991 President Bush made a commitment to address a few of these concerns in the trade negotiations, while speeding up bilateral cooperation with Mexico. Based on existing differences, these commitments effectively split the US environmental movement and strongly affected further transnational ENGO activism. They also marked the start of the debate's second phase, which revolved around Mexico-US environmental cooperation and the incorporation of environmental provisions in NAFTA. After NGO discussions had dominated the first phase of the NAFTA environment debate, the Bush administration and to a lesser extent the Mexican government actively participated in the second phase by producing analyses, proposals and plans.

When the trade negotiations were completed in August 1992, the outcome was denounced by both critical and moderate ENGOs. In the context of internal US political circumstances, incoming President Clinton convinced Mexico and Canada to negotiate a supplemental environmental agreement. In the third phase of the NAFTA environment debate, between October 1992 and November 1993, private sector organizations became involved too. The main topic was the authority of the regional environmental commission that would be created, and in particular trade sanctions were a sensitive issue. Major tensions arose among NAFTA proponents as there was no support for these proposals outside the Clinton Administration. After the completion of the supplemental agreements on the environment and labour standards in August 1993, there was continuing uncertainty as to whether the resistance in the US would impede NAFTA's becoming effective, and proponents of NAFTA united again in their intensified coordinated lobbies in Washington DC. The debate's third phase ended with the ratification of the NAFTA package by the US Congress in November 1993.

The split between moderate and critical environmental organizations had a determining influence on the second and third phases of the NAFTA environment debate. Instead of the initial two contrasting positions of environmental organizations and proponents of free trade, a third and intermediate position came from moderate ENGOs who accepted or applauded free trade as the route for development, while posing certain environmental demands. Politically, moderate organizations also operated between critical NGOs and government agencies. Especially in the US, moderate organizations participated in governmental and congressional processes, reaping the benefits of the pressure created by critical groups. Within Mexico, the NAFTA process was largely a government affair, but the limited NGO input was also dominated by moderate organizations who were occasionally allowed restricted participation in NAFTA discussions and negotiations. Critical organizations in Mexico, the US and Canada, on the other hand, attempted to establish strong ties with various non-environmental organizations, such as unions, organizations for local development, human rights groups, and women organizations. These different political strategies were also evident at the transnational level. The transnational relations of moderate groups had a rather temporary, coalitional character, whereas critical environmental organizations formed a more structural alliance that in the end developed a joint alternative to NAFTA.

While ENGOs were successful in having the environment integrated into the trade negotiations and the NAFTA package, the moderate-critical divide, which was continuously fed by the US government, allowed the three governments to ignore the more fundamental issues raised by critical groups. Endorsement of environmental concessions and provisions by the main moderate US organizations was sought in order to convince the majority of US Congress. As a consequence of this situation, and of the regional inequalities in general, US perceptions and concerns dominated in the transnational debate. In Mexico, the main environmentalist concerns were uncontrolled industrialization, deepened inequalities, and rapid exploitation of natural resources. The latter was also of concern to Canadians, who additionally wanted to safeguard their stringent environmental legislation. Similarly, a major US concern was the legal and political obstacles to stringent environmental legislation, as well as more problems of ecological degradation in the border region, and the import of toxic goods. In addition, Mexico's weak environmental policy enforcement added to the US fear of relocation of plants to Mexico. As we have seen, typical US issues were to a larger extent addressed in the NAFTA debate as well as in the NAFTA package than Mexican and Canadian concerns. Nevertheless, the debate rendered the environment a legitimate and indispensable issue in North American politics.

These national differences raise questions of the durability of the transnational relations established during the NAFTA environment debate. The development of the NAFTA plan was a political moment that encouraged transnational relations and initiatives which had not been achieved at the level of civil society in North America before. However, to speak of a coming into being of something like a regional civil society seems very premature. For Mexico, NAFTA implied the consolidation of the transnationalization of production, finance and the state, compared to which the transnational counter-movement was still fragile. Predominantly, the NAFTA plan and the NAFTA environment debate produced a basis for transnational relations which may be activated rapidly again.

Implications of the NAFTA package

The NAFTA environment debate gave rise to several arrangements, including the environmental provisions in the trade agreement, Mexico-US environmental programmes, and the supplemental environmental agreement. This NAFTA package is progressive when compared to GATT's environmental provisions, and therefore serves as an international example of how the environment can be integrated in free trade agreements. NAFTA arrangements encourage environmental cooperation between its member countries, and allow for a few limitations on free flows of goods and capital for the sake of environmental protection. Although the neoliberal integration scheme of NAFTA implies more influence of market forces and less government control, the NAFTA package stimulates some joint government efforts and secures certain regional avenues for NGO participation. In the event of new accessions to NAFTA, the supplemental agreements do not apply, but negotiations will have to address environmental concerns.

Mexico-US environmental issues were largely dealt with via NAFTA-linked bilateral arrangements, and a large number of these arrangements focus on the border region. While this focus will benefit that region, the impact of the NAFTA package on the rest of Mexico will remain rather limited. Especially the absence of funding arrangements for regional environmental initiatives is a lost opportunity for improving Mexico's situation. The more influential elements of the package for Mexico as a whole are part of the supplemental agreement. Its provision on enforcement of environmental policy was directed at Mexico, and even though it is unlikely that the ultimate penalty of trade sanctions will ever be used, the dispute settlement arrangement at this point and the negative publicity that such a case would involve render policy enforcement of greater priority to the Mexican government. However, this does not necessarily imply a constant protection of existing environmental legislation and institutions, as resources for environmental protection in Mexico have decreased since the end of the NAFTA debate.

The creation of the Commission for Environmental Cooperation (CEC) is the most far-reaching element of the NAFTA package, but whether the commission will be basically an institution for analysis, or instead become a booster of political and policy integration at the regional level depends largely on the three governments. Monitoring policy and the environment, and encouragement of the regional debate are the main tasks of the commission, but the extent of these activities is not certain. The CEC's role thus depends on the priority of the environment in regional politics, which has been rather low since the commission's creation. Nonetheless, the environmental commission makes a crucial contribution through an ongoing closer monitoring of Mexico's environmental performance.

CHANGES IN MEXICO'S ENVIRONMENTAL POLITICS

Let us now return to the question of how the transnational NAFTA environment debate has affected environmental politics in Mexico. As chapter 6 analysed the immediate effects, we shall here turn to the long-term impact. To start with, Mexico's environmental performance is likely to be the subject of external scrutiny in the long run as well. With the NAFTA debate the Mexican government was faced with criticism that could not be as easily averted or silenced as Mexican environmentalist protests before. This criticism linked to NAFTA's destiny even surpassed the regional level, resulting in worldwide attention to Mexico's environmental problems and policy. Apart from CEC's regular policy monitoring, external attention may be easily attracted again in the case of failures. Less than before can Mexico's environmental image be built on a few symbolic projects. Environmental protection will thus remain of a more priority to the Mexican government.

The NAFTA debate also extended the involvement of external actors within Mexico's environmental politics. Several US organizations increased their presence in Mexico in the form of environmental projects or support for Mexican (government and non-governmental) environmental projects. In addition, since improving Mexico's environmental performance became of interest for all NAFTA proponents, the Mexican government received considerable finan-

cial support. This support was predominantly an extension of earlier involvement of the US government and the World Bank. At the political level, apart
from external attention and possible criticism, involvement of external actors
may shift policy priorities and produce innovations. The attention to economic
instruments in environmental policy is a good example of this influence. Moreover, like the international peso crisis relief, the NAFTA environment debate has
demonstrated that international integration intensifies external willingness to
contribute to solving national problems.

Another political change in which the NAFTA environment debate played a
role concerns Mexico's private sector. Mexican business organizations with
transnational interests hardly developed their own position in the debate, as they
largely followed the Mexican government. Nevertheless, through the debate and
the interaction on environmental issues with US counterparts, the environment
gradually became incorporated in the agenda and activities of major Mexican
business organizations. Far from being a priority for the private sector as a whole,
the NAFTA debate did advance environmental consciousness among businessmen as well as activities with respect to environmental protection in several corporate organizations, which in the long run may have considerable effect.

For Mexican ENGOs, the NAFTA debate's effect involved better access to the
transnational political arena. New cross-border relations were established during the debate. These new relations and the external criticism on Mexico's environmental policy hardly contributed to more political influence at the national level of Mexican environmental organizations in general. Moderate
ENGOs to a certain extent benefited from more formal consultation channels,
but participation remained marginal. In this context, it was important that
Mexican groups learned how to attract attention for their political demands
outside Mexico. The NAFTA debate contributed to their visibility and credibility abroad, even beyond North America. This may come in handy in case of
serious government negligence or major failures.

However, more decisive than the opportunities created by the NAFTA debate
for transnational attention to Mexican ENGOs is their position in national
politics and the relation between state and civil society in Mexico in general.
The lack of democracy, a lack which cannot be compensated by indirect transnational politics, continues to dominate the political situation in Mexico. Irre-
spective of the success or failure of the CEC or other NAFTA environmental
arrangements, democracy and options for public participation in Mexico's
decision-making on the environment continue to be necessary if the Mexicans
are to assume their own responsibility for the environment. More political
room for Mexico's ENGOs is crucial for raising further environmental knowledge and consciousness, monitoring policy results, and inciting the govern-

ment to deal with the environmental problems that are most urgent for the Mexican population. So far, however, Mexico seems to have fallen into a political impasse, in which neither the PRI, the opposition nor NGOs are able to improve their position and fundamentally change the political system.

THE FUTURE OF MEXICO'S ENVIRONMENTAL POLICY

Besides the political effects, how did the transnational NAFTA environment debate affect Mexico's environmental policy? From a short-term perspective, if only considering the immediate impact, the effect might be described as two steps forward and one step back. The Mexican government responded actively to the environmental criticism expressed in the debate. The transnational political pressure on Mexico for implementation of its environmental legislation outweighed earlier activities of national ENGOS, as the risk of losing NAFTA gave Mexico enough motivation to make an effort. Between 1991 and1993 several initiatives were taken to change Mexico's poor enforcement record. Helped by other major NAFTA proponents such as the US government and the World Bank, the environmental institutional structure was reformed, personnel were recruited, trained and equipped, and legislation was elaborated. Apart from external support, these improvements were based on a multiplication of the federal resources for the environmental agencies, reflecting the increased priority of the environment for the Mexican government. However, not all of the progress that was made during the NAFTA debate was structural. In interviews, several high-level Mexican government officials revealed that shortly after the NAFTA debate the environmental budget went down, that environmental protection lost part of its urgency for the government as a whole, and that the environmental agencies are still isolated within the government. In short, a considerable share of the progress of Mexico's environmental policy made in the context of the NAFTA debate proved of limited durability.

The fact that the NAFTA environment debate reinforced the Mexican government's narrow approach of environmental protection is another reason to question the government efforts during the debate. There was a striking preponderance of trade-related issues and US concerns in the NAFTA environment debate, as a result of which several Mexican issues were ignored. Focusing on pollution caused by the industrial sector implied a neglect of many other problems and the largest share of Mexico's territory. Several factors explain the narrow environmental focus of the NAFTA debate. First, the debate was a free trade debate, and although its proponents could not keep the environmental issue off the table they managed to restrict its focus. Second, the domination of US interests and moderate groups was evident throughout the whole debate and resulted in limited attention to Mexican problems which would not negatively affect the US. Third, the debate's narrow focus was partly caused by the strategy of the moderate wing of the US environmental movement in accepting the narrow environmental approach of the three governments and denouncing proposals by critical organizations for a North American development initiative which would comprehensively deal with environmental issues.

Moreover, the NAFTA approach towards Mexico's development problems was narrow. During the debate, proponents managed to establish a general idea of economic growth as the solution to Mexico's problems, with market forces leading the way. There was little attention to the nature of the development problems of Mexico, and the agreement does not provide for development funding like, for instance, the European Union. The Mexico-US border has become the subject of support for bilateral institutions, which assume some responsibility for the development of the region, in particular its infrastructure. A more profound concern for sustainable development in Mexico, let alone North America, was absent. However, this is the immediate result of NAFTA's aim: creating a zone of free trade and investment with a minimum of political and policy integration. Regional support for backward regions or regulating the exploitation and use of natural resources do not fit into such a neoliberal scheme. North American asymmetries and Mexico's resistance to regional institutions with supranational authority are likely to hinder such initiatives in the future.

In the medium and long run, then, NAFTA is likely to be detrimental to Mexico's options for sustainable development. The narrow approach of NAFTA's environmental package and the absence of development support are lost opportunities for sustainable regional integration. The Mexican government primarily needs to find ways to deal with the ongoing economic crisis and social misery, which may still produce a political crisis. A few steps towards political democratization have temporarily relieved some citizen dissatisfaction and improved the international image of Mexico, but the development issue is far from solved. Contrary to ideas of matching development and environment solutions, the alleviation or solution of social and economic problems will most likely come at the cost of attention to and resources for the environment. The beneficial socio-economic effect of growth brought by regional integration is likely to come only after a long time lag and considerable environmental damage. And if claims of NAFTA proponents that economic growth produces the resources necessary to cover environmental protection and social needs do materialize in the long run, Mexico will "achieve" the same ambiguity as the US, combining stringent environmental norms with extremely wasteful consumption patterns.

References

Adler Hellman, Judith. 1991. *Mexican Popular Movements, Clientelism, and the Process of Democratization*. Paper prepared for the CEDLA / CERLAC joint workshop on Social Movements and Power Relations: The Latin American Experience, Amsterdam, 13-15 November.

Aguilar Zinser, Adolfo. 1993. "Authoritarianism and North American Free Trade: The Debate in Mexico" in: Ricardo Grinspun and Maxwell A. Cameron (eds), *The Political Economy of North American Free Trade*, New York: St. Martin's Press.

Alba Vega, Carlos. 1993. "El empresariado mexicano ante el Tratado de Libre Comercio en América del Norte" in: Gustavo Vega Cánovas (ed.), *Liberación Económica y Libre Comercio en América del Norte*, México: El Colegio de México.

Alexander, Carol, and Ken Stump. 1992. *The North American Free Trade Agreement and Energy Trade*. Washington: Greenpeace.

Alfie, Miriam. 1991. "Ecología y Tratado de Libre Comercio". *El Cotidiano* 43, 57-62.

—. 1995. "La realidad del movimiento ecologista en México". *El Cotidiano* 70, 14-8.

Alonzo, Anne L. 1992. *Mexico*. Paper presented at Loyola Law School Symposium: Free Trade and the Environment in Latin America.

Alvarez Béjar, Alejandro, and Gabriel Mendoza Pichardo. 1993. "Mexico 1988-91. A Successful Economic Adjustment Program?". *Latin American Perspectives* 20 (3) 32-45.

AMCHAM. 1993. *Environmental Compliance and Enforcement in Mexico: A Corporate View*.

Anderson, Sarah, John Cavanagh, and Sandra Gross. 1993. *NAFTA's corporate cadre. An analysis of the USA*NAFTA State Captains*. Washington: The Institute for Policy Studies.

Arías, José, and Luis Barquera. 1988. *¿Laguna Verde nuclear? ¡No, gracias!* México DF: Claves Latinoamericanas.

Arídjis, Homero (Grupo de los Cien). 1993. *Mexico's environmental movement and its influence on the NAFTA negotiations*. Paper.

Arídjis, Homero, et al. 1992, April 10. Letter of 20 Mexican ENGOs to President Carlos Salinas de Gortari.

Aspe, Pedro. 1993. *Economic Transformation the Mexican Way*. Cambridge, MA: The MIT Press.

Atkeson, Timothy. 1992. "The Mexican-U.S. Border Environmental Plan". *Journal of Environment & Development* 1 (1) 143-9.

Audley, John J. 1995. *What Environmentalists Got in* NAFTA: *Environmental Participation in Trade Policy.* Paper presented at the 36th annual International Studies Association Conference, February 21.

Audley, John J., and Eric M. Uslaner. 1994. "NAFTA, the Environment, and American Domestic Politics". *North American Outlook* 4 (3) 23-58.

Bailey, John. 1994. "Centralism and Political Change in Mexico: The Case of National Solidarity" in: Wayne A. Cornelius, Ann L. Craig, and Jonathan Fox (eds), *Transforming State-Society Relations in Mexico. The National Solidarity Strategy*, San Diego: Center for U.S.-Mexican Studies.

Barba Pírez, Regina. 1993. "La Unión de Grupos Ambientalistas en el proceso de negociación del Tratado de Libre Comercio", *Frontera Norte* 5 (10) 117-132.

Barkin, David. 1990. *Distorted Development. Mexico in the World Economy.* Boulder: Westview Press.

—. 1991. "State Control of the Environment: Politics and Degradation in Mexico". *Capitalism Nature Socialism* 2 (1) 86-108.

—. 1992. "El impacto ambiental del Tratado de Libre Comercio en el campo mexicano" in: Cuauthémoc González Pacheco (ed.), *El Sector Agropecuario Mexicano al Tratado de Libre Comercio*, México DF: Instituto de Investigaciones Económicas, UNAM.

—. 1993. "Salinastroika and Other Novel Ideas". *Economic and Political Weekly*, March 20-27, 531-7.

—. 1994. "Las Organizaciones No Gubernamentales Ambientalistas en México" in: Alberto Glender and Víctor Lichtinger (eds), *La diplomacia ambiental, México y la Conferencia de las Naciones Unidas sobre Medio Ambiente y Desarrollo*, México DF: Secretaría de Relaciones Exteriores and Fondo de Cultura Económica.

Barkin, David, and Stephen Mumme. 1992. US *Environmental NGOs in Mexico: Their Orientation, Structure and Impact.* Paper for the ISA Conference in Acapulco, Mexico, March.

Barry, Tom, and Beth Sims. 1994. *The Challenge of Cross-Border Environmentalism. The U.S.-Mexico Case.* Albuquerque, NM: Resource Center Press and Bisbee, AR: Border Ecology Project.

Barton Bray, David. 1995. "Peasant Organizations and 'The Permanent Reconstruction of Nature': Grassroots Sustainable Development in Rural Mexico". *Journal of Environment & Development* 4 (2) 185-204.

Bath, C. Richard. 1991. *The Impact of the Proposed U.S.-Mexico Free Trade Agreement on the Border Environment.* Paper.

Bielschowsky, Ricardo A., and Giovanni Stumpo. 1995. "Empresas transnacionales y cambios estructurales en la industria de Argentina, Brasil, Chile y México". *Revista de la* CEPAL 55, 139-64.

Bizberg, Ilán. 1990. "La Crísis del corporativismo mexicano". *Foro Internacional* XXX (4) 694-735.

—. 1993a. "Los efectos de la apertura comercial sobre el mercado laboral y las relaciones industriales en México" in: Gustavo Vega Cánovas (ed.), *Liberación Económica y Libre Comercio en América del Norte*, México DF: El Colegio de México.

—. 1993b. "Modernization and corporatism in government – labour relations" in: Neil Harvey (ed.), *Mexico: Dilemmas of Transition*, London: British Academic Press.

Blanco Mendoza, Herminio. 1994. *Las negociaciones comerciales de México con el Mundo.* México DF: Fondo de Cultura Económica.

Brañes, Raúl. 1994. *Manual de derecho ambiental mexicano.* México DF: Fundación mexicana para la educación ambiental and Fondo de Cultura Económica.

Bustamante, Jorge A. 1991. "El Consejo Asesor del Tratado de Libre Comercio" in: Mario Ojeda Gómez et al., *Hacia un Tratado de Libre Comercio en América del Norte,* México DF: Secretaría de Comercio y Fomento Industrial.

Caballero U., Emilio (ed.). 1991. *El Tratado de Libre Comercio. México, EUA, Canadá. Beneficios y Desventajas.* México DF: Editorial Diana.

Calva, José Luis. 1991. *Probables Efectos de un Tratado de Libre Comercio en el Campo Mexicano.* México DF: Distribuciones Fontamara.

—. 1993. *La Disputa Por La Tierra, La reforma del Artículo 27 y la nueva Ley Agraria.* México DF: Distribuciones Fontamara.

Carabias, Julia, and Enrique Provencio. 1994. "La política ambiental mexicana antes y después de Rio" in: Alberto Glender and Víctor Lichtinger (eds), *La diplomacia ambiental, México y la Conferencia de las Naciones Unidas sobre Medio Ambiente y Desarrollo,* México: Secretaría de Relaciones Exteriores and Fondo de Cultura Económica.

Cárdenas, Cuauhtémoc. 1991. "Speech for the Convention of the B.C. Federation of Labour in Vancouver, 30 November 1990". *The Pro-Canada Dossier* 29.

—. 1992. "Free Trade, the Environment, and the Need for a Social Charter". *Loyola of Los Angeles International and Comparative Law Journal* 15 (1) 71-8.

Carmona Lara, María del Carmen. 1991. "Derecho Ecológico" in: *El Derecho en México, Una visión de conjunto* Tomo III, México DF: UNAM, Instituto de Investigaciones Jurídicas.

Carruthers, David V. 1996. "Indigenous ecology and the politics of linkage in Mexican social movements". *Third World Quarterly* 17 (5) 1007-28.

Castañeda, Jorge G. 1993. "The Clouding Political Horizon". *Current History* February, 59-66.

Castañeda, Jorge G., and Carlos Heredia. 1992. "Another NAFTA: What a Good Agreement Should Offer". *World Policy Journal* IX (4) 673-85.

Centeno, Miguel Angel. 1994. *Democracy within Reason. Technocratic Revolution in Mexico.* Pennsylvania: Pennsylvania State Press.

Centeno, Miguel Angel, and Sylvia Maxfield. 1992. "The Marriage of Finance and Order: Changes in the Mexican Political Elite". *Journal of Latin American Studies* 24 (1) 57-85.

CNI (Community Nutrition Institute). 1991. *Brief of Community Nutrition Institute concerning negotiation of a North American Free Trade Agreement.* Presented to the Trade Policy Staff Committee Office of the United States Trade Representative, Washington, August 12.

Coll-Hurtado, Atlandita. 1993. "Recursos naturales y desarrollo sustentable" in: José Luis Calva (ed.), *Alternativas Para el Campo Mexicano,* Tomo II, México DF: Fontamara, PUAL-UNAM and Fundación Friedrich Ebert.

Commins, Margaret M. 1994. *The New Regional Agenda of American Trade Politics: Explaining U.S. Support for the NAFTA.* Paper presented at the 35th Annual Convention of the International Studies Association, Washington, April 1.

Cook, Maria Lorena, Kevin J. Middlebrook, and Juan Molinar Horcasitas (eds). 1994. *The Politics of Economic Restructuring. State-Society Relations and Regime Change in Mexico*. San Diego: Center for U.S.-Mexican Studies.

Coote, Belinda. 1995. *NAFTA. Poverty and Free Trade in Mexico*. Oxford: Oxfam Publications.

Cornelius, Wayne A., and Ann L. Craig. 1991. *The Mexican Political System in Transition*. San Diego: Center for U.S.-Mexico Studies.

Cornelius, Wayne A., Ann L. Craig, and Jonathan Fox (eds). 1994. *Transforming State-Society Relations in Mexico. The National Solidarity Strategy*. San Diego: Center for U.S.-Mexican Studies.

Correa, Eugenia. 1993. "Mexico and financial services in NAFTA". *Mondes en developpement* 21 (84) 19-23.

—. 1994. "Apertura, liberalización y reestructuración del mercado financiero". *Mondes en developpement* 22 (87) 21-27.

Corro Barrientos, Bernardo. 1991. "Apertura comercial de México y nueva proyección mundial de Estados Unidos". *Comercio Exterior* 41 (7) 676-81.

Cox, Robert W. 1983. "Gramsci, Hegemony and International Relations: An Essay in Method". *Millenium* 12 (2) 162-175.

—. 1987. *Production, Power and World Order. Social Forces in the Making of History*. New York: Columbia University Press.

—. 1991. "The Global Economy and Social Choice" in: Daniel Drache and Meric S. Gertler (eds), *The New Era of Global Competition. State Policy and Market Power*, Montreal and Kingston: McGill-Queen's University Press.

CPI (Center for Public Integrity). 1993. *The Trading Game. Inside Lobbying for the North American Free Trade Agreement*. Washington.

Cronin, Patrick. 1994. *Domestic versus international influences on state behavior: trade liberalization in Mexico*. Paper presented at the Latin American Studies Association XVIII International Congress, Atlanta, Georgia, March 10-12.

Cypher, James M. 1990. *State and Capital in Mexico. Development Policy Since 1940*. Boulder: Westview Press.

Davis, Diane E. 1992. "Mexico's new politics: changing perspectives on free trade". *World Policy Journal* IX (4) 655-71.

De la Garza Toledo, Enrique. 1994. "The Restructuring of State-Labor Relations in Mexico" in: Maria Lorena Cook, Kevin J. Middlebrook and Juan Molinar Horcasitas (eds), *The Politics of Economic Restructuring. State-Society Relations and Regime Change in Mexico*, San Diego: Center for U.S.-Mexican Studies.

Demmers, Jolle, and Barbara Hogenboom. 1992. *Popular Organization and Party Dominance. The Political Role of Environmental NGOs in Mexico*. Amsterdam: University of Amsterdam, Master thesis.

Dillon, John. 1993. "The Petroleum Sector under Continental Integration" in: Ricardo Grinspun and Maxwell A. Cameron (eds), *The Political Economy of North American Free Trade*, New York: St. Martin's Press.

Dresser, Denise. 1991. *Neopopulist Solutions to Neoliberal Problems. Mexico's National Solidarity Program*. San Diego: Center for U.S.-Mexican Studies.

—. 1994a. "Bringing the Poor Back In: National Solidarity as a Strategy of Regime-Legitimation" in: Wayne A. Cornelius, Ann L. Craig and Jonathan Fox (eds), *Transforming State-Society Relations in Mexico. The National Solidarity Strategy*, San Diego: Center for u.s.-Mexican Studies.

—. 1994b. "Embellishment, Empowerment or Euthanasia of the PRI? Neoliberalism and Party Reform in Mexico" in: Maria Lorena Cook, Kevin J. Middlebrook and Juan Molinar Horcasitas (eds), *The Politics of Economic Restructuring. State-Society Relations and Regime Change in Mexico*, San Diego: Center for u.s.-Mexican Studies.

—. 1995. *Preaching to the Unconverted: Political Constraints to Economic Adjustment in Mexico*. Paper presented at the XIX International Congress of the Latin American Studies Association, Washington, September 28-30.

Eden, Lorraine, and Maureen Appel Molot. 1993. "De la integración silenciosa a la alianza estratégica: la economía política del libre comercio en América Latina" in: Gustavo Vega Cánovas (ed.), *Liberación Económica y Libre Comercio en América del Norte*, México: El Colegio de México.

Embassy of Mexico. 1992. *Mexico Environmental Issues. Fact Sheets*. Washington.

—. Undated a. *NAFTA: A Partnership for Growth and Competitiveness*. Brochure.

—. Undated b. *Mexico/United States Free Trade. Fact Sheets*. Brochure

EPA. 1991, November 22. *Evaluation of Mexico's environmental laws and regulations. Interim report on EPA findings*. Office of General Counsel, International Activities Division.

—. 1992. *Summary. Environmental Plan for the Mexican-U.S. Border Area*.

Ezcurra, Exequiel. 1995. "Las Manifestaciones de impacto ambiental. Un análisis crítico". *Industria* junio, 33-8.

Faber, Daniel. 1992. "The Ecological Crisis of Latin America, A Theoretical Introduction". *Latin American Perspectives* 19 (1) 3-16.

Fernández Jilberto, Alex E., and Barbara Hogenboom. 1996. "Mexico's integration in NAFTA: Neoliberal Restructuring and Changing Political Alliances" in: Alex E. Fernández Jilberto and André Mommen (eds), *Liberalization in the Developing World, Institutional and economic changes in Latin America, Africa and Asia*, London and New York: Routledge.

—. 1998. "The Politics of Open Regionalism and Neoliberal Economic Integration in Latin America: The Case of Chile and Mexico" in: Alex E. Fernández Jilberto and André Mommen (eds), *Regionalization and Globalization in the Modern World Economy. Perspectives on the Third World and Transitional Economies*, London and New York: Routledge.

Fox, Jonathan, and Luis Hernández. 1992. "Mexico's Difficult Democracy: Grassroots Movements, NGOs, and Local Government", *Alternatives* 17, 165-208.

Gallardo, Juan. 1991. "La coordinadora de organismos empresariales para el comercio exterior" in: Mario Ojeda Gómez et al., *Hacia un Tratado de Libre Comercio en América del Norte*, México DF: Secretaría de Comercio y Fomento Industrial.

Gallardo C., Sofía. 1993. "El debate sobre el Acuerdo de Cooperación Ambiental". *Estados Unidos: Informe Trimestral* invierno, 34-48.

—. 1994. *Diferencias y posiciones en el movimiento ambientalista frente al Tratado de Libre Comercio de América del Norte*. Paper for LASA conference, 9-12/III/94.

GAO (United States General Accounting Office). 1991. *U.S.-Mexico Trade. Information on Environmental Regulations and Enforcement.* Report to the Chairman, Committee on Commerce, Science and Transportation, U.S. Senate.

—. 1992. *U.S.-Mexico Trade. Assessment of Mexico's Environmental Controls for New Companies.* Report to the Chairman, Committee on Commerce, Science and Transportation, U.S. Senate.

Garrido, Celso. 1994. "Grupos privados nacionales en México, 1987-1993". *Revista de la CEPAL* 53, 159-75.

Garrido Noguera, Celso, and Enrique Quintana López. 1987. "Financial Relations and Economic Power in Mexico" in: Sylvia Maxfield and Ricardo Anzualda M. (eds), *Government and private sector in contemporary Mexico*, San Diego: Center for U.S.-Mexico Studies.

Gestrin, Michael, and Alan M. Rugman. 1994. "The North American Free Trade Agreement and foreign direct investment". *Transnational Corporations* 3 (1) 77-95.

Gil Villegas M., Francisco. 1994. "La política de protección al medio ambiente en México durante el gobierno de Carlos Salinas de Gortari" in: Antonio Yúnez-Naude (ed.), *Medio Ambiente, problemas y soluciones*, México DF: El Colegio de México.

Gilbreath, Jan. 1992a. *Planning for the Border's Future: The Mexican-U.S. Integrated Border Environmental Plan.* U.S.-Mexican Occasional Paper No. 1, U.S.-Mexican Policy Studies Program, LBJ School of Public Affairs, The University of Texas at Austin.

—. 1992b. "Financing Environmental Infrastructure on the Texas-Mexico Border: Will the Mexican-US Border Plan Help?". *Journal of Environment & Development* 1 (1) 151-75.

Gilbreath, Jan, and John Benjamin Tonra. 1994. "The Environment: Unwelcome Guest at the Party" in: M. Delal Baer and Sidney Weintraub (eds), *The NAFTA Debate. Grappling with Unconventional Trade Issues*, Boulder and London: Lynne Rienner Publishers.

Gill, Stephen. 1990. *American Hegemony and the Trilateral Commission.* Cambridge: Cambridge University Press.

—. 1993. "Neoliberalism and the shift towards a US-centred transnational hegemony" in: Henk Overbeek (ed.), *Restructuring hegemony in the global political economy*, London and New York: Routledge.

Gill, Stephen, and David Law. 1993. "Global hegemony and the structural power of capital" in: Stephen Gill (ed.), *Gramsci, historical materialism and international relations*, Cambridge: Cambridge University Press.

Globerman, Steven. 1994. "The Economics of NAFTA" in: Alan M. Rugman (ed.), *Foreign Investment and NAFTA*, Columbia: University of South Carolina Press.

Godau Schucking, Rainer. 1985. "La protección ambiental en México, sobre la conformación de una política pública". *Estudios Sociológicos* III (7) 47-83.

Gómez, Leopoldo, and John Bailey. 1990. "La transición política y los dilemas del PRI". *Foro Internacional* XXXI (1) 57-87.

Góngora Soberanes, Janette. 1991. *El ecologismo en México.* Paper.

González Martínez, Alfonso. 1994. "Las luchas ecológico-sociales en México: prospectivas" in: María Pilar García-Guadilla and Jutta Blauert (eds), *Retos para el desarrollo y la democracia: movimientos ambientales en América Latina y Europa*, México: Fundación Friedrich Ebert de México and Caracas: Editorial Nueva Sociedad.

Government of Canada. 1992. *North American Free Trade Agreement, Canadian environmental review.*

Government of Mexico. Undated. *A better Mexico * a better environment.* Brochure.

Gregory, Michael. 1992. "Environment, Sustainable Development, Public Participation and the NAFTA: a Retrospective". Prepublication copy, scheduled to appear in *Journal of Environmental Law and Litigation*, Summer 1992.

Grinspun, Ricardo, and Robert Kreklewich. 1993. *Consolidating neoliberal reforms: "free trade" as a conditioning framework.* Paper, York University (to be published in *Studies in Political Economy*).

Grossman, Gene M., and Alan B. Krueger. 1991. *Environmental impacts of a North American free trade agreement.* Discussion Papers in Economics, Woodrow Wilson School, Princeton University, Princeton, New Jersey.

Guillen, Arturo. 1994. "El proceso de privatización en México". *Mondes en Developpement* 22 (87) 29-39.

Günther, Regina Andrea. 1989/90. *Umweltpolitik und Umweltsituation in Mexiko unter besonderes Berücksichtigung von Mexico City.* Mimeo, Diplomarbeit, FU, Berlin.

Haber, Paul. 1994a. "Political Change in Durango: The Role of National Strategy" in: Wayne A. Cornelius, Ann L. Craig and Jonathan Fox (eds), *Transforming State-Society Relations in Mexico. The National Solidarity Strategy*, San Diego: Center for U.S.-Mexican Studies.

—. 1994b. "The Art and Implications of Political Restructuring in Mexico: The Case of Urban Popular Movement" in: Maria Lorena Cook, Kevin J. Middlebrook and Juan Molinar Horcasitas (eds), *The Politics of Economic Restructuring. State-Society Relations and Regime Change in Mexico*, San Diego: Center for U.S.-Mexican Studies.

Harvey, Neil. 1993. "The Difficult Transition: Neoliberalism and Neocorporatism in Mexico" in: Neil Harvey (ed.), *Mexico: Dilemmas of Transition*, London: British Academic Press.

Heredia, Blanca. 1992. "Profits, Politics, and Size: The Political Transformation of Mexican Business" in: Douglas A. Chalmers, Mario do Carmo and Atilio A. Boron (eds), *The Right and Democracy in Latin America*, New York: Praeger.

Heredia, Carlos A., and Mary E. Purcell. 1994. *La polarización de la sociedad mexicana: una visión desde la base de las políticas de ajuste económico del Banco Mundial.* Washington: The Development GAP.

Heredia Zubieta, Carlos. 1991. *Las organizaciones no gubernamentales y el medio ambiente ante el Tratado de Libre Comercio.* Ponencia en la Mesa Redonda 'El Tratado de Libre Comercio y el Medio Ambiente', UNAM, México DF, 3/XI/91.

Hernández Lezama, Luis Fernando. 1994. "El ambiente y la salud humana" in: Alberto Glender and Víctor Lichtinger (eds), *La diplomacia ambiental, México y la Conferencia de las Naciones Unidas sobre Medio Ambiente y Desarrollo*, México: Secretaría de Relaciones Exteriores and Fondo de Cultura Económica.

Hernández Rodríguez, Rogelio. 1991. "La reforma interna y los conflictos en el PRI". *Foro Internacional* XXXII (2) 222-49.

Hogenboom, Barbara. 1996. "Cooperation and polarisation beyond borders: the trans-nationalisation of Mexican environmental issues during the NAFTA negotiations". *Third World Quarterly* 17 (5) 989-1005.

—. 1997. "Mexico: Open Regionalism and the Politics of a Transnationalizing State". *International Journal of Political Economy* 26 (3) 12-31, special issue: The Political Economy of Open Regionalism in Latin America, edited by Alex E. Fernández Jilberto and Barbara Hogenboom.

Houseman, Robert F., and Paul M. Orbuch. 1993. "Integrating Labor and Environmental Concerns into the North American Free Trade Agreement: A Look Back and a Look Ahead". *The American University Journal of International Law and Policy* 8 (4) 721-815.

Hudson, Stewart. 1992. "Trade, Environment and the Pursuit of Sustainable Development" in: Patrick Low (ed.), *International Trade and the Environment*, Washington: The World Bank, World Bank Discussion Paper 159, 55-64.

Hufbauer, Gary Clyde, and Jeffrey J. Schott. 1993. *NAFTA. An Assessment.* Washington: Institute for International Economics.

Human Rights Watch and NRDC. 1992. *Defending the Earth: Abuses of Human Rights and the Environment.*

Hustis, Brenda S. 1993. "The Environmental Implications of the North American Free Trade Agreement". *Texas International Law Journal* 28 (3) 589-632.

Jarque, Carlos M. 1994. "Cuentas Nacionales y medio ambiente" in: Alberto Glender and Víctor Lichtinger (eds), *La diplomacia ambiental, México y la Conferencia de las Naciones Unidas sobre Medio Ambiente y Desarrollo*, México: Secretaría de Relaciones Exteriores and Fondo de Cultura Económica.

Jessop, Bob. 1992. *Changing Forms and Functions of the State in an era of globalization and regionalization.* Paper presented to EAPE Conference, Paris, 4-7 November.

Kamp, Dick (Border Ecology Project). 1991. *EPA-SEDUE Integrated Border Environmental Plan Public Hearing.* Testimony.

Keck, Margaret, and Kathryn Sikkink. 1995. *Transnational Issue Networks in International Politics.* Paper presented a the XIX International Congress of the Latin American Studies Association, Washington, September 28-30.

Kehoe, Timothy J. 1994. "Assessing the Economic Impact of North American Free Trade" in: M. Delal Baer and Sidney Weintraub (eds), *The NAFTA Debate, Grappling with Unconventional Trade Issues*, Boulder and London: Lynne Rienner Publishers.

Kelly, Mary E. 1991. *Remarks before U.S. Environmental Protection Agency regarding Draft Integrated Border Environment Plan.* Texas Center for Policy Studies.

—. 1993a. "Review of the NAFTA Environmental Side Agreement: Does it Meet Expectations?" *Frontera Norte* 5 (10) 133-48.

—. 1993b. "Cross-Border NGO Relations in the Environmental Arena". *Enfoque* (Center for U.S.-Mexican Studies, University of California, San Diego) Spring.

Kelly, Mary E., and Dick Kamp. 1991. *Mexico-U.S. Free Trade Negotiations and the Environment: Exploring the Issues*, discussion paper, research by Jan Rich, Texas Center for Policy Studies and Border Ecology Project.

Kolk, Ans. 1996. *Forests in International Environmental Politics. International Organisations, NGOs and the Brazilian Amazon.* Utrecht: International Books.

Krasner, Stephen D. 1993. "Bloques económicos regionales y el fin de la guerra fría" in: Gustavo Vega Cánovas (ed.), *Liberación Económica y Libre Comercio en América del Norte*, México: El Colegio de México.

Krugman, Paul. 1993. "The Uncomfortable Truth about NAFTA". *Foreign Affairs* 72 (5) 13-9.

—. 1995. "Dutch Tulips and Emerging Markets". *Foreign Affairs* 74 (4) 28-44.

Kürzinger, Edith, et al. 1990. *Umweltpolitik in Mexiko: Die Rolle der Nicht-Regierungs-organisationen.* Berlin: Deutsches Institut für Entwicklungspolitik.

Land, Geoffrey. 1993. "North American Free Trade and the Environment: Border Environmental Groups and the NAFTA". *Frontera Norte* 5 (10) 99-115.

Latapí, Pablo. 1992. "El 'liberalismo social' en el Informe". *Proceso* 836, 9/XI/92, 40-1.

Lee, Thea. 1992. "NAFTA and the environment: a critique of Grossman and Krueger". Washington: Economic Policy Institute.

Leff, Enrique. 1994. "El movimiento ambiental y las perspectivas de la democracia en América Latina" in: María Pilar García-Guadilla and Jutta Blauert (eds), *Retos para el desarrollo y la democracia: movimientos ambientales en América Latina y Europa*, México: Fundación Friedrich Ebert de México and Caracas: Editorial Nueva Sociedad.

Legorreta, Jorge. 1994. *Efectos ambientales de la expansión de la Ciudad de México*. México DF: Centro de Ecología y Desarrollo.

Levy, Santiago, and Sweder van Wijnbergen. 1992. *Mexican agriculture in the free trade agreement: transition problems in economic reform.* OECD Development Centre, Technical Papers no. 63.

Loaeza, Soledad. 1994. "Political Liberalization and Uncertainty in Mexico" in: Maria Lorena Cook, Kevin J. Middlebrook and Juan Molinar Horcasitas (eds), *The Politics of Economic Restructuring. State-Society Relations and Regime Change in Mexico*, San Diego: Center for U.S.-Mexican Studies.

London Environmental and Economics Centre. 1992. "Case Study for Mexico" (based on a study directed by Juan Carlos Belausteguigoitia) in: David Reed (ed.), *Structural Adjustment and the Environment*, Boulder: Westview Press.

Luna, Matilde. 1992. "Inconsistencias de la modernización: el caso del Consejo Coordinador Empresarial". *El Cotidiano* 50, 136-41.

Lustig, Nora. 1992. *Mexico. The Remaking of an Economy.* Washington: The Brookings Institution.

—. 1995. "México y la crisis del peso: lo previsible y la sorpresa". *Comercio exterior* mayo, 374-82.

Macdonald, Laura. 1994. "Globalising Civil Society: Interpreting International NGOs in Central America". *Millenium* 23 (2) 267-85.

Maihold, Günther. 1989. "Umweltprobleme als Thema der Aussenpolitik: Mexiko-USA". *Verfassung und Recht in Übersee*, 392-413.

Margulis, Sergio. 1991. *Back of the Envelope Estimates of Environmental Damage Costs in Mexico*. World Bank, Latin American and the Caribbean Region, Internal Discussion Paper, report no. IDP-0104.

Márquez, Miguel, and Roberto López. 1988. "The Impact of Oil Exploitation on the Environment" in: Miguel S. Wionzcek, Oscar M. Guzmán and Roberto Gutiérrez (eds), *Energy Policy in Mexico. Problems and Prospects for the Future*, Boulder and London: Westview Press.

Meacham, Charles E. 1993. "Foreword" in: Beatriz Boza (ed.), *The North American Free Trade Agreement: Provisions and Implications*. Association Internationale des Jeunes Avocats.

Moguel, Julio. 1994. "The Mexican Left and the Social Program of Salinismo" in: Wayne A. Cornelius, Ann L. Craig and Jonathan Fox (eds), *Transforming State-Society Relations in Mexico. The National Solidarity Strategy*, San Diego: Center for U.S.-Mexican Studies.

—. 1995. "Salinas's Failed War on Poverty" in: Fred Rosen and Deidre McFadyen (eds), *Free Trade and Economic Restructuring in Latin America—a NACLA Reader*, New York: Monthly Review Press.

Molina, David J. 1993. "A Comment on Whether Maquiladoras Are in Mexico for Low Wages or to Avoid Pollution Abatement costs". *Journal of Environment & Development* 2 (1) 221-41.

Molinar Horcasitas, Juan, and Jeffrey A. Weldon. 1994. "Electoral Determinants and Consequences of National Solidarity" in: Wayne A. Cornelius, Ann L. Craig and Jonathan Fox (eds), *Transforming State-Society Relations in Mexico. The National Solidarity Strategy*. San Diego: Center for U.S.-Mexican Studies.

Montesinos, Rafael. 1992. "Empresarios en el nuevo orden estatal". *El Cotidiano* 50, 108-14.

Moody, Kim. 1995. "NAFTA and the Corporate Redesign of North America". *Latin American Perspectives* 22 (1) 95-116.

Morris, Stephen D. 1995. *Political Reformism in Mexico. An Overview of Contemporary Mexican Politics*. Boulder and London: Lynne Rienner Publishers.

Mouzelis, Nicos. 1995. "Modernity, Late Development and Civil Society" in: John E. Hall (ed.), *Civil Society. Theory, History, Comparison*, Cambridge: Polity Press.

Mumme, Stephen. 1988. *Apportioning Groundwater beneath the U.S.-Mexico Border*. San Diego: Center for U.S.-Mexican Studies.

—. 1992. "System Maintenance and Environmental Reform in Mexico, Salinas' Pre-emptive Strategy". *Latin American Perspectives* 19 (1) 123-43.

—. 1993. "NAFTA and the Future of Mexico-U.S. Border Environmental Management". *Frontera Norte* 5 (10) 85-98.

Mumme, Stephen P., C. Richard Bath, and Valerie J. Assetto. 1988. "Political development and environmental policy in Mexico". *Latin American Research Review* 23 (1) 7-33.

Mumme, Stephen P., and Roberto Sánchez. 1990. "Mexico's Environment Under Salinas: Institutionalizing Policy Reform". *Review of Latin American Studies* 3 (2) 44-81.

Mumme, Stephen P., and Dimitris Stevis. 1995. *NAFTA and International Social Policy*. Paper prepared for the 36th Annual International Studies Association Convention, Chicago, Illinois, 21-25 February.

Newman, Gray. 1995. "In theory and in practice". *Business Mexico* special edition: 40-3.

NRDC, INAINE and Grupo de los Cien. 1991. *Comments on the Draft Review of U.S.-Mexico Environmental Issues*.

NWF. 1991. *Comments on the Draft Review of U.S.-Mexico Environmental Issues*.

Ortiz, Edgar. 1994. "NAFTA and Foreign Investment in Mexico" in: Alan M. Rugman (ed.), *Foreign Investment and NAFTA*, Columbia: University of South Carolina Press.

OTA (Office of Technology Assessment, U.S. Congress). 1992. *U.S.-Mexico Trade: Pulling Together or Pulling Apart?* Washington: U.S. Government Printing Office. ITE-545.

Palan, Ronen P. 1994. "State and Society in International Relations" in: Ronen P. Palan and Barry Gills (eds), *Transcending the State-Global Divide. A Neostructuralist Agenda in International Relations*, Boulder: Lynne Rienner Publishers.

Pastor, Robert A. 1990. "Post-Revolutionary Mexico: The Salinas Opening". *Journal of InterAmerican Studies and World Affairs* 32 (3) 1-22.

Pastor, Manuel, and Carol Wise. 1994. "The origins and sustainability of Mexico's free trade policy". *International Organization* 48 (3) 459-89.

Van Pelt, Laura J. 1994. "Countervailing Environmental Subsidies: A Solution to the Environmental Inequities of the North American Free Trade Agreement". *Texas International Law Journal* 29 (1) 123-47.

Peña, Devon. 1993. "Letter From Mexico. Mexico's Struggle Against NAFTA". *Capitalism, Nature, Socialism* 4 (4) 123-8.

Peña Ramírez, Jaime. 1991. *Estado, Ecología y Movimiento Social. Evolución reciente.* Paper presented at the XXI Coloquio de Antropología e Historia Regional sobre Sociedad y medio ambiente en México, El Colegio de Michoacán, August 7-9.

Peón Escalante, Ignacio. 1991. "Repercusiones ambientales del Tratado y propuestas para la negociación" in: RMALC, *Libre Comercio o Explotación Libre*, México DF.

Peres Núñez, Wilson. 1990. *From globalization to regionalization: the Mexican case.* OECD Development Centre, technical papers no. 24.

Peterson, M.J. 1992. "Transnational Activity, International Society and World Politics". *Millenium* 21 (3) 371-88.

Phillips, David. 1993. "Dolphins and GATT" in: Ralph Nader et al., *The Case Against Free Trade. GATT, NAFTA and the Globalization of Corporate Power*, San Francisco and Berkely: Earth Island Press and North Atlantic Books.

Poder Ejecutivo Federal. 1989. *Plan Nacional de Desarrollo 1989-1994*. México.

Poitras, Guy, and Raymond Robinson. 1994. "The Politics of NAFTA in Mexico". *Journal of InterAmerican Studies and World Affairs* 36 (1) 1-35.

Public Citizen. 1993. *NAFTA's Bizarre Bazaar. The Deal Making that Bought Congressional votes on the North American Free Trade Agreement.*

Puga, Cristina. 1992. "Medianos y pequeños empresarios: la díficil modernización". *El Cotidiano* 50, 126-9.

—. 1994. *Los industriales mexicanos en una época de cambio (La negociación del TLC).* Paper presented at the XVIII Congress of the Latin American Studies Association, Atlanta, March.

Quadri de la Torre, Gabriel. 1989. "Una breve crónica del ecologismo en México" in: Günther Maihold and Leonardo Meza (eds), *Ecología: motivo de solidaridad*, México DF: Friedrich Ebert Stiftung.

—. 1994. "La política ambiental en México. Necesidades y prioridades" in: Alberto Glender and Víctor Lichtinger (eds), *La diplomacia ambiental, México y la Conferencia de las Naciones Unidas sobre Medio Ambiente y Desarrollo*, México: Secretaría de Relaciones Exteriores and Fondo de Cultura Económica.

Quadri de la Torre, Gabriel, and Enrique Provencio Durazo. 1994. *Partidos políticos y medio ambiente, Experiencias internacionales y perspectivas para México*. México DF: El Colegio de México.

Rebolledo, Juan. 1993. *La reforma del Estado en México*. México: Fondo de Cultura Económica.

Redclift, Michael. 1989. *Sustainable Development, Exploring the contradictions*. London: Routledge.

Restrepo, Iván. 1993. "Comisión Ambiental del TLC: tares y posibles atribuciones". *La Jornada* 12/VII/93, 6.

Ritchie, Mark. 1993. "Agricultural Trade Liberalization: Implications for Sustainable Development" in: Ralph Nader et al., *The Case Against Free Trade. GATT, NAFTA and the Globalization of Corporate Power*, San Francisco and Berkely: Earth Island Press and North Atlantic Books.

RMALC. 1991. *Libre Comercio o Explotación Libre*. México DF.

—. 1992. *Memoria de Zacatecas. 25, 26 y 27 de octubre de 1991. La opinión pública y las negociaciones del Tratado de Libre Comercio: Alternativas ciudadanas*. México DF.

—. 1993a. *Propuesta de RMALC para la creación de una comisión ambiental de América del Norte (CAAN)*, 7/VI/93.

—. 1993b. *Declaración de prensa sobre la terminación de las negociaciones de los acuerdos paralelos al TLC*, 14/VIII/93.

—. 1993c. "Nuestro balance de la negociación formal sobre el Tratado de Libre Comercio" in: El Fisgón, *¡Me lleva al TLC! El Tratado retratado*, México DF: Grijalbo.

Robinson, David. 1994. "Wasted Potential. Mexico's eco-biz grounded by lack of financing". *Business Mexico* December, 4-6.

Rodarte, Humberto. 1992. "Environmental Protection in Mexico". *Loyola of Los Angeles* 15 (1), 79-86.

Romero, José. 1994. "Energía, emisiones y precios relativos" in: Antonio Yúnez-Naude (ed.), *Medio Ambiente, problemas y soluciones*, México DF: El Colegio de México.

Romero Lankao, Patricia. 1994. "Ciudad de México: problemas socioambientales en la gestión del agua" in: Antonio Yúnez-Naude (ed.), *Medio Ambiente, problemas y soluciones*, México DF: El Colegio de México.

Ros, Jaime. 1992. "Free Trade Area or Common Capital Market? Notes on Mexico-US Economic Integration and Current NAFTA Negotiations". *Journal of InterAmerican Studies and World Affairs* 34 (2) 53-91.

Rosas, María Cristina. 1995. *Crisis del multilateralismo clásico: política comercial externa estadounidense y zonas de libre comercio*. México DF: Universidad Nacional Autónoma de México.

Rosen, Howard. 1994. "Adjustment and Transition Mechanisms for a U.S.-Mexico Free Trade Agreement" in: M. Delal Baer and Sidney Weintraub (eds), *The NAFTA Debate, Grappling with Unconventional Trade Issues*, Boulder and London: Lynne Rienner Publishers.

Rousseau, Isabelle. 1992. "Le liberalisme social ou la politique du juste milieu". *Problèmes d'Amérique latine* 5, 29-44.

Rugman, Alan M., and Michael Gestrin. 1994. "NAFTA's Treatment of Foreign Investment" in Alan M. Rugman (ed.) *Foreign Investment and NAFTA*. Columbia: University of South Carolina Press.

Russell, James W. 1992. "Free trade and concentration of capital in Mexico". *Monthly Review* June, 23-30.

Salas-Porras, Alejandra, and Francisco Vidal Bonifaz. 1992. "La élite corporativa mexicana enfrenta la apertura económica. Nuevos patrones de control corporativo". *El Cotidiano* 50, 116-25.

Sánchez, Roberto. 1991a. "Environment: Mexican Perspective" in: Sidney Weintraub, Luis Rubio F. and Alan D. Jones (eds), *U.S. Mexican Industrial Integration. The Road to Free Trade*, Boulder: Westview Press.

—. 1991b. "El Tratado de Libre Comercio en América del Norte y el Medio Ambiente de la Frontera Norte". *Frontera Norte* 3 (6) 5-28.

—. 1993. *The North American Free Trade Agreement and the Environment: Challenges and Alternatives for Canada, the United States, and Mexico*. Paper presented at the conference Mexico and the NAFTA: Who will benefit?, University of London, Institute of Latin American studies, May 12-14.

Sánchez Rodríguez, Roberto. 1990. *El Medio Ambiente como Fuente de Conflicto en la Relación Binacional México-Estados Unidos*. Tijuana, BC: El Colegio de la Frontera Norte.

Sanderson, Steven E. 1986. *The Transformation of Mexican Agriculture. International Structure and the Politics of Rural Change*. Princeton, NJ: Princeton University Press.

Sándoval, Juan Manuel. 1991. "Los nuevos movimientos sociales y el medio ambiente en México" in: Martha Schteingart and Luciano d'Andrea (eds), *Servicios Urbanos, Gestión Local y Medio Ambiente*. México DF: El Colegio de México.

SECOFI. 1993. *Mexico Canada. Forging a new relationship*.

SEDESOL. 1992a. *México. National Report on Environment (1989-1991) for the United Nations Conference on Environment and Development. Summary*.

—. 1992b. *Los instrumentos económicos aplicados al medio ambiente / The economic instruments in environmental protection*. Instituto Nacional de Ecología. Serie monografías no. 2.

—. 1993. *México. Informe de la Situación General en Materia de Equilibrio Ecológico y Protección al Ambiente 1991-1992*.

—. 1994a. *México. Informe de la Situación General en Materia de Equilibrio Ecológico y Protección al Ambiente 1993-1994*. Instituto Nacional de Ecología.

—. 1994b. *Normas Oficiales Mexicanas en materia de protección ambiental*. Instituto Nacional de Ecología.

—. 1994c. *Aplicación de la ley. Resultados y Programa 94*. Procuraduría Federal de Protección al Ambiente.

—. Undated a. *El Tratado de Libre Comercio y el medio ambiente. Carpeta informativa*. Oficinas del C. Secretario, Coordinación General de Asuntos Internacionales.

—. Undated b. *Protecting the Environment. Mexico's Public Works Program for the Border Region*. Brochure.

SEDUE. 1983. *Informe de labores 1982-1983*.

—. 1986. *Informe sobre el estado del medio ambiente en México*.

—. 1989. *Programa Nacional para la Protección del Medio Ambiente 1990-1994.*

—. Undated. *Evaluación del impacto ambiental por el incremento de la actividad eco-nómica por efecto del Tratado de Libre Comercio. Actividades de competencia federal. Modalidad general. Versión borrador para revisión.* Draft report.

SEDUE and EPA. 1991. *Integrated Environmental Plan for the Mexico-U.S. Border Area (First Stage, 1992-1994).* Working Draft.

Sherwood Truitt, Nancy (ed.). 1992. *Forum of the Americas. Open Trade and Investment: A Vision and an Agenda for the Americas.* San Francisco: ICS Press.

Shrybman, Steven. 1993. "Trading Away the Environment" in: Ricardo Grinspun and Maxwell A. Cameron (eds), *The Political Economy of North American Free Trade*, New York: St. Martin's Press.

Sierra Club et al. 1993. *Analysis of the U.S. proposal for an environmental side agreement to the North American Free Trade Agreement: Omissions and ambiguities.* Washington 8/VI/93.

Silva-Herzog F., Jesús. 1991. "Mexico and the World: Opportunities and Risks in the 1990s" in: Riordan Roett (ed.), *Mexico's External Relations in the 1990s*, Boulder and London: Lynne Rienner Publishers.

Sklair, Leslie. 1989. *Assembling for Development. The maquila industry in Mexico and the United States.* Boston: Unwin Hyman.

—. 1991. *Sociology of the Global System.* New York: Harvester Wheatsheaf.

—. 1992. "The Maquilas in Mexico: a Global Perspective". *Bulletin of Latin American Research* 11 (1) 91-107.

Smith, Peter H. 1993. "El impacto político del libre comercio en México" in: Gustavo Vega Cánovas (ed.), *Liberación Económica y Libre Comercio en América del Norte*, México: El Colegio de México.

Spalding, Mark J. 1995. "Resolving International Environmental Disputes. Public Partici-pation and the Right-to-Know". *Journal of Environment & Development* 4 (1) 141-54.

Stern, Marc A. 1993. "Mexican Environmental Policy Revisited". *Journal of Environ-ment & Development* 2 (2) 185-196.

Székely, Alberto. Undated. *NAFTA's "environmental" component and North America as an ecological region.* Draft paper.

Székely, Gabriel. 1991. "Forging a North American Economy: Issues for Mexico in the 1990s" in: Riordan Roett (ed.), *Mexico's External Relations in the 1990s*, Boulder and London: Lynne Rienner Publishers.

TCPS (Texas Center for Policy Studies). 1990. *Overview of Environmental Issues Associ-ated with Maquiladora Development Along the Texas: Mexico Border.*

—. 1992. *A response to the EPA/SEDUE Integrated Border Environment Plan.*

Teichman, Judith. 1992. "The Mexican State and the Political Implications of Eco-nomic restructuring". *Latin America Perspectives* 19 (2) 88-104.

—. 1993. "Dismantling the Mexican State and the Role of the Private Sector" in: Ricardo Grinspun and Maxwell A. Cameron (eds), *The Political Economy of North American Free Trade*, New York: St Martin's Press.

—. 1995. *Neoliberalism and the Transformation of Mexican Authoritarianism.* Paper for the workshop on Mexico in the Post-NAFTA Era, York University, September 22-24.

Ten Kate, Adriaan. 1993. *Industrial Development and the Environment in Mexico.* Policy Research Public Economics Working Papers, Policy Research Department, The World Bank, WPS 1125.

Thorup, Cathryn L. 1991. "The Politics of Free Trade and the Dynamics of Cross-Border Coalitions in the U.S.-Mexican Relations". *Columbia Journal of World Business* XXVI (11) 12-26.

Tirado, Ricardo. 1992. "Los dirigentes del Consejo Coordinador Empresarial". *El Cotidiano* 50, 130-5.

Toledo, Alejandro. 1992. "Economía y ecología: las dos dimensiones de la globalidad" in: Cuauthémoc González Pacheco (ed.), *El Sector Agropecuario Mexicano al Tratado de Libre Comercio,* México DF: Instituto de Investigaciones Económicas, UNAM.

Toledo Patino, Alejandro. 1994. "México: un balance económico del gobierno de Carlos Salinas (1988-1994)". *Mondes en Developpement* 22 (87) 55-87.

TPCC (Trade Promotion Coordinating Committee). 1994. *Mexico. Environmental Technologies Export Marking Plan.* U.S. Department of Commerce, International Trade Administration, Environmental Trade Working Group.

UGAM. 1993. *NAFTA and the environment: Round II.* Letter, March.

Umlas, Elizabeth. 1995. *Environmental Networking in Mexico: The Comité Nacional para la Defensa de los Chimalapas.* Paper for the 1995 meeting of the Latin American Studies Association, September 28-30.

—. 1996. *Environmental Non-Governmental Networks: The Mexican Case in Theory and Practice.* Dissertation presented to the Faculty of the Graduate School, Yale University.

United Nations. 1996. *1995 International Trade Statistics Yearbook. Volume I.* New York.

U.S. Council of the Mexico-U.S. Business Committee. 1993, July. *Analysis of Environmental Infrastructure Requirements and Financing Gaps on the U.S./Mexico Border.* Washington.

U.S. President. 1991. *Response of the Administration to issues raised in connection with the negotiation of a North American Free Trade Agreement.* Transmitted to Congress by the President on May 1.

—. 1992. *Report of the Administration on the North American Free Trade Agreement and actions taken in fulfillment of the May 1, 1991 commitments.*

—. 1993. *The NAFTA, Expanding U.S. Exports, Jobs and Growth. Report on Environmental Issues.*

USCIB (United States Council for International Business). 1993. *Updated Statement on the Cooperative Efforts of the U.S. and Mexican Business Communities to Address Labor and Environment Issues in the NAFTA.*

USTR. 1992a. *Review of U.S.-Mexico Environmental Issues.*

—. 1992b. *Summary of environmental provisions.*

Valdés Ugalde, Francisco. 1994. "From Bank Nationalization to State Reform: Business and the New Mexican Order" in: Maria Lorena Cook, Kevin J. Middlebrook and Juan Molinar Horcasitas (eds), *The Politics of Economic Restructuring. State-Society Relations and Regime Change in Mexico,* San Diego: Center for U.S.-Mexican Studies.

Velasco Arregui, Edur. 1994. *Productivity and Employment in the Mexican Industrial Restructuring.* UAM-Xochimilco, paper.

Vidal, Godofredo. 1992. "Expectativas económicas del TLC". *El Cotidiano* 50, 30-5.

Vidal, Gregorio. 1993. "Los grupos financieros en México, la restructuración del capital y la integración de la economía mexicana a la norteamericana". *Mondes en developpement* 21 (84) 9-17.

Wallach, Lori. 1993. "Hidden Dangers of GATT and NAFTA", in: Ralph Nader et al., *The Case Against Free Trade. GATT, NAFTA and the Globalization of Corporate Power*, San Francisco and Berkely: Earth Island Press and North Atlantic Books.

Weintraub, Sidney. 1990. *A Marriage of Convenience. Relations between Mexico and the United States.* New York and Oxford: Oxford University Press.

Whitehead, Laurence. 1991. "Mexico and the 'Hegemony' of the United States: Past, Present, and Future" in: Riordan Roett (ed.), *Mexico's External Relations in the 1990s*, Boulder and London: Lynne Rienner Publishers.

Wiarda, Howard. 1994. "The U.S. Domestic Politics of the U.S.-Mexico Free Trade Agreement" in: M. Delal Baer and Sidney Weintraub (eds), *The NAFTA Debate. Grappling with Unconventional Trade Issues*, Boulder and London: Lynne Rienner Publishers.

Wionczek, Miguel S. 1985. *Industrialization, Foreign Capital and Technology Transfers. Mexican Experiences 1930-1985.* New Delhi: Research and Information System for the Non-Aligned and other Developing Countries.

World Bank. 1989. *Mexico: Environmental Issues and Strategy Paper.* Latin America and the Caribbean Region Office.

—. 1992a. *Staff Appraisal Report. Mexico Environmental Project*, no. 10005-ME.

—. 1992b. *World Development Report 1992. Development and the Environment.* Oxford University Press.

—. 1993. *Country Strategy Paper Mexico.*

—. 1994a. *Mexico Northern Border Environment Project.* Staff Appraisal Report, no. 12603-ME.

—. 1994b. *OED Précis, World Bank Relations with Mexico* no. 71, June. Operations Evaluation Department.

Yanner, Keith. 1995. *The Salience of NAFTA in the 1994 Mexican Presidential Election.* Paper to the International Studies Association Annual Meeting, Chicago, February 22-25.

Zagema, Bertram. 1991. *Dancing on the volcano. Ecological crisis and ecological movements in Mexico City.* Catholic University of Nijmegen, Third World Centre, Occasional Paper 24.

List of Interviews[1]

AMCHAM, Mexico City, 10/v/94 and 18/v/94.

American Embassy, Mexico City, 25/x/95.

BEP, Bisbee AR, 17/IV/94.

Canadian Environmental Law Association (CELA), Toronto, 3/III/95 and 19/IX/95.

CEC, Montreal, 1/III/95.

Center for International Environmental Law (CIEL), Washington DC, 29/IX/95.

Center for U.S.-Mexican Studies, San Diego CA, 19/IV/94.

Centro de Ecología (Centre of Ecology), *Universidad Nacional Autónoma de México* (National Autonomous University of Mexico, UNAM), Mexico City, 19/v/94 and 24/v/94.

Centro de Estudios del Sector Privado para el Desarrollo Sostenible (Private Sector's Study Centre for Sustainable Development, CESPEDES), Mexico City, 25/x/95.

Colegio de la Frontera Norte, Tijuana, 15/IV/94.

Comisión Nacional para el Conocimiento y Uso de la Biodiversidad (National Commission for the Knowledge and Use of Biodiversity, CONABIO), Mexico City, 19/v/94.

CTC, Washington DC, 31/VIII/93.

Department of Foreign Affairs and International Trade, Ottawa, 21/IX/95.

Embassy of Mexico, Ottawa, 20/IX/95.

Embassy of Mexico, Washington DC, 29/IX/95.

Environmental Committee of the Tijuana-San Diego Region, San Diego CA, 21/IV/94.

Environmental Technology Export Council (ETEC), San Diego CA, 22/IV/94.

Environment Canada, Ottawa, 20/IX/95.

EPA, Washington DC, 27/IX/95, 27/IX/95 and 27/IX/95.

Equipo Pueblo, Mexico City, 5/IV/94.

Foundation for Border Progress (FBP), San Diego CA, 22/IV/94.

Greenpeace Canada, Toronto, 23/IX/95.

Greenpeace USA, Washington DC, 10/IX/93.

Grupo de los Cien (Group of Hundred), Mexico City, 9/VIII/93.

---

1 As many of the interviewees requested or expected confidentiality, this list contains the interviewees' affiliations and the date of interview. In some cases, interviewees had moved to another job since the NAFTA debate. What has been marked here is the affiliation that was of relevance to the debate. The places marked are those of the institutions, and not necessarily the place where the interview took place.

Institute for Policy Studies (IPE), Washington DC, 7/IX/93.
NAFTA Office, Embassy of Mexico, Washington DC, 7/IV/94, 11/IV/94 and 29/IX/95.
NRDC, Washington DC, 12/IV/94.
NWF, Washington DC, 30/VIII/93.
Programa de Acción Forestal Tropical (Tropical Forest Action Plan, PROAFT), Mexico
    City, 25/V/94.
Public Citizen, Washington DC, 1/IX/93.
RMALC, Mexico City, 23/V/94.
San Diego State University, San Diego CA, 19/IV/94.
SECOFI, Mexico City, 9/VIII/93 and 9/V/94.
Secretaría de Medio Ambiente, Recursos Naturales y Pesca (Ministry of Environment,
    Natural Resources and Fisheries, SEMARNAP), Mexico City, 4/X/95, 12/X/95, 17/X/95
    and 17/X/95.
Secretaría de Relaciones Exteriores (Ministry of Foreign Affairs, SRE), Mexico City, 10/
    VIII/93 and 5/X/95.
SEDESOL, Mexico City, 6/VIII/93, 26/VIII/93, 7/IV/94, 9/V/94, 9/X/95, 13/X/95, 16/X/95
    and 19/X/95.
Sierra Club, Washington DC, 9/IX/93.
Skadden, Arps, Slate, Meagher & Flom, Washington DC, 28/IX/95.
UGAM, Mexico City, 17/V/94 and 17/V/94.
U.S. Council of the Mexico-U.S. Business Committee, Washington DC, 11/IV/94 and
    19/IV/94.
USTR, Washington DC, 8/IX/93 and 12/IV/94.
World Bank, Mexico City, 16/V/94.
World Bank, Washington DC, 8/IV/94 and 11/IV/94.

Samenvatting

In juni 1990 werd bekend gemaakt dat Mexico en de Verenigde Staten (vs) streefden naar de totstandkoming van een bilateraal vrijhandelsverdrag. Het plan trok de aandacht omdat er sprake was van een uitzonderlijke situatie van vergaande economische integratie tussen een ontwikkelingsland en een aangrenzend geïndustrialiseerd land. Canada besloot zich bij het plan aan te sluiten, en zo begonnen de onderhandelingen voor het Noord-Amerikaans Vrijhandelsverdrag (NAFTA). Tegelijkertijd kwam er ook een politiek en maatschappelijk debat op gang over de mogelijke milieu-effecten van regionale vrijhandel. Het gebrek aan implementatie van Mexico's milieubeleid stond daarin centraal.

Belemmeringen voor een breed Mexicaans debat over NAFTA waren de overheidspropaganda en de structurele onderdrukking van politieke partijen en niet-gouvernementele organisaties (NGOs) die kritiek hebben op Mexico's dominante partij, de PRI, en haar beleid. Om dezelfde redenen waren Mexicaanse milieu-organisaties voorheen zelden in staat geweest invloed op hun regering uit te oefenen. Het NAFTA plan bracht een grote verandering teweeg in het politieke krachtenveld ten aanzien van Mexico's milieubeleid. Amerikaanse en Canadese milieu-organisaties kregen aandacht voor de problemen en het falende beleid in Mexico, en organisaties uit de drie landen begonnen samen te werken. Bovendien was er in de vs grote bezorgdheid dat Mexico's minder strenge toezicht op naleving van milieuregels een groot concurrentievoordeel zou betekenen voor aldaar producerende bedrijven. Doordat deze kwesties in het Amerikaanse Congres zoveel weerklank kregen dat de verwezenlijking van NAFTA onzeker werd, kwam de Mexicaanse regering voor het eerst onder grote druk te staan om haar milieubeleid te verbeteren.

In tegenstelling tot de officiële onderhandelingen over het vrijhandelsverdrag was het NAFTA milieudebat niet alleen een aangelegenheid van staten, maar raakte een groot aantal andere politieke actoren betrokken. Een reeks van Mexicaanse, Amerikaanse en Canadese NGOs, vakbonden, organisaties van het bedrijfsleven, oppositiepartijen, en ook de Wereldbank speelden een rol. Van-

wege de actieve deelname van veel niet-staatsactoren in de grensoverschrijden-
de politieke strijd over NAFTA wordt in deze studie gesproken van het *transnationale* NAFTA milieudebat. De vraag die hierin centraal staat is *hoe het transnationale NAFTA milieudebat van invloed is geweest op Mexico's milieupolitiek en
milieubeleid.*

Het onderzoek levert een bijdrage aan discussies over regionalisering en mon-
dialisering, en de relatie tussen economische integratie en politieke transnationalisering. In het algemeen kan worden gesteld dat door voortgaande liberale economische integratie nationale democratische mechanismen minder effectief
dreigen te worden. Alhoewel er nieuwe, transnationale kanalen voor politieke
beïnvloeding ontstaan zijn er op regionaal en mondiaal niveau nog nauwelijks
structurele mogelijkheden voor politieke invloed van de civiele maatschappij. In
deze case-study, die voortbouwt op ideeën uit de politieke economie, wordt in-
gegaan op de politieke implicaties van Mexico's toetreding tot NAFTA.

Terwijl de transnationale aandacht voor Mexico's milieu en milieubeleid
nieuw was, waren de plannen voor de Mexicaanse deelname aan NAFTA slechts
een volgende stap in het proces van Mexico's economische en politieke transnationalisering. Economische integratie met de VS in de vorm van handel heeft
een lange geschiedenis. Directe Amerikaanse investeringen en industriële export werden vooral gestimuleerd vanaf de jaren zestig in Mexico's noordelijke
grensgebied (met het zogeheten *maquiladora* programma), dat tot een snelle industrialisering maar ook tot enorme milieuschade leidde. Vanaf de jaren zeventig werd Mexico steeds afhankelijker van buitenlands financieel kapitaal (via
overheidsschulden en bankkredieten), en sinds 1989 door de liberalisering van
de Mexicaans aandelenmarkt. Mexico's economische transnationalisering raakte in een stroomversnelling door het beleid van neoliberale herstructuring dat
in het midden van de jaren tachtig in gang werd gezet door een groep techno-
craten in de PRI. Privatisering, liberalisering en inkrimping van overheidssubsi-
dies waren de centrale onderdelen van dit beleid. NAFTA consolideert Mexico's
neoliberale ontwikkelingsmodel door middel van een structurele externe economische en politieke inbedding.

Het neoliberale ontwikkelingsmodel en de technocratische dominantie van
Mexico's staat-partijsysteem hadden aanzienlijke consequenties. Een aantal
grote bedrijven had succes, maar veel kleinere bedrijven kwamen in de problemen. Gecombineerd met de opeenvolgende economische crises die Mexico
doormaakte, had het nieuwe ontwikkelingsmodel tot gevolg dat de inkomens-
verdeling polariseerde en grote delen van de bevolking verarmden. Op ogen-
schijnlijk tegenstrijdige manieren poogde de technocratische elite ondanks haar
impopulaire economische beleid aan de macht te blijven. Aan de ene kant
kwam er een groot sociaal ondersteuningsprogramma genaamd Solidariteit, en

werd een zekere politieke liberalisatie en decentralisatie in gang gezet die de ruimte voor oppositiepartijen en NGOS enigszins vergrootte. Aan de andere kant werden de autoriteit en de autonomie van de president en de bureaucratie verder uitgebreid. Van werkelijke democratisering was geen sprake (hoofdstuk 1).

De toenemende maatschappelijke bezorgdheid in Mexico over milieudegradatie viel samen met de neoliberale herstructurering en de slechte economische omstandigheden. Onder invloed van de toenemende mondiale aandacht voor milieuproblemen had de Mexicaanse overheid al in het begin van de jaren zeventig formeel een milieubeleid ontwikkeld, maar dit werd nauwelijks uitgevoerd. Incidentele lokale milieuprotesten werden veelal genegeerd of onderdrukt. In de loop van de jaren tachtig bleek dit echter steeds minder goed mogelijk te zijn vanwege het groeiende aantal milieu-organisaties en hun toenemende maatschappelijke steun. De president en federale overheidsinstanties poogden grip te krijgen op de milieubeweging om te voorkomen dat deze oncontroleerbaar zou worden. Door een combinatie van samenwerking, coöptatie en repressie bleef de kritiek op het milieubeleid meestal beheersbaar.

Dat het milieubeleid voor de Mexicaanse regering weinig prioriteit had werd gecamoufleerd door de formele regels, retoriek en enkele prestigieuze projecten voor Mexico Stad en natuurgebieden. Deze aanpak leverde Mexico zelfs een "groen" internationaal imago op, en ten tijde van president Salinas (1988-1994) veel buitenlandse milieuleningen. In werkelijkheid was er echter sprake van een beperkte, gefragmenteerde wettelijke basis voor beleid, en werd wetgeving niet of slechts gedeeltelijk geïmplementeerd. Verreweg de meeste aandacht was gericht op industriële vervuiling en bedreigde plant- en diersoorten, waardoor andere problemen, zoals de degradatie van natuurlijke hulpbronnen, werden verwaarloosd. Milieu-instanties kregen de budgetten noch de autoriteit ten opzichte van andere overheidsinstellingen om hun taken tot uitvoering te kunnen brengen (hoofdstuk 2).

Naar aanleiding van de vrijhandelsplannen kwamen Mexico's milieuproblemen en het gebrekkige beleid onverwachts in de schijnwerpers te staan. Dit was zeker niet de bedoeling van de voorstanders van het verdrag, die uit waren op volledige liberalisering van de regionale stromen van goederen, diensten en kapitaal, ten behoeve van uiteenlopende economische en politieke belangen. Milieu-organisaties en academici brachten echter naar voren dat vrijhandel milieubescherming op verschillende manieren negatief beïnvloedt. Milieu-regels die eisen stellen aan import en export van goederen kunnen in het kader van vrijhandelsverdragen onwettig worden verklaard. Ten aanzien van Mexico's milieu was er bovendien bezorgdheid over de versnelde economische groei die NAFTA teweeg zou brengen, en de mogelijkheid dat vervuilende productieprocessen van de VS naar Mexico zouden worden verplaatst (hoofdstuk 3).

Het NAFTA milieudebat kan worden ingedeeld in drie fases. In de eerste fase, die de periode juni 1990 tot en met april 1991 besloeg, zetten milieu-organisaties in de drie betrokken landen het debat over NAFTA en milieu in gang. Mexicaanse organisaties stelden ongecontroleerde industrialisering, de effecten van grotere sociaal-economische ongelijkheid, en een snelle exploitatie van natuurlijke hulpbronnen voor de Amerikaanse markt aan de orde. Dit laatste was ook een punt van grote zorg voor Canadese groepen. Daarnaast waren Canadese en Amerikaanse organisaties bezorgd over de toekomst van nationale en lokale milieuregels die strenger waren dan de Mexicaanse. In de VS trok de extreme vervuiling aan de Mexicaanse kant van de grens veel aandacht. Zowel nationaal als transnationaal gingen milieu-organisaties samenwerken met elkaar en met andere NGOS. Dit gevarieerde gezelschap bracht de mogelijke milieu-effecten van regionale economische integratie onder de aandacht van het brede publiek.

Op 1 mei 1991 deed president Bush daarop een aantal toezeggingen aan het Amerikaanse Congres met betrekking tot NAFTA en milieu. Behalve een paar kleine concessies aan de eisen van milieu-organisaties wilde Bush de meeste milieu-aangelegenheden buiten NAFTA houden en bilateraal met Mexico regelen. Deze toezeggingen veroorzaakten een breuk tussen gematigde en kritische milieu-organisaties en dit markeerde het einde van de eerste fase van het milieudebat. Tijdens het verdere debat zouden de verschillen tussen deze twee typen organisaties een belangrijke rol blijven spelen en worden uitgebuit door voorstanders van het verdrag. Kritische organisaties streefden naar een verdrag dat, in plaats van vrijhandel, regionale duurzame ontwikkeling en democratie zou stimuleren. Gematigde groepen concentreerden zich daarentegen op waarborgen die milieuschade als gevolg van vrijhandel zouden moeten voorkomen. Daarnaast verschilden de organisaties in hun politieke strategieën. Gematigde groepen hadden redelijk goede toegang tot de regeringen, maar hun transnationale relaties met NGOS bleven vrij beperkt en ad hoc. Kritische groepen bouwden brede nationale netwerken op om politieke invloed te krijgen, en deze netwerken gingen transnationale verbanden aan met elkaar. Wat betreft de transnationale relaties van milieu-organisaties in het NAFTA milieudebat kan daarom worden gesproken van een transnationale coalitie van gematigde organisaties, en een transnationale alliantie van kritische organisaties (hoofdstuk 4).

Nadat bleek dat de kritiek van milieu-organisaties, in combinatie met de tegenstand van vakbonden, een serieuze bedreiging vormde voor de goedkeuring van NAFTA in het Amerikaanse Congres, kwamen NAFTA voorstanders in actie. In eerste instantie reageerden vooral de Mexicaanse en Amerikaanse presidenten en overheidsinstanties op milieucritici, maar later raakten ook organisaties uit het bedrijfsleven in de twee landen betrokken, en droeg de Wereldbank een steentje bij. Tussen deze verschillende instellingen werden transnationale banden gelegd, die het karakter van een alliantie hadden. In hun gezamenlijke pro-NAFTA lobby werd de recente vooruitgang in Mexico's milieubeleid benadrukt. Tegenover de kritiek van milieu-organisaties werd gesteld dat NAFTA goed was voor het milieu omdat de extra economische groei meer geld voor milieubescherming zou opleveren. Vrijhandel zou ook tot meer samenwerking op het terrein van milieu leiden, en enkele NAFTA milieuregels en -fondsen zouden milieuschade helpen voorkomen.

Opvallend aan de positie van voorstanders van NAFTA ten aanzien van het milieu was de beperkte benadering. De Mexico-VS grensregio en industriële vervuiling stonden centraal, terwijl aan veel andere kwesties geen aandacht werd besteed. Deze nauwe interpretatie van de aan NAFTA verbonden milieuproblemen was vooral het gevolg van de dominantie van de Amerikaanse invalshoek. In de VS bestond primair angst voor verdere vervuiling van het grensgebied, en voor een verplaatsing van industrie en banen, omdat in Mexico milieuregels minder streng werden toegepast (hoofdstuk 5).

De tweede fase van het NAFTA milieudebat liep van mei 1991 tot en met september 1992. Tijdens deze periode van onderhandelingen over het vrijhandelsverdrag draaide het debat om de milieubepalingen van NAFTA en de bilaterale milieu-initiatieven van Mexico en de VS. Kritische groepen eisten een milieu- en sociaal handvest, gematigde groepen stelden een reeks milieuwaarborgen voor, maar de NAFTA voorstanders wilden een vrijhandelsverdrag zonder milieurestricties. Het uiteindelijke verdrag omvatte slechts een aantal zwakke milieubepalingen, die zowel door de kritische als vrijwel alle gematigde milieugroepen werden afwezen. Ook nadat de drie regeringen de toezegging deden dat er een regionale milieucommissie zou worden opgericht, was er nauwelijks enige steun voor NAFTA onder milieu-organisaties en leek de kans op goedkeuring van het verdrag door het Amerikaanse Congres klein.

Van oktober 1992 tot en met november 1993, tijdens de derde en laatste fase van het NAFTA milieudebat, stond het zogenaamde milieuzijverdrag centraal. Dit idee kwam uit de koker van de nieuwe Amerikaanse president Clinton, die hoopte dat samen met een arbeidszijverdrag het totale "NAFTA pakket" aanvaardbaar zou zijn voor het Congres. De invulling die Clinton aan het milieuzijverdrag wilde geven was een compromis tussen zeer uiteenlopende posities. Kritische milieu-organisaties wilden dat de zijverdragen duurzame ontwikkeling zouden garanderen en zetten een transnationaal alternatief voor NAFTA op papier. Gematigde groepen legden de nadruk op het oprichten van een sterke, supranationale milieucommissie. Dit was ook een belangrijk onderdeel van Clintons voorstel, die het nodig leek om handelssancties als ultiem dwangmiddel bij milieu-conflicten op te nemen, om goedkeuring van het Congres te krijgen. Het Amerikaanse voorstel viel echter slecht bij de Mexicaanse en de

Canadese regering, en werd ook door het bedrijfsleven in de drie landen afge-keurd. Na lang onderhandelen werden de regionale milieucommissie en de handelssancties wel deel van het zijverdrag, maar in zeer afgezwakte vorm. Daarnaast werden er door Mexico en de VS afspraken gemaakt voor de oprich-ting van een grens-milieucommissie en een ontwikkelingsbank voor die regio. Ook de milieufondsen die door de Wereldbank werden vrijgemaakt waren voornamelijk voor het grensgebied met de VS bedoeld. Gematigde Amerikaan-se milieu-organisaties spraken hun steun voor het NAFTA pakket uit, maar de meeste anderen keurden het af. In november 1993 ging het Amerikaanse Con-gres met een kleine meerderheid van stemmen met het NAFTA pakket akkoord.

Het economische en politieke overwicht van de VS was een bepalende factor in het transnationale NAFTA milieudebat. De VS zetten Mexico erg onder druk om het formele milieubeleid ook uit te voeren. In het kader van de zeer onge-lijke machtsverhoudingen en vanwege het feit dat de Mexicaanse regering erg gespitst was op het vrijhandelsverdrag, accepteerde zij tijdens de onderhande-lingen over milieubescherming meer dan haar lief was. In vergelijking met Mexicaanse milieu-organisaties waren Amerikaanse groepen rijker, professio-neler en invloedrijker. Deels bracht de regionale asymmetrie Mexicaanse en Canadese groepen nader tot elkaar, maar Mexicaanse groepen maakten ook veel gebruik van de nieuwe betrekkingen met Amerikaanse organisaties. Soort-gelijke spanning en samenwerking ontstond tussen organisaties van het be-drijfsleven, alhoewel de Mexicaans-Canadese link bij deze actoren veel zwakker was.

Het transnationale NAFTA milieudebat zorgde ervoor dat binnen korte tijd het milieubeleid prioriteit kreeg voor de Mexicaanse regering. Milieubudgetten stegen sterk, er werden nieuwe milieunormen vastgesteld en er vonden institu-tionele hervormingen plaats. Op basis van beperkte informatie kan de voor-zichtige conclusie worden getrokken dat tussen 1991 en 1993 de implementatie van Mexico's milieubeleid op een aantal punten verbeterde. Inhoudelijk had het NAFTA milieudebat tot gevolg dat de nadruk op industriële vervuiling werd versterkt en het grensgebied met de VS aanzienlijk meer aandacht kreeg dan voorheen. Wat betreft de nationale politieke verhoudingen ten aanzien van het milieu veranderde er weinig. Kritische milieugroepen werden nog steeds ge-marginaliseerd en de invloed van gematigde groepen nam maar weinig toe. Het gebrek aan openheid van overheidsinstanties en aan openbare toegang tot in-formatie duurde voort (hoofdstuk 6).

De tweespalt tussen gematigde en kritische organisaties, die tijdens het mi-lieudebat geregeld werd gevoed door de NAFTA voorstanders, en met name de regeringen, had belangrijke consequenties. Enerzijds konden gematigde groe-pen, wegens hun relatief goede betrekkingen met de regeringen, en hun grotere bereidheid tot het doen van concessies, de vruchten plukken van de politieke druk die kritische organisaties creëerden. Anderzijds was het door de breuk gemakkelijker voor NAFTA voorstanders om de meer fundamentele kwesties die kritische groepen naar voren brachten te negeren. Desondanks hebben de activiteiten van de milieubeweging uit de drie landen een grote bijdrage geleverd aan de milieu-inhoud van het NAFTA pakket. Bovendien vormde het NAFTA plan de aanleiding voor een ongekende transnationale samenwerking tussen politieke actoren uit de drie landen, die in de toekomst weer snel geactiveerd kan worden. Het zou echter overdreven zijn om te spreken van de totstandkoming van een regionale civiele maatschappij.

Door voorstanders wordt NAFTA geroemd als het groenste vrijhandelsverdrag ter wereld, maar in werkelijkheid zitten er grote mazen in de milieubepalingen van het NAFTA pakket. Vergeleken met GATT is er inderdaad een stap vooruit gezet, zoals op het terrein van samenwerking tussen de lidstaten en enige beperking van vrijhandel ten behoeve van milieubescherming. De meeste van deze beperkingen hebben evenwel een vrijwillig karakter. Sancties kunnen alleen worden opgelegd aan een land dat zijn eigen milieuwetgeving niet uitvoert, en de procedure voor een dergelijke afstraffing is zo gecompliceerd dat de kans erg klein is dat er ooit een sanctie zal worden opgelegd. Daarnaast hebben Mexico en de VS bilaterale regelingen voor milieubescherming in het grensgebied getroffen, maar voor milieuproblemen in de rest van Mexico is in het kader van NAFTA geen geld vrijgemaakt. Alhoewel de invloed van NAFTA's milieucommissie afhangt van de bereidheid van de drie regeringen, was haar oprichting het meest vergaande onderdeel van het NAFTA pakket. Zij zal in ieder geval het regionale milieudebat blijven stimuleren en ervoor zorgen dat er een zeker extern toezicht is op Mexico's milieubeleid.

De invloed van het transnationale NAFTA milieudebat op Mexico's milieupolitiek is gerelateerd aan de wereldwijde aandacht die in dat kader ontstond voor Mexico's milieuproblemen. Het debat heeft er in ieder geval aan bijgedragen dat de Mexicaanse regering minder dan voorheen haar milieu-imago kan baseren op een paar symbolische projecten. Een ander effect is de vergrote steun van externe actoren, zoals NGOs, regeringen en de Wereldbank, voor milieubescherming in Mexico. Voor het Mexicaanse bedrijfsleven was het milieudebat een kleine doch niet te verwaarlozen impuls voor bewustwording. Alhoewel Mexicaanse milieu-organisaties door het NAFTA debat belangrijke externe relaties opbouwden, nam hun politieke invloed in Mexico zelf nauwelijks toe. Los van de milieubepalingen in het NAFTA pakket, zijn binnen Mexico democratisering en participatie van maatschappelijke organisaties in besluitvorming over het milieu noodzakelijk, willen Mexicanen zelf verantwoordelijkheid kunnen nemen voor milieubescherming.

Op korte termijn had het NAFTA milieudebat een positief effect op Mexico's milieubeleid en werd er ook in de uitvoering vooruitgang geboekt. Achteraf bezien bleek een aanzienlijk deel van deze vooruitgang evenwel van korte duur. Tevens versterkte het debat de beperkte benadering van de Mexicaanse regering ten aanzien van Mexico's milieuproblemen. Economische groei werd, niet alleen in verband met het milieu, maar ook met Mexico's ontwikkeling, gepresenteerd als de oplossing voor alle problemen. In het NAFTA debat en in het verdrag zelf is er vrijwel geen aandacht voor de aard van de Mexicaanse ontwikkelingsproblemen, noch voor de mogelijkheden voor duurzame ontwikkeling geweest. Wellicht dat op lange termijn de ingezette koers van regionale economische integratie de verwachte positieve sociaal-economische effecten zal sorteren, maar deze strategie om de meest dringende sociale en economische problemen in Mexico op te lossen zal dan wel ten koste zijn gegaan van het milieu.

Index

Series **Environmental Studies**

Nico Nelissen, Jan van der Straaten and Leon Klinkers (eds.)
Classics in Environmental Studies
An Overview of Classic Texts in Environmental Studies

Arthur P.J. Mol
The Refinement of Production
Ecological Modernization Theory and The Chemical Industry

Martijntje Smits (ed.)
Polymer Products and Waste Management
A Multidisciplinary Approach

Ans Kolk
Forests in International Environmental Politics
International Organisations, NGOs and the Brazilian Amazon

Barbara Hogenboom
Mexico and the NAFTA Environment Debate
The Transnational Politics of Economic Integration

Bas Arts
The Political Influence of Global NGOs
Case Studies on the Climate and Biodiversity Conventions